NEW VOICES

AT THE

CROSSROADS

JOSEPHINE O'BRIEN

ISBN: 978-1-905451-96-8

A CIP catalogue for this book is available from the National Library.

This book was published in cooperation with

Choice Publishing & Book Services Ltd, Drogheda, Co Louth, Ireland

Tel: 041 9841551 Email: info@choicepublishing.ie

www.choicepublishing.ie

dedicated
to travellers everywhere
to those who travel because they want to
to those who travel because they have to

acknowledgements

to everyone who gave me of their time, their narratives and their insights into life in Ireland

to friends and family who read, discussed and listened to my concerns about this project

to dara for her work on the book cover

Contents

Afghanistan – Nasruddin 5
Angola – Dassy 12
Bahrain – Mustafa 17
Bangladesh –Mufti 25
Bolivia – Roberto 29
Bosnia – Haris 37
Brazil – Marcia 42
China – Cheng, Chu 56
Colombia – Dolly 64
Congo – Junior 71
France – Pascal 83
Germany – Ulrike 87
India – Sujada, Puri, Sudanash, Siraj 93
Iran – Mohammed 141
Iraq – Mustafa 144
Israel – Joseph 154
Japan – Sena, Shin 163
Korea – Penny 168
Kurdistan – Zhyan, Howre 176
Lebanon – Abdullah 188
Libya – Ibrahim 195
Lithuania – Ewa 205
Malaysia – Raj 210
Mauritius – Jennyfer 214
Nigeria – Chenidu, Abimola 222
Pakistan – Tauseef, Afdal 232
Poland – Iwona, Magda, Olivia, Paul 238
Romania – Ovidiu 253
Slovakia – Lucia 267
Somalia – Fatima 271
South Africa – Shaheed 274
Spain – Monica 281
Sudan – Oliver, Magdi, Yahya 293
Turkey – Serhat 305
Turkmenistan – Azat 317
Ukraine – Inna 331
Venezuela – Rafael 339
Zimbabwe – Dambudzo 344

Introduction

I grew up in small town Ireland in a society so homogenous and interconnected that people could trace their longitudinal and lateral genealogy to the 32nd degree. We were the stuff that geneticists dreamed of – a purity in cell structure that might possibly reach all the way back to the Phoenicians! The down side of this was the lack of diversity, the sameness of thought, beliefs, and cultural features. Conformity was an unconscious given and suspicion an expected reaction to any apparent deviations from the norm. Those who enjoyed the comfort of the known remained at home while others sought the new and the unfamiliar. I have spent most of my adult life in pursuit of difference – wandering as many other Irish did, have done and will continue to do for no other reason often than the sheer excitement of experiencing the different. We have gone in search of strangers and made ourselves at home living among them, learning from them, and becoming a part of their worlds.

For centuries, Ireland experienced emigration, exodus of its people in search of sustenance and survival abroad. The incoming stranger bode ill and understandably, given our history an air of suspicion and paranoia developed about the foreigner. Times have changed, and so should our perception of ourselves and others. Our identity is changing, absorbing an otherness that has much to contribute. The reality of who we are and what we have become needs to be explored anew. Donne's words that 'No man is an island, entire of itself; every man is a piece of the continent, a part of the main' echo across the island. We can no longer close our eyes to the world outside. In our globalized world of the 21st century, our interconnectedness and interdependence challenge us every day. We cannot live in a world where we ignore the values, beliefs and cultures of others, in particular those who come to live among us. We need to acknowledge that we are diminished by the pain and suffering of others and that we can be enhanced by the changing face and diversity of our country.

Ireland has become a diverse and exciting place. The narratives of the new voices are all around us on the streets, in the workplace and even in our homes. These voices tell a story that can hurt as well as compliment. We may be reminded of facts we have forgotten about ourselves. Not everyone who comes encounters the famous Irish welcome. We learn of the intense marketing of Ireland that has been conducted by Irish entrepreneurs especially in the field of 'education' to attract students to the country with the promise of work for them and the anticipation of foreign fees for the institutions. There are the paradoxes of the person refused citizenship three times but called upon to do voluntary translation for a fellow countryman as the government has no other option.

In general, people were willing to talk and to share their stories. Many have made and continue to make amazing contributions to Irish society and economy. People are involved in all kinds of professional activities including education, health care, social work and technology. Some are involved in voluntary work helping by visiting the elderly, doing charity work in the inner city and taking care of the religious needs of communities. These narratives reflect the worlds of just a small number of people and nationalities I encountered in my wanderings around Dublin. It is time we acknowledged the divergence and the changing face of our island, accept it and turn it into a positive feature of Irish society.

Since I began collecting these narratives, the face of Ireland has changed again. The global downturn has threatened to reduce the prosperity we have grown accustomed to. The challenge to remain open and positive is even greater.

Afghanistan

Afghanistan's story is high profile news. The tragic events that make up the country's recent history have forced refugees to travel far in search of security and a home. Some of these have made their way to Ireland where they have settled. **Nasruddin** *is from Herat in Afghanistan and he illustrates an aspect of Afghani culture that has been overlooked or forgotten in recent times. I saw this side of the country when I visited before the troubled times of Russian and American invasions and mujahedeen resistance.*

I am originally from Herat in southern Afghanistan where I grew up and finished high school. Then I moved to Kabul where I worked in the Ministry of Telecommunications. While I was working there, I attended Kabul University and took a degree in Literature. I continued working in telecommunications for some time but eventually migrated to Iran. It was difficult for me to move to Iran because the Afghani government brought in a law saying that educated people could not leave the country. Eventually I managed to get a passport by saying that I was a shopkeeper and in this way was able to move from Herat to Iran.

I speak Dari and Farsi, the language of Iran. I found employment in Iran in the Afghani Consulate where I worked for nine years. I also worked as a teacher with Afghanis. I did not have any documentation and so was not recognized as a refugee or as an asylum seeker. I could not get an ID card from the Iranian authorities. I told them that I was a government employee and that I had a problem. During the Taliban time in Afghanistan, it was very difficult for me because I did not have any papers.

The United Nations eventually helped me to sort out my situation. They sent all my papers to Geneva and from there, they were sent to Ireland where my family and I were accepted as refugees. When I arrived in Ireland in 2000, there were about three Afghani families here. While I had been living in Iran, I had been very busy. I had gathered a number of singers and musicians who had left Afghanistan because of pressure on them there and I organized a society and association for them. The result was that I wrote a book about Afghani music that was published in Iran.

When I came here, I found a country with culture and friendly Irish people. I had good impressions of the place. At first after our arrival, there was not any house for me and my family and we were put in a B & B for 6 months. An Irish lady who worked 3 nights in the reception was a journalist, and she was organizing a multi-media festival that involved Ireland, UK and USA. She asked me to attend. At that time, it was difficult for me because my English was not so good and they wanted information about Afghani culture and music. There was only limited time to prepare but I was able to present some information about Afghani calligraphy in the city museum. I found that many people were interested in these topics.

I was invited to talk to different groups and meet different people and so I thought it was better to set up a small cultural organization for Afghanis. I did so in the name of Afghan people and although the community is very small, we are able to organize some activities. There was no funding but I met many people and got to know the country. It was a good opportunity because I was able to attend the different cultural festivals. I was able to give a picture of Afghani society to Irish people. Most of the people here are not aware of Afghanistan. They ask me why I have come here. A journalist from Castlebar who interviewed me asked me how I felt about culture. I asked him what he meant and he replied: *'You are here and you are wearing a suit and a tie and in Afghanistan you had a turban and other clothes – how do you feel about this?'* I said: *'These things are not new to us'.* I was surprised that a journalist did not seem to know anything about our country. As you saw when you travelled there in the past, Afghanistan was a developed country.

I went to an exhibition once in Temple Bar and I saw four to five large pictures on the wall. One picture was of people wearing traditional clothes and sitting on a cart. Another picture showed people fighting while a third showed a woman riding a cow. I felt angry and said this is not all there is to Afghani culture. We have a good culture and heritage but it was a good opportunity for me to see other people's impressions. Later, I exhibited a number of pictures that helped Irish people increase their awareness of Afghanistan.

There are about 15 – 16 families here now; the number of Afghanis is increasing. We also have a number of Afghani asylum seekers, most of whom are single. Some are not in Dublin but in hostels around the country. In 2006, some (about 40 of the 300 here) of these went on hunger strike. They cannot get any status and their cases have been under review for 2 years. They are depressed because they do not have the right to work. In many conferences and meetings, I have suggested that it is better to make them busy. I told people that when I was in Iran there were one and a half million refugees and they were allowed to work. Consequently, the Iranian authorities could benefit through their physical labour for the construction work in the country. These refugees helped build Iran and contributed to its development. I do not think it is necessary that the government employ them as doctors or engineers but they should use them and have them work. These people got depressed;

they went into the Cathedral where they said they were going to kill themselves.

For us and the other families things are good here but not so for the asylum seekers. The people who went on strike were not threatened with deportation but it is just that their cases are in process and are taking time. Some people advised them that it was not good to stay in the church because people wanted to pray there so they left. They could not get any papers and are still waiting.

I was a refugee for 3 years in Ireland before I got Irish citizenship. My family is comfortable here. I have four children. One of my sons studied in Iran and when we came here he studied Computer Science in DIT. He works with a multinational computer company and he has just been transferred to the USA. He also travels to Canada and Australia with the company. My wife was working as a teacher but she has not been well and is taking some time off. She had some work experience in Afghanistan with teaching small children and when we got here she had an interview. She thought she would not get the job because her English might not be good enough but they hired her because of her experience. The educational system she had studied under in Afghanistan was similar to the English system. My daughter is training to be a Montessori teacher and my son is in DCU. I have one son in school still. I work as a translator and I want to translate my own work on Afghan music into English. My book is about traditional music in Herat and I want to launch this book with a video cassette. There was an English professor in Afghanistan in the 1970s by the name of Professor John Bailey; he and his wife trained in Herat and lived there for about two and a half years. His wife learned how to sing traditional Afghani music and he learned how to play some of the instruments. He also wrote a book about the music of Afghanistan and about some of the professional musicians. The book was written in English and published in Cambridge. I want to translate that book into Farsi. I have some references from Professor Bailey's book in my work.

I have another book also about calligraphy and painting in Herat and I am waiting to publish this in Afghanistan. I am optimistic about the country. There are a lot of people who are educated now and with a lot of experience about the political process in Afghanistan. People know what to do. They know who the enemy is and they know who is working. As I see it, people do not like the Taliban and they do not like Communists. People do not like those who brought these forces into our country and destroyed it. We do not want the terrorism of the Taliban and their suicide bombers. They are creating problems and running away. There are international forces in our country but if they are not there we cannot secure our country. We would have the same problem as before and we would have the Taliban back again. Sometimes when they suggest decreasing the number of international troops, people say 'No'. Afghan people see this as a good chance for us. When Russia and the Communist regime invaded our country, nobody invited them. These people now came through the invitation of the United Nations in Afghanistan.

Now there appears to be problems between the tribes. Thirty years ago, we had the same tribes in the country: Dari, Pashtu, Tajik, Baluch, Hazaara and we also had Hindus, Jews and Buddhists. These people all integrated well. People did not have any problem with each other. Afghanistan at that time was multicultural. Everybody had his rights, for example, a Sikh could do military service. We had people from Russia, from Kazakhstan, from Uzbekistan – they were refugees sometimes but they integrated. The problems we have now come from the political parties because the parties have identified with separate tribes and look for power for their own tribes. They bring people from the same tribal background together and then they start to fight. In the past we did not have this problem and we did not hear talk of tribes. Nowadays I think people are beginning to understand this feature of the political parties. During the Taliban times, people did not know what to do because the Taliban are Muslim just like the rest of the population. People felt they could not go against the Taliban because they share the same religion as they do. So they said to people in Herat, *'Oh Herati people, these Taliban are Pashtun and you are not Pashtun'.* They found that using the tribe was a way to get support to oppose the Taliban.

We still have difficulty with Hamid Karzai. In the Parliament, we have Communists and we have Mujahedeen and these people fought and killed each other in the past but now they have set up a society to unite against the government. This is bad and people ask them how they can unite when they were killing each other. We do not believe them. The Communists are already divided into two groups and the Islamic parties are divided into several groups so how can they all come together. They are uniting just against the government. I think if the parties leave Hamid Karzai alone he will work very well but they are making problems for him. We know that the Iranian authorities are expelling about 5,000 Afghanis from Iran. The Afghani Minister for Foreign Affairs and Immigration had to go to the Parliament but they said, *'We don't want them here, make them go away'.* The Minister told them that he had already sent a letter to the Iranian Ministry of Foreign Affairs and to the United Nations and there was not anything else he could do. These kinds of situations are making the government weaker.

Some of the Ministers have lived and studied abroad and they bring ideas from countries such as Germany, where people know how to work and how to run the system. These ministers understand the European system and they are very active and forceful. The local chiefs want to push them back because they are afraid that these educated ministers are taking their places and they want to control things themselves. This is Karzai's problem and people say Karzai should not bring these people in. However, I say democracy works in this way; if people want them they should be there. Some people feel that some of the people who are in government are criminals and they should be brought before a tribunal. These people destroyed the country and they killed millions of people. This is the problem that Karzai has. Without such people, there would not be a problem.

Another problem is drug production. People are very poor and are worried about how to make a living but drugs are not the right way. They are forbidden under Islamic law. Years ago, if somebody grew hash he was put in prison. It was a sinful thing to do. Now we have the same religion but people are very poor. If they were supported in some way, they would not grow the poppy. So there is still a long road to travel.

Angola

Angola, a country rich in oil, diamonds and other minerals was one of the many secondary locations in which the superpowers acted out the Cold War. Recent events have brought some stability to the country. Meanwhile, Angolans have been scattered all over the world. I met **Dassy** *on Dorset Street where he was running an internet cafe.*

Growing up in Angola meant different things to different people. The chances were there but it depended on whether or not people could take them. I grew up in a country at war but I did have the chance to go to primary school. We did not notice the war too much as most of the fighting was in the south and I grew up in the north. By the time the war reached the north, I was already in the capital Luanda and here the war never made as much of an impact as in the countryside. People moved from one province to another and then came to the capital.

After primary school, I had a chance to do a professional course, a two-year apprenticeship as an electrician. Then I went abroad to study computer courses in programming in Russia in 1988. The government sponsored me and I was one of the lucky ones who benefited from this program. After my computer courses ended, I wanted to learn some English because most material to do with computing is in English.

I decided to move to one of the English speaking countries. I lived in the UK for two years until I learned of the IT boom in Ireland. Sometime in 1996 or 1997, I moved to Ireland. I did a short course in hardware management and maintenance of PCs and after that I got a job with Compaq that later became Hewlett Packard. I worked with them for four years and at the same time I started a business myself. I left HP and started to run my own internet café. I wanted the challenge of managing a business and wanted to test myself to see if I could do it. It has been great, though there are some difficulties. When you come to a new country, the systems are different. The taxation system is different here. The rents are very high and so on but we are struggling and trying to move upwards.

I still have family in Angola. People say things have changed there today. We are no longer involved in a war. We are waiting for elections to be held, but for some reason all African leaders find ways out of holding elections. They always manage to postpone the elections. It was supposed to be next year. Let us see what happens. We need a democracy back home. Then people can speak up; people can have a decent life.

It wasn't easy coming to Ireland and it is still not easy. We are in a different country and we have to focus and try to ignore those who ignore us. Everyone knows exactly why you are here and what you are doing. You can be judged just by the colour of your skin. Some people see you as a very stupid person who has come into Ireland. Of course, if they sit with you and talk and if they have the maturity and the open-mindedness to see how the world moves, they will understand that the world is not just one country. The world is made up of many countries and people have to move from one country to another, to learn new cultures and try to make life better for themselves. They should not think that Ireland is the most beautiful place in the world. From history itself, people know that Irish people have had to move to the UK, to England, to the United States. People are white here and you don't really notice it but in a political sense you know how much you had to suffer under the British people. The treatment was bad. I heard that there were hotels that you could not go into. There were signs that said 'No Blacks, No Irish, No Dogs'. People who have already lived this type of story should be much wiser when people come into their country. People have gone through this kind of story themselves.

Africa is a continent that belongs mostly to black people. The white man came to Africa. We never invited anyone but at the same time, we never rejected anyone. You guys came and we opened our arms and we received you with both hands. Why is it always so complicated for a black man to move? In Ireland at the beginning, it was very complicated. As time moves on, we are hopeful that things are getting better and everyone is much more integrated. In the case of ignorant people, we just ignore them as well. If you use the theory of ignoring those who ignore you or do not want to know about you it is better. If you know yourself, you do not want another person to tell you who you are. I know who I am, where I am coming from, and what I am doing. It is difficult for me to accept someone coming in and judging me and telling me 'you are this or you are that' when I know very well who I am. No one can know better than me who I am. There are many opportunities in Ireland. People just have to come and take them. They should not abuse the system of course. They should try to do things in the right way and they will find many opportunities.

My children are in school here and though there can be problems they are comfortable. I had a very tough period when my first child started school. The teacher would always come up with complaints and tell me, *'Your son did this to that child and your son did that to that child'*. She never said that someone did something to my child. I asked myself if it is possible that my son does something and the other child never does anything to him. I got mad with the teacher once and I went to the principal and said enough is enough. I asked them to write a report for everything that my child does wrong and everything that is done to my child. We tend to go into the war of words and get stuck in 'you said this' and 'I said that'. However, if everything is written down, I have that as proof. No one has touched my son in an entire year and things have calmed down. He has moved on and now he is in a different class and has never had the same problem again. It was just a person who was having difficulty accepting people from a different culture. I would not say it was the teacher's first year but it just happened and maybe she did not interact well with my son. I do not think my son was the only one making trouble. I will accept that he was perhaps a difficult child at that time but he was not the only one. Can you believe that he is the only one who starts a fight and no one fights against him? These situations created difficulties and interfered with integration. Some people tend to take advantage because they know the system better than we do. They know we are foreigners, and that we may be very scared of everything. That is why sometimes people tend to take advantage of us.

I speak about seven languages. I speak Portuguese because we were colonized by the Portuguese. I speak Congolese, the main language spoken in my tribe. I speak Linguala, the language spoken in the north of my country and in the Democratic Republic of Congo. I speak a little French because I lived in the Congo for a little while. I speak Russian because I studied in Russia and I speak English. This was one of my dreams to speak English and when I started my computing course and learned English, it was a dream come true. I can also understand a bit of Spanish and Italian because they are close to Portuguese and all are derived from Latin.

Angola is a very wealthy country but the wealth is no use if you have as many problems as Angola has. What we have here in

Ireland in terms of a social welfare system is better. The country is organized. You do not have any of the natural wealth of minerals and oil that Angola has, but you have a well-organized system and people can live from the effort of the other person. In Angola, it does not happen like that. If you do not do your very best, you cannot live because there is nothing from the government. They invest the money more in defence, in the army, in fighting instead of investing it in education that can make a better Angola tomorrow. Hopefully, Angola will try to follow the path of European countries. People need to be taken care of and that is their very first basic human right. We hope there is enough for every Angolan to live well. You cannot explain why one person there is very rich and you have nothing. It is not the fault of the poor person because the government has not given him even a basic education so that he can start something in life. A person deserves at least a good primary education and then he can get some professional training.

We all come from different backgrounds with different levels of education but now we are trying to do our best in Ireland after going through the proper channels to be legal here. It happened to the Irish as it is happening to us now. Your story is history but ours is happening now.

Bahrain

*Bahrain in the Arabian Gulf has close medical ties with Ireland through the College of Surgeons and sends many students to study medicine, thus contributing to the Irish economy. I first met **Dr Mustafa** at a mosque in Milltown. He has a doctorate in Nursing and works in a private clinic in Dublin.*

I come from Bahrain, a small island in the Middle East. The diameter of the country is 24 kilometres only – a very small island in the middle of what they call the Arabian or Persian Gulf. Our income in the past came from fishing and pearl diving. Since petroleum was found in Bahrain, it has been different. Now we have oil and Bahrain is a rich country. Because of the location of the country, Bahrain is a very special place for everyone going through the region. People had to transit through the island, so Bahraini people got to know different nationalities early on in our history. We are used to different cultures and people from all over the world as they pass through. We are open-minded as we get to see more foreigners. That is why they say people from Bahrain are not extreme as people from some of the neighbouring countries can be. If you compare other groups of people with us, you will see the difference. Bahraini people are always very friendly like Irish people and they welcome any nationalities without reserve. They are open-minded and welcoming to strangers.

I came to live in Ireland because I found the same kind of behaviour from the Irish people as in Bahrain. I first came here in 1995 to study. I am a nurse, which used to be unusual for an Arab man but more males are fighting for the job now because it is secure. Once you finish your training, you can get a job anywhere in the world. I got my first nursing certification from the College of Health

Sciences in Bahrain. The World Health Organization has recognised this College for a long time. When I came here in 1995 to do my postgraduate courses I had no problem entering college here without any conditions while others who came from Oman, for example, had problems. They graduate as nurses in Oman but they repeat nursing before they do postgraduate study because the World Health Organization does not yet recognize their qualifications. We had nursing degrees in Bahrain before Ireland had. In 1995, when I was doing my theatre courses here I was the only one with a degree. The others had a hospital certificate or diploma. So I was considered highly qualified at that stage. The Nursing Board recognized my qualification. Bahrain is far ahead of most of the other countries that are now doing the same. Ireland opened a branch of the College of Surgeons last year in Bahrain and classes are interchangeable. You can do the first year in Bahrain and then come over and continue in Ireland.

I came here to do my postgraduate in theatre on a scholarship from Bahrain. At the same time, I did a diploma in management. When I first came, I really liked Dublin. I did not feel like I was in a foreign country because people were so friendly. I never noticed anyone who was not happy, and I really liked it. I went back home in 1996 to work in theatre for about three years. Then I decided to come back here to continue my studies. When I arrived for the second time in 1999, I noticed the difference even from the first week. The people were not as they used to be especially the younger generation. The older generation was still OK but even they were changing and they did not accept foreigners. They do not consider you as an equal, as if they feel they are superior though they have nothing more than you do. I do not know what changed here.

I tried to analyse this one. I think what that makes them behave in this way is similar to what made the English people do so in the past. Ireland has money now especially after joining the EU. People come to Ireland. There are refugees from Romania and several other places. There is no problem for the refugees to come here but some of them may abuse the system. This may make the Irish take a negative view of all foreigners. They do not differentiate between who is doing what, between who is a refugee and who is not. I do not blame the Irish in a way for that but I think they need to know more. In the past, they treated everyone as if all were doctors though they were not but now even when you are a doctor or a professional they treat everyone as a refugee. That is really something that hurts. In the past, I would not hesitate to send my kids to play outside but now I think I would be more conservative. I cannot trust anybody just walking outside. I, myself, have not had any experience with racism but I can feel it. Irish people are good at hiding what they feel so they might have some racist feelings against you but they never let them out. This is good in one way because they don't hurt you directly. However, at the same time you know how they feel because you have been living with them for a long time. So you feel that you are sitting among people and they are not welcoming you. I am sure that one day they will realize what they are doing. Once they come over to the Middle East or wherever they go outside of Ireland they are always welcome though they are not doing anything special. In Bahrain, we welcome all the foreigners as equal with the citizens. Some Irish have worked in Bahrain and in the Gulf and they realize they like the people there. But when you sit with Irish people, you find a very conservative attitude and they make sure they don't have that much contact with you, which is surprising. .

I went on and did my Master's and PhD in Ireland, studying and working at the same time. When I started, I remember I was the only male and only foreigner in the place. Now you can see a lot of Indians, Filipinos, and South Africans in all the hospitals. They feel like foreign hospitals and not Irish. When I started, I was the only foreigner but I didn't feel foreign but now if you are Irish in the hospitals you will feel that you are foreign, especially in some of the public hospitals. I did some of my study in the College of Surgeons and some by correspondence. That is how I could work and study at the same time. For the time being, I will stay in Ireland. I am happy enough in Ireland and I can do all that I want to do. I think that it is wise to stay for some time to practice whatever input and experience you have gained from being here. My family has settled in well and my kids are happy in school. They don't even want to change school. I want to move to another house but they do not want to change school so they will have to travel by bus to keep the same school as they are very happy there.

Bahrain is a mixture of Sunni and Shii'ah Muslims. The Shii'ah make up about 75% of the population. Among the normal people, we live and work together, we are well integrated; they marry us and we marry them. There is no problem whatsoever. There are some issues to do with work; some of the government jobs such as the military were not easily available to Shii'ah. It depended on the bosses. If the boss is Sunni, the first question he would ask is 'Are you Sunni or Shii'ah?' If you are Shii'ah then you don't get the job. They always tried to show that the Shii'ah had no loyalty to the country. In fact, it is the other way round; we are very loyal and those worries are false. However, you find racism everywhere. It could be that they are worried about a closer Shii'ah connection with Iran but they have no reason to be. Even when there was a problem in Bahrain, you never heard anyone say 'we want to go to Iran'.

Some people have issues with the Shii'ah and that is why they keep raising it but if you go through history and look at the country you will see the king in favour of the Shii'ah. There is an independent Shii'ah Ministry and Shii'ah Ministers. Maybe there are difficulties at the top level but at the normal, lower levels there are no problems. We all live together and we visit each other. We pray in the same mosques and we go to the same places. It is just a minor thing anyway and it rarely happens now.

In 1995 for about one and a half years, there was trouble. But as soon as the king became Emir on his father's death, he proved that he is really with the people and not against them. He does not differentiate between the Shii'ah and Sunni and that is why everybody likes him and supports him. He issued new orders and now it is difficult to differentiate between Sunni and Shii'ah. Since the change of Bahrain from an emirate to a kingdom, the only thing I have noticed is that all the Ministers can be changed now by voting in the Parliament while in the past nobody could change anything unless the Emir changed it himself. We did not have a Parliament at that stage but now because it is a kingdom we have a Parliament. We have a Constitution and even the media are more open. Anyone can criticise any minister in the newspaper whereas in the past, there was no democracy and if you criticized anybody you would be put in jail straightaway. People have the right to defend themselves openly and in the media, with no pressure from anybody.

I worked in the public health care sector in Ireland before coming to the private sector. Compared with the public, we manage to do quite a lot in the private system. The public system is very messy and we only do trauma cases, seriously urgent cases. It is very hard to do any elective surgery like knee replacements because it requires a lot of effort and post operative treatment. The problem of cancellations often arises; it seemed every time we planned to do a major case it was cancelled for some reason or other. The private hospitals are smaller and more efficient though money oriented. The work load is definitely far greater than in the public because you can do five joints a day in a small hospital while in the public you can do about one joint a month. The reason is that the power in the public hospitals is distributed among so many bosses; there are so many heads and you have to go through all these people. This is supposed to be a routine procedure and patients are waiting. When you want to prepare the patient for theatre, the surgeon cannot ask the nurse to bring the patient. Everybody works by herself/ himself. There are many people involved in management and fewer people to do the actual work. That is the way the workload is distributed and so the hospital ends up doing only the emergency cases and the other cases are cancelled.

In the private hospital the patient is insured; they get full attention from the time they enter the hospital until they leave; they get the best quality work and whatever they require. I think that is what makes the private hospital much better. Here you pay but you get the best results. In the public sector, you pay the minimum but you get nothing. There is too much bureaucracy but in private hospitals there are not too many people involved and when the order comes, it goes through to the concerned people. They do the work efficiently and quickly because as they say in the private system time is money. The good thing as well in the private hospital is we do not recruit people here for training. People who work in private hospitals have the skills; they do not need any training so you don't have to tell them twice what they have to do. When you give your order, it goes through smoothly because you have people who know how to do it in the right way. In the public system, you find people who have just graduated and they must be trained. Some of these people need time and effort to learn. In private hospitals, you do real work because you keep working and you do not play for one hour. If you do not work, you do not get money. In the public, if you don't come to work nobody reports you and you get your salary at the end of the month. They just think of putting in the eight hours and then going home. Of course, this is not true for everyone. Sometimes if there are ten people for an operation in the public hospital, you push them back and you end up doing only three in your eight hours. You say my day is over and you go home. Then there are five more to do; you keep pushing them back and the number of people waiting keeps expanding. In private, you are tied and you have to keep doing everything efficiently. You don't waste time and that is why the patient gets the best treatment. At the end of the day you feel you have done a good job.

The system in Bahrain is not similar to Ireland. Bahrain is a small country and we have only a few public hospitals sponsored by the government. The government sends all the nurses and doctors to be trained. Most of our surgeons were trained in Ireland. They are exposed to different kinds of cultures and they are able to deal with all the work in the public system, because the population of Bahrain is very small and the workload is a lot less.

I hope that one day the Irish people will realize that wherever you walk in a street there are bound to be different kinds of people, not all of whom are refugees. Even the refugees are not all bad so I hope people will at least try to understand. When you have refugees here, it is a sign that the country is doing very well and you should accept the people who have had disasters in their countries. You should remember that the Irish people used to go all over the world and they were accepted so I ask that there be an understanding of others. One day we received and now we are giving back to others. But the Irish people are friendly and they share this with Bahraini people. We are both agricultural countries surrounded by the sea and this makes us aware. It is still true that wherever you go you find people welcoming and they want to help you. In 1995, the first year I came to Ireland, everybody was helpful. One day I was in the College of Surgeons and I wanted to go for prayers. There was one old lady working there and I asked her if she knew where I could pray in the college. ' She took me; she walked for more than 15 minutes to show me the place. I did not realize that she would walk all that way; I thought she would tell me where to go but no she went herself to show me where the place was. I felt so welcome, so overwhelmed that this old lady walked with me though she could not walk very well.   I wonder if I ask the question now will people have the same attitude.

Bangladesh

*Bangladesh is generally seen as a country that is on the receiving end of end and more than their fair share of natural disasters. We should remember, however, that the Bangladeshi diaspora can be found all over the world and contribute to the development of many countries. It is interesting to note how they are contributing to the Irish economy. I met **Mufti** in the restaurant where he does part-time work as a waiter.*

I am from Bangladesh, from the southeast of the country, Changpuri in the Diadong division. I lived there until I was 12 and then moved to Dhaka where I started my secondary schooling and prepared for the leaving certificate. I lived in Dhaka for ten years and then I moved to Ireland for university. In Dhaka, I studied the same kind of things you guys study here in Ireland for the Junior and Leaving Certificates. We study science and commerce; I was in the science group so I studied Physics, Chemistry, Biology, Mathematics and such subjects. I came to Ireland to study and I am in DIT now. I did two years of Computer Studies but I didn't like it so I changed to Business Studies. I am in my second year. This is an undergraduate course and I am just finishing my exams right now. The whole course takes four years.

I have been in Ireland for five and a half years but I have had many problems with the study here. It is very expensive – €10,000 euro for the course fees. That is why it has been very difficult for me to go back to Bangladesh because €10,000 is a lot of money. I went home this year in January because my Dad passed away and I stayed for 18 days. My Mum, my brother and my sister and all my relatives are in Bangladesh. I am the only one here.

25

The weather is the big difference between Ireland and Bangladesh. Here it is much colder than my country. The culture and religion are also different. In Bangladesh, many of the people are Muslim and we are used to praying five times a day. They say Dhaka is the capital of mosques. There are four or five mosques here in Dublin and I go sometimes. The one in Moore Street is mainly for Pakistanis but other Muslims go also. The mosques in South Circular Road and Clonskeagh are maintained by the Gulf people. I can read Arabic but I can't speak it.

When I first came, my English was not great so I had to take a three-month course. Then I had an exam and I passed so I moved on to the college. The biggest difficulty is the expense. Dublin is a very expensive city, probably the most expensive city in Europe. You have to get a job; you can work for 20 hours when you are a student. You earn €300 – 400 but this goes very quickly. You need at least €800 a month here for all the expenses. You have rent and fares, food and all those expenses. The minimum you can live on I think is about €600.

At the beginning, life was very tough for me and I did not get a job for two and a half months. Nowadays it is not so tough because people are used to students being able to work part time. When I first came in 2001, Irish people did not know that foreign students were allowed to work 20 hours a week and we had some difficulty. Everybody knows now so it is easy. Every year we have to renew our visa and that costs €100. If you apply to study in the UK, you get a 4-year visa; in Australia, you get 3 years. I know one of my friends got a 10 day visa here by mistake. He asked the authorities to change it as it was their mistake. They told him to come back after 10 days and renew it and he had to pay another €100. This charge just started last year so the Irish are making a lot of money out of visas. This is bad but the country is following the UK in making students pay for visas. Ireland is following the UK in many things but the UK gives a long visa for the length of the course.

It is better to have a degree from an English speaking country to get a good job back in my own country. You will be valued more if you have such a degree. When I go back to Bangladesh, I can get a better job than most people who have not studied abroad. You also get good experience in life because here you have to learn to survive and work. In my country students don't work; their parents take care of their education. This is a big difference between your country and my country. In Bangladesh, parents look after their children well and look after their education even if they are 25 or 26. I think there are very few families here that give that kind of support to their children. I think it will be easy to get a good job in the business or banking sectors when I go back to my country. It is worth going through this trouble to get the degree.

Many of the restaurants that appear Indian in Dublin are actually run by Bangladeshis. The food is basically the same. In Bangladesh, we use rice more than anything else whereas Indians eat chapattis and rotis. The same ingredients are used for the main dishes.

There have been many political problems in Bangladesh but now the Caretaker Government is putting things right. It is bringing a lot of stability and is trying to get rid of corruption. The Caretaker Government is trying to get Hasina and Khaldia for corruption, which is a huge problem in my country. Nowadays people are happy; there is no 'hartal' (strike) and life is getting better.

Dhaka is a crowded city with 20 million people. The population of Bangladesh is 140 million in a country about double the size of

Ireland. There is a tourist industry but the political problem interferes. We have the longest beach 'Cox's Beach' 760 km and we have 'the Sunderabans', a very big mangrove forest and some very good hill areas. When we have a good government, tourism will improve. 10 – 12% of the people of the country are Hindu, Buddhist and Christian and they all live comfortably side by side. We celebrate all the festivals of each religion.

I think there are about 10,000 Bangladeshis living here mostly in Dublin but there are some around the country. There are 500 – 600 living and working in a furniture factory in Killarney. Our garment industry in Bangladesh is huge and most of our foreign currency comes from this. Most of the brand name clothes in Ireland and the UK come from Bangladesh. There are sometimes problems with shipments and with wages. There are often electricity problems in the country but the caretaker government is trying to solve this. We have our own gas in the southeast and we use this for transport and cooking. It is also used in generating electricity. We had cyclones in the country in 1988 and 1991 when 100,000 people died. Now things are better because they know how to deal with it and move people before the cyclone happens. Only two people died in the tsunami.

I have many Irish friends. I have travelled around the country and I lived in Louth for a year when I first came. I travelled to Kerry and Killarney. This is probably better than most other European countries not as cold as other countries and the people are nice.

Bolivia

*There are very few Bolivians in Ireland. In fact, **Roberto** is the only Bolivian I have met here. He is studying in Dublin.*

My name is Roberto Chavez from Bolivia. I was born in 1978; both my parents are Bolivian. Bolivia is a little country in South America and is very volatile both economically and politically. Although it is one of the poorest countries in Latin America, you can have a good quality of life there because it has a lot of natural resources and everything is extremely cheap. The natural resources are in the hands of the multinationals but the government is trying to nationalise them. However, the way it is doing this I would say is unfriendly. It is giving a very bad image to the country for further foreign investment. Bolivia has a lot of tin, the price of which was low but it rising again. The main resource is natural gas; we have some oil but I would say that natural gas is more important. We don't tend to industrialise anything; we just export commodities. We are very dependent on international prices.

Most people are farmers. The majority of people in the country are indigenous though there are some people of European, mainly Spanish origin. You can clearly see the different positions of people of European/ Spanish origin and the indigenous people. In times of economic downturn you see great rivalry between these two groups. Our current president, Evo Morales, is the first indigenous president of Bolivia. He is a very populist president who is trying to show to the world and the Bolivian people that he can do good things for the country but in my view, he is not doing it in the right way. He is scaring off investment and he uses very strong language especially when he is talking about the developed world. He is very Hugo Chavez in his approach. Indigenous people have the same opportunities as people of European origin and the same rights. But the country itself is very poor so you can see people from both groups in the same difficult situations. When you go to the countryside things are even worse.

I am from Cochabamba, a city in the middle of the country. The capital is La Paz and the economic capital is Santa Cruz with Cochabamba somewhere in between. I went to primary and secondary school there and I did a Bachelor's degree in Economics. I did a Master's in the UK and now I am doing a PhD here in Ireland. I usually go back to Bolivia once a year. My family still lives there but they are not too happy with the economic situation so they are trying to send as much money as they can out of the country – sometimes to the USA but like a lot of families mostly to countries around the region like Brazil and Argentina. They are investing in real estate just to secure the value of the money. You never know what can happen in the country.

Bolivia was a comfortable, secure place to grow up in. The economy in the past was much better. We have had as many presidents as years of independence and also a lot of dictators. Every year it seemed there was another – in 200 years of independence we have had 190 presidents. One guy would push out the other – that was up to about 20 years ago but since that time things have become a bit more stable. The government now is elected in a sense but things are a little strange. The president may be elected with a majority of 51% but you can see a lot of irregularities. For instance, when you go to the countryside, which is the area that gives the most support to this government, people, can have two to three IDs so they can vote a number of times. But the government can say that you the people elected us so there is no excuse. There are UN monitors for the elections but it is very difficult to really observe what is going on especially in the countryside.

I decided to go to the UK to do the MA because I wanted to develop my career more and to study. I wanted to go to the USA but that was around September 11th and I changed my mind. I was always interested in learning more English. I had taken English in school but I could not speak it very well so I decided to go to the UK. My father supported me while I was there. I was also able to work part time. I was accepted in a good university in my field where I spent two years learning English and finishing the MA. Then I went to Switzerland and did an internship with an NGO for 6 months and I really liked the work but I could not enter the organization full time because I did not have a PhD.

I moved back to my country and I worked with the European Union. It was very difficult for me to get this type of job and it takes 6 months to a year to get a job with this money. I stayed for 9 months until the project ended. There are a lot of NGOs and EU organizations in Bolivia who are trying to develop the place especially with the coca leaves. The coca leaves are very valuable right now and are used for many things including medicine and of course for cocaine though that is not the main product. The image we have outside is that the coca leaf is cocaine but that is not the case. The coca leaf was used 2,000 years ago in the Inca civilization as a sort of stimulant and is deeply rooted in our culture and civilization. Though Bolivia does not have the reputation for drugs that Columbia has, it still exports drugs. I remember when I was doing my first degree, one of the professors looked at the macroeconomic figures and asked us what we thought 'others' which earned the country billions was (about 10% of our GDP). It was cocaine. They could not list it as such but this money was not coming from industry, from the government, from exports and they believed that it was from cocaine.

The problem is that growing the coca leaves is more profitable for the farmers than the type of projects that the European Union or the USA would like the farmers to be involved in. The president of the coca-growing region happens to be the president of the nation right now. He had a lot of power and organized a lot of demonstrations before the elections and though people didn't like him very much they decided to vote for him. It was really a case of 'If you can't beat him, join him.' Now people realize that it was a big mistake. Even the poor people are recognizing this because they thought they could get as much from him as they did in the past but I think he is not coping properly with all the sectors. He is not a well-educated guy. To be honest I am not against him; in the past I supported him and I was happy when he was elected because I thought he would be a good change in the country because we, the indigenous people, are in the majority. I think he had to leave school when he was 10 years old. He is a very good leader with his own people but not as a national leader because he thinks that the industrial sector (middle and small businesses) and academics are not to be trusted. He is very communist in a way. The countryside and the peasants are not going to support the whole economy. The image that he presents to the world like Hugo Chavez in Venezuela is different to the image they have at home. I went to speak on this point in DCU but I think they did not agree with me because of socialist ideological views. I think it is very important to let the world know that the image these leaders give is very anti-American, socialist but things are not happening, as they should in their own countries. There is also a lot of corruption especially now that the price of oil is so high. People like Hugo Chavez are getting a lot of money from the oil and they are giving money away in the streets just so they will be elected again and also to the public sector. They are not using the money wisely and if there is a downturn in the future, I do not know what is going to happen.

After working back in Bolivia for 9 months I decided to leave because I knew that it was going to be difficult to get a good job again. I needed funding so I started writing to the European countries. I was not interested in the USA. I applied to the UK, Spain and Finland. I was not familiar with Ireland though I had heard about it. I read about this Celtic Tiger thing and heard that the economy was growing. I thought it might be less difficult to get funds here especially in my area. The government was giving a lot of support to industry here and they were working with the universities to improve the economic sector. My application was accepted here and in Spain but Spain did not provide funding. I got the funding here from UCD and came to Ireland. The research proposal was about something new – the management tool in vogue these days – and it is now being used by all the multinationals and the middle-sized enterprises. It is a practice-based tool that should improve performance. My area is operations management and if you could compare it to much more developed areas in economics or psychology it is under-developed. Companies are using this tool now and it is very practical, useful and fashionable among scholars and industrial people. It is used in the small companies here in Ireland. Let us take one sector for example, the electronic sector, a sector that contributes a lot to the GDP in Ireland. This sector is non-regulated and therefore it is expected that the multinationals and indigenous industries are using this management tool. It is a very good way of achieving best performance in management. I think my research will help me but I think it will also help industry in Ireland. It is a very practically oriented area and I would like to contribute to the industry here. I don't want my thesis to just sit on a library shelf.

I think it is a win-win situation and that is why I got my scholarship. I am quite happy also to contribute positively to a country that has given me this opportunity.

I have been in Ireland two years now. It is a very nice country, developed if you compare it with my country but not very developed if you compare it with other European countries. It has a lot of facilities and I think policy makers are doing a good job at least in the economic and communications sectors. They are using the resources very wisely in terms of attracting a lot of multinationals. In terms of the economy, this is very good but I am not sure how long it is going to be like this. In terms of society you can see there are a lot of people coming from all over the world. I think that may be difficult for Irish people because they are not used to all these foreigners. I can tell that everyone is not quite comfortable with this especially when these new people get jobs instead of them. I, myself, have not had any experience of racism and I feel very comfortable here. I think in this way it is different to other European countries. Ireland is a very friendly country compared with the UK. It is, however, very expensive compared to other European countries but it is easy to get a job and a good wage. That compensates for the expense. I have a student visa, which allows me work 20 hours a week during term time and 40 hours a week during holidays. I have only been working part time because I have to concentrate on my research. I renew the visa every year and that is quite straightforward – I just get a letter from my university and submit it with my papers. It used to be free but now we pay €100 – perhaps the government realises it can make money out of this. There are a lot of people here who seem to have a lot of money and who do not need to worry about how much they spend. I noticed this when I was working in one of the stores in Dublin. People only seem to care about having the latest fashions and buying as much as they can. I have been wondering where they get the money. Some of these people look very uneducated, rough and rude. It seems to happen when people who have been poor get money. Sometimes they can change overnight. The same thing can happen in my country.

I cannot perceive much politics here. People do not seem to be concerned about politics and I never hear them speak about it. In my country everything is politics – you talk politics with your mother, your father, your sister, with everybody. It can get very boring but it is how things are. Here when you approach a person you speak about the weather; in my country you speak about politics. Perhaps it is because it is a total disaster in Bolivia and everyone is unhappy with it whereas here everyone is somewhat happy with the economy. The difference is perhaps here you have already achieved economic success; in my country, people do not know what it is like to have a good economic situation. It is difficult to tell them to share what they do not have. That is why I believe that even though .economic globalization can result in an uneven society if it is managed well it can benefit everybody. It may not be everybody but I think the majority will benefit. Capitalism rewards people who have drive but there are also people who have problems. Not everybody is the same and for that reason I think governments should have some policies to protect these people. The difference between Ireland and Bolivia is that here you are already thinking three to four steps ahead and thinking in terms of quality but in my country, we are still thinking of survival. I think you can get development with a wide support from the different economic sectors, not just at the national level but through small and medium enterprises, through adding value to their different businesses.

We need a very big change in the way we are running Bolivia. I would say we need new leaders, young leaders and new parties. We just have traditional parties and we need a new way of thinking. We have 92 – 93% literacy level in my country though there are some indigenous people spread throughout the countryside who are not educated. We have potential; we have the resources but we need leaders. We need smart and wise people who will work for the good of the country. Even if you are against the USA, you do not need to say it to the world. You need to be a little crafty. I am not very warm; I am not very cold. I see myself in the middle and you know they say the worst people are those in the middle. I think you finally get what you want.

I just read a book by an interesting writer and he said that what we need in Latin America are boring predictable governments. Governments in Latin America tend to offer the people change every four years and people believe them. They do not need to be extremely socialist or extremely right wing. You should not divide the country; you should just run the country. Be predictable and do the best for your country. Have good relations with the countries that surround your own. I would not call Chile a successful country because of what happened with Pinochet, the dictatorships and the killing of so many people. But a good example is Brazil which they now call the 'Giant of Latin America' and the president Lula is very intelligent. He is not very well educated but he is a very good leader. Although, he did not finish school he is doing things in the right way. He deals with the multinationals in a very interesting way. The big American multinational 'Merck' invests heavily in Brazil. Brazil has a huge problem with AIDS, but the drugs are extremely expensive. Lula told 'Merck' – well sorry we are not going to buy your drugs and we are going to buy generic drugs from India. So although the government invites in multinationals he is able to make a choice. I think that is a very smart way; he is doing what is best for the people.

36

Bosnia

*Ireland has had associations with Bosnia that go back to the early 1990s when the first Bosnian refugees arrived in the country. I met **Haris** in the Bosnian Community Centre in Pierce Street, Dublin where he works.*

I was born in Sarajevo, the capital of Bosnia in 1974 and lived in Bosnia-Herzegovina until 1996 after the war and the peace agreement. I got an opportunity to come to Ireland because my aunt was already here. She came in 1992 as a refugee. I decided to come here for six months or maybe a year and then I ended up staying. That was ten years ago. When I came to Ireland, I was quite fortunate because I had English and it was much easier to adapt, to integrate here. I got a job with the Bosnian Community Centre as a part time worker. I worked in that position for two years and in September 1998, I was appointed to a full time position as a Community officer. I am still here.

I grew up in the former Yugoslavia; at that time Bosnia was part of that country but it separated in 1992 when the war started. Before that, Yugoslavia was a country that most people associated with the Soviet Union but it was completely independent and was not a member of either the Eastern or Western bloc. Yugoslavia was one of the group who established the non-aligned movement. It was a socialist country but not a dictatorship as some people wanted to portray it. We had a lot of freedom. People could vote and could travel. Many Yugoslavs went to Germany to work in the 1950s and 1960s. At that time, it was easy to travel freely anywhere in the world with a Yugoslav passport. In fact, the passport was equivalent to an Irish passport today because you could travel to any country without a visa.

According to my parents, life was very good and they could afford many things. Having a car was common and everybody had a house or an apartment because the state would give you a place to live. The company where a person worked would buy apartments and then give them to the workers. The companies all had a management committee that was made up of the workers so there was worker input regardless of the fact that the state was the owner of the company. Some workers took jobs in the underdeveloped countries in Africa, Asia and even Iraq where the Yugoslavs were building roads. At that time Yugoslavia had very big companies. The country was rich with industry and natural resources. However, when Tito died, the politics of Yugoslavia changed and in 1991 the country fell apart. Slovenia and Croatia wanted independence and so did Bosnia-Herzegovina and Macedonia. The war happened in 1992. Now we have over a million displaced Bosnians scattered around the world. Some people might say this is not a bad thing generally because those people will go back one day and help the Bosnian state to generate growth. This was the case in Ireland also where Irish people came back to the country, helped the growth of the economy and now Ireland is quite well off. Most Bosnians in Ireland who are middle-aged or elderly intend or hope to go back because they miss home and all they left behind. The younger generation is different. Many of them were born here. They are well integrated. They go to school here, to colleges and universities. Most of them will stay because they are Irish anyway and do not know Bosnia at this stage.

Our Bosnian/ Irish community is a mixed community with about 1800 people. The Irish government invited the Bosnians here because of the war. The first group came in September 1992 from the refugee camps in Vienna. Then four groups of sick and wounded were evacuated to Ireland. They were offered the right to stay. Some people brought their families and now the total number is between 1700 and 1800. You can say that the Bosnian community is one of the most settled immigrant communities in Ireland. Some people have been here for 13 years.

Today when you hear the word Muslim, you connect it with Iran or one of those countries. Bosnian Muslims are different because they are more open-minded and many may not even practice their religion. Most of the young people in particular would not be fanatically religious. The media portrayed the people of Bosnia wrongly. They always referred to them as the Muslims and separated people according to religion. In Bosnia, everybody suffered during the war irrespective of religion. Of course, there are fanatics on all sides but generally, the people would not be that religious. A very small number may have been radicalized but that is purely because of the war. If you go to Sarajevo, capital of Bosnia, you will not know what religion people belong to and everybody sits together side by side. Religion is not that radical and not that visible. You may see some women who are covered and there are some religious schools but women are not covered as you see in the Arab countries or Afghanistan. They are covered as you see women cover when going into the church. The Bogomils accepted Islam during the period of the Ottoman Empire. Islam was quite open at that time and that is why people from other religions became Muslims. It was to the people's advantage to become Muslims because in that way they got work and a better standard of living. It was very good for the economy of the country. At the same time Christians were cut off from Rome and were open to influences from other cultures.

For myself, I decided to come here because I did not like the way things were after the war. This was my first proper trip abroad and at that time in Bosnia it was a very difficult situation in terms of employment and salary. It will take some time before the political situation in Bosnia sorts itself out. We hope that in the next five to seven years we will become members of the European Union. Bosnia is not a big country and has a population of only four million people. All the people who are abroad generate income for the country. They say that the Bosnian diaspora send home about €3 billion a year directly or indirectly. We are hoping that all of this will improve the country over the next ten years.

There are industries in Bosnia and we still have big companies that pick up some jobs worldwide with contacts from the former Yugoslavia. We have a very large steel industry. We also have electricity from the many rivers with dams. Agriculture is quite important. Volkswagen has factories and exports to central and eastern Europe. There are also many small industries.

At the moment, Ireland is definitely home for me and I am used to the people and way of life. People are working hard here to make a better life but eventually you feel homesick. I go there every year once or twice. Attitudes of Irish people towards the Bosnian community vary. Ireland was for a long time completely isolated from the world but now many people are coming here and some of them abuse the system. I am not saying that everybody is coming to abuse the system and I know the Bosnians appreciate everything that has been done for them. They are working very hard to improve their lives. Many of them now have Irish passports and they feel part of Ireland. They work here and their children go to school here. Some of them have married Irish. This is a very settled community and they do not feel isolated in the way that other communities might. They have integrated quite well. It was easier for them because when they first came, there were no other refugees in

Ireland. You know around 1997 the Bosnians were accused of many things here but now the focus is on other communities and nobody bothers the Bosnians anymore. They leave us alone to live a normal life and now it is someone else. Hopefully, all this will change over time.

I work here full time helping Bosnians and at the same time trying to preserve the Bosnian culture. We have an art exhibition on the 6th of April in Temple Bar. Two Bosnian sculptors are coming to present their work and a gift will be given to the Lord Mayor of Dublin as a gift from Sarajevo to Dublin. We hope to develop stronger links between Dublin and Sarajevo so this meeting will be political in the sense that we want to present Bosnia in a better light. We will invite the media as well. These artists are famous in Bosnia and their work illustrates the unity of Sarajevo, a city that was divided during the war. The bridge is a symbol of this unity. We will also show a film set in Sarajevo. It won an award at the Berlin Film Festival and is a great movie. Those artists are now based in Sarajevo and will be in Dublin for five days. Hopefully, we will have some CDs on Sarajevo and the culture of Bosnia. We will also have some Bosnian wine, which is quite good.

Brazil

*According to the 2006, census there are 4,388 Brazilians in Ireland, most of whom work in the meat industry in counties Galway and Roscommon. Many of these live in Gort in Co Galway changing a town from which young people emigrated to a thriving, vibrant multi cultural centre. I met **Marcia** in Dublin.*

My name is Marcia Brincas. I am Brazilian and my ancestry is a mix of French, Portuguese, Italian and probably indigenous people. In my 30's, I decided to change my life a little bit and get some experience overseas.

I come from a town called Florianopolis, located in the South of Brazil, with more than 30 beaches and an economy based on tourism and public services. The population is approximately 300,000. Professionally speaking, in the last few years I have been working as an environmentalist and social developer, but my degree is in Business Administration with a specialization in Public Administration and Leadership for Civil Society. After finishing university and working in different positions in companies and NGO's in Brazil, I decided to experience a different life. I had an interesting corporate career in Sao Paulo. I was not in my home town, but I was happy and passionate about my work. However, having spent four years working more than 10-12 hours per day and not enough time for myself, I decided to give myself a gift, discover different sides of life and go abroad with the only certainty that I wanted to learn English, do a Master's Degree and learn from different cultures and situations.

I had several options on where to go, but I decided to come to Ireland. And here I am, living again in this interesting country, full of changes and happy that I can describe my experience here. Talking about Ireland is not an easy task, as everyone has different points of view. People complain a lot about the "miserable weather". People have shown me different aspects of Irish society in my short time here and these people have influenced me. Another challenge is talking about different periods in Ireland: the Ireland of the past, the Celtic Tiger and perhaps the future of a sustainable Ireland. Although, I have traveled through most of Ireland, from very small villages to big cities, I can talk better about Dublin where I have been living most of the time since I arrived. What I know, indeed, is that Ireland has changed considerably during the last 20 years.

My history in Ireland started properly in 2005 when I came here for the first time to study English. Until 2005, I just knew Ireland as a place about which I had read on the internet, in newspapers, but I had very little information. Generally, I would say that I had much more information about the negative things, for instance, the IRA and the conflicts between the North and South, often completely incorrect information. So, being in Ireland was a time for lots of discoveries about the true history of Irish culture. At the same time, it was a good time to see my own country in a different perspective, from outside, from other minds and eyes, and be able to evaluate and appreciate the good things that we have in Brazil.

I first started to be interested in Ireland when I received a folder/invitation to participate in a Third Sector Conference in Trinity College in 1998. I just looked at the picture of Trinity College in the folder and my imagination flew away to a distant place, very far from Brazil. I saw Ireland with nice landscapes and rural areas, flowers, green fields, very traditional people and places. I also imagined old towns and castles, people singing Celtic songs, the incomparable sound of the Irish flute and the uillean pipes, all in a unique context. Then I met an Irish guy in Sao Paulo, who was working as a consultant in a Brazilian mechanics industry, and when I told him that I was thinking of studying English abroad he said: " Why don't you go to Ireland? We have lots of similarities with Brazil: we love music, beer and football, and people are very friendly". That conversation made me much more curious and motivated me to come here, more than New Zealand or Australia which I was thinking of at the time. Another good advantage was that it was/is considerably easier to travel from Ireland to other Europeans countries and I really would like to visit different countries in Europe.

I read about Irish society and culture. I found some key words used to describe the country - Emerald Island, Mystic Island, Celtic music, political and religious conflicts and Irish dance. My curiosity increased. Some of those descriptions that I read in books and on the internet are true. Ireland still has emerald colors in its fields and gardens, even with so many grey days. I still notice the drawings and Celtic symbols around Dublin and places that I have visited. We also can find some nice Irish music in different parts of Dublin and Ireland. So, even with so much change, if we are interested in looking for traditional Irish music sessions, food and landscape we can find them. Irish people are really very friendly; they love beer, especially Guinness. They also like football. I think Gaelic football is more interesting than normal football, and hurling, the traditional Gaelic sport. Indeed they have music in their blood/soul.

We really did not learn about Irish history. I was surprised to hear of 800 years of British colonization, such a long time of domination! I am surprised that Ireland keeps its national policy on the Irish language on the public signs and national/foreign documents as an official language, even though English is spoken in most places. The effort to preserve Irish is seen in different projects on radio and television channels. We can see around the country that the vocabulary is included in the day-to-day language. One day, I met an old guy at the bus stop. We started to chat a bit and he asked me what brought me to Ireland and I told him the culture and to learn English. He looked me a little upset and answered me " English? You should come here to learn Irish, our official language, not English, you know!" I apologized to him and told him that people coming to learn English in Ireland was a positive thing because it is a good opportunity to learn about the country and its culture, helping to project the image of Ireland overseas. A few days ago I was in the public library and I saw a book and an Irish dictionary on the table, a nice indicator that people are still keeping the language alive!

The first time I was here, in 2005, walking around O' Connell Street and the city centre, I saw so much diversity around the city, people from everywhere, and I was very surprised. Sometimes I had an impression that there were more foreign than Irish people. However, with time, I started to understand some reasons why so many different people are in Ireland. One reason why immigrants came here, was definitely the economic boom and not for the culture at all. I had an opportunity to witness some signs of this prosperity during 2005 and 2006, two years before the "so-called" recession arrived in Europe and consequently in Ireland. At that time, you could walk around the streets and observe the clothes shops, the internet cafes, restaurants, full of people. If we looked through some windows in the top of some high buildings, the city was like a future movie with lots of construction and cranes. A funny thing was that we could find lots of coins along the sidewalks and people used to give more money to the artists around the streets, even change to beggars. Different shops were opening everyday and also art galleries were being created in different parts of Dublin.

It was also a time when there were many English schools promising overseas students an easy way to find jobs in Ireland while studying here. I was at a fair about 'English Study Abroad '(2005), in Sao Paulo, and we were told that in Ireland we could work and study easily. This fact attracted many Brazilians to Ireland in addition to curiosity about the country. I did not know at that time that there was already a big Brazilian community attracted by the meat factories in Ireland. But in Goiania, a town in the countryside of Brazil, people know about Ireland.

I would like to talk a little now about my experiences that include good and not so good times. As soon as I arrived here (May 2005), I had a not so friendly approach from the British Immigration in London but I finally started my life in Ireland. I decided to live with people who could speak English, and not with Brazilians. I found a host mother (a widow) for one month with a very nice place in Northwood Park, Santry a few minutes from the airport. I lived with her, and her kids used to visit her very often with her grandchildren, but it was very expensive. I stayed only one month and I moved to a small flat, sharing a room in a flat in Bolton Street, for €350 a month. After paying €150 to a host mother and after €40 per day in DCU for a student room, that option in Bolton Street seemed good, especially as I didn't need transport. I shared with a European couple and for me it was so different being with people from other countries. In fact it was good at the beginning, but as soon as I started to figure out that they were subletting the flat, things started to change. After getting the extra money that I had paid, I just left there.

I worked as a volunteer for a few months in an organization called Sustainable Ireland and from my network there I found a good place to live, paying much less and with my own room. It was a nice Georgian house in Gramthan Street. The only problem was that the price of the house was cheaper because the heating did not work and for 8 years more or less the landlord had not done any repairs in the house as he was expecting to sell it. For this reason the guys who were living there before got a fair price in exchange for repairing everything. Despite spending some freezing nights in a cold room without heating, and managing with the old things in the house that didn't work, the location was good. I really had a great time in Ireland. I was living with two Irish guys, one guy from Chicago and a Polish girl, so it was a good time to improve my English. It was hard to find a place to live at that time. I visited different flats and I saw places with very crazy people. Others were dirty and I could not afford the comfortable ones. I was studying and also trying to look for a job and my money was running out. It was not a good time for me in a foreign country and the winter was starting.

As soon asmy English started to get better I put more effort into looking for jobs and some opportunities started to appear. That time I could not be a more "sustainable" consumer, by buying fair trade and local products. I would prefer to be an aware consumer but I had to go to the cheapest prices at Tesco, Lidl and Aldi, even though I knew that those supermarkets are not very ethical and helpful to local development. As soon as I started to be financially stable I had better options to shop. In this case, I have to say that some shops in Dublin were very helpful to the foreigners here, especially the charity shops. The first job was a few hours a week as a kitchen assistant in a kind of a "posh" Casino near Grafton Street. The environment was not bad, but after two weeks I found myself asking what I was doing there. So, next step was to look for another job. A few weeks later I got a few hours working in Guinness Store House. It was new for me, especially as I had always worked in offices with defined positions. Working in catering was completely different but I saw it as a way into Irish culture as well and I accepted it as a kind of learning. Perhaps, the best advantage was to improve my English through working with Irish people and talking with tourists there. In 2006, I worked also in the coffee shop of Amnesty International. After that, I got an opportunity to work in a retail shop with a nice Irish couple. I had a great 6 months working there. It was my best time in Ireland.

I went back to Brazil for almost two years to stay close to my family and to go back to the market and my normal job and career. However, the idea of getting my Master's was still in my mind. I realized that I was losing my English and all my investment and time in Ireland was being lost, so I decided that I should come back and pursue my aims. Now (2008), I am back and pursuing a better English level. All my networks from before have been very important. The friendship and good heart of some nice people that I met before were essential to my stay in Ireland this time. Otherwise, I could not stay here for more than one month. One of my Irish friends received me as a guest for more than two months in his nice house near Harold's Cross. It was a very nice demonstration of kindness. Right now, I am also in a very cozy place, just in the city centre in very fair conditions.

In a general way, I can see some changes in the places where I lived around the city. It is clear that the prosperity is not the same as it was two years ago although the country is still much healthier than it was 20 years ago and still developing. Right now, we can see the opposite movement – many migrants leaving the country, due to the recession. Consequently, some commercial places have closed or are being closed, for example, internet cafes, restaurants and coffee shops. Some IT companies are cutting down some jobs not just in Dublin but also in Cork, Galway and Limerick. We can also observe something different in the architecture of the city. In some places, we have modern architecture and new buildings are taking the place of old ones and empty spaces giving a new face to Ireland. The docks is the most visible site of those changes. Some places are just abandoned or closed, perhaps because the entrepreneurs are waiting for the prices of the properties to go down.

It's a pity that economic development does not always mean social and environmental development. Ireland faces a big challenge in trying to solve its social problems such as drugs and alcohol together with social welfare, and education. In addition, there is the environment where the challenge is linked to consumption and waste. Sometimes I get a negative impression with all the rubbish in the streets, especially if we walk in the early morning after people have had a late night in the pub. Walking around the canals in Dublin – with nice green sites in the middle of the urban spaces, trees, swans and ducks - we see the signs of the lack of respect for the environment. On the beaches of Bray and Wicklow, we see lots of cans and plastic bottles stuck in the middle of the stones, in the same way that we see rubbish in yards of abandoned houses in different streets in Dublin. I know, I don't come from a country where the cities are the best example of urban ecology. This is especially true of Sao Paulo, but Brazil is a developing country.

The problem with alcohol is serious. Drink companies increase their profits and there is no effective program to minimize the impact of the alcohol industries on people's lives. It is not the fault only of those companies/industries but all society, migrants and foreigners who live here. Those companies should contribute to the solution of the drink problem.

Nowadays, walking around the city centre, near O'Connell Street, we still see many migrants. It is a strange atmosphere, and a little sad sometimes. We see big queues in the evenings at the bus stop and the tired faces of foreigners and Irish people. For sure they are not the wealthy ones who got money during the economic boom in Ireland. They are probably the ones working hard to pay their basic expenses. However, on each face I realize a feeling of hope or expectation that things will be better in the future - for Ireland and Europe as a whole. An interesting fact that I have noticed is the intermixing of foreigners with Irish and in many cases as couples. This will help break down the social barriers in the country.

I really wish Ireland a good future. Irish people are nice in a general way and have a nice and respectable history. Since I have been here I have visited almost all the Irish museums and have learnt about some famous Irish writers that I never knew before as well as artists, good film makers, cultural producers and indeed famous singers, all from a small country, with only around 4 million inhabitants. That's great! With all the struggles for hundreds of years, Ireland has kept her artistic soul alive. I like to learn what is behind the Irish symbols of harp, swans, shamrock. Most people are likely have forgotten those. The same happens with the historical past of the country in the lyrics of Irish songs, just to quote some: Fields of Athenry, Rare Auld Times and Stolen Child. In some other songs we have the funny side of Ireland, the way that they joke about themselves about the drunken stories, just to provoke a good laugh about their own lives.

I think that as a foreigner, I am very into Irish culture, maybe more than some Irish. I know lots of places where you can find Irish music sessions. I know some good musicians and also famous writers. I have been traveling all over Ireland to different places and I read, learnt about different times in Irish history. I know the lyrics of some Irish songs. I like to go to traditional pubs, just sit down beside the musicians and try to learn new songs and sing together. That is such a good thing to do here in Ireland. It makes our hearts happy and is good for our souls, probably more than "Guinness is good for *us*!". I know some poems (not by memory but at least the name of some of them), and a little about some famous Irish myths. I like Guinness (although I am not a good drinker!) and I have been at a final of a hurling match (not yet in the Gaelic Football).

I do think Gaelic football is more interesting than the mercenary Brazilian football. People sometimes are surprised about my opinion but it's true. It is nice to know that people still play for pleasure and to keep the traditions alive. The players of hurling and Gaelic football have some advantages as citizens, but they don't get paid properly in the way that professional football players do. I think that is interesting. We would say in Portuguese that they play with "garra", a word which means play with heart and full of energy representing their provinces or towns, or in other words their identities. I like the emotion when watching a hurling or Gaelic football match, just to see people singing national songs and holding their hands strongly to their chests, in a sign of proud feeling for what they represent. They sing and play with heart.

51

I have done some Irish dancing but not as much as I wanted. It was enough for a tourist see me in a pub and think that I was Irish. If you like to dance, move your body and use up lots of energy, do Irish dance! I consider myself a good dancer, but, contrary to what people think not all Brazilians dance, especially the samba. I have to say that no matter how good you are in dance, try some "river dance" ; that is a good challenge. It requires extremely good physical preparation in addition to learning the steps, and it can keep your body very fit! I had a few opportunities to practice the other traditional dances where all the family dance together and it is really nice to see couples and all the family getting involved in dancing.

The influence of the Catholic religion is intrinsic to Irish culture. We walk around Dublin or Ireland and we see churches in the middle of the cities (some Catholic, some Protestant). Saint Patrick's Day is still celebrated in Ireland and 90% of the population is Catholic. Over the years, Catholicism has given Irish society its values. Most of these have been lost because of changes, the diversity of population and also because of the mistakes of the Catholic Church itself. Now we see part of the new generation (and not so new generation), with different values, sometimes positive and sometimes just as a way to avoid religion. It sounds like they had an "overdose" of rules in the past that don't make sense anymore. Now the Catholic churches and even the Protestant ones are not as full as in the past. This is a good time for thinking about the importance of the role of religion in this society, a very polemic subject to talk about.

In contrast, we can see different religions being introduced. I see it in a positive way. In Brazil we have approximately twelve different religions, from Christian ones, to African, western, and evangelical. Even though Catholicism is still predominant, the diversity makes us more open to discuss different kinds of polemic subjects, with more respect between people from different religions and ethnic groups. Our problem has always been the big difference between rich and poor people (a shameless and sad problem to be solved), and I would say that inside this we can also see some kind of racism too. It is not so clear but it exists.

There are plenty of Brazilians in Ireland right now and Gort is a special case. It is a kind of "Brazilian" town in the middle of Ireland with about three thousand Brazilians living there. I think about the hope those people have in their minds, just to get some different opportunity and to be in a different country. I also see young people in Dublin, some students and some others just trying different styles of life and experience like myself. I wonder sometimes how aware we are about how worthwhile it is to leave our countries and be in a different place and how valuable it is to adapt to living in Ireland and experience the culture. I wonder how they are managing with the new social circumstances that are being created. A good question to bear in mind is what the Irish culture is right now. One day, I was in a public library, one of great and organized places that I like most in Dublin and there was an Egyptian guy who asked me why I had come to Ireland. I said to study English and I had chosen Ireland because of its history and culture. He asked me which culture and it made me think about this. He was asking an interesting question, I really think that the culture that I was talking about was a culture that perhaps doesn't exist anymore. I can see the Irish keeping the language, good music, food, signs from the Celtic culture, but thinking better about it, what is the real culture right now? What is the identity? In which direction is Ireland heading right now?

I think sometimes that at the beginning, all those changes in the country were very different and had a big impact on local people, some positive, others negative. On the one hand, it was also a good opportunity for Ireland to become more multicultural. On the other hand, others, perhaps the older people, have started to feel put out by this situation - too many different people in their country. In many cases, this circumstance created a kind of discrimination in relation to foreign people. I personally felt it myself when an old lady asked me once where I came from and why I was in Ireland. She wanted to know if I was looking for a job and in a negative way tried to tell me that there are no jobs here anymore. Another case was a Brazilian that I met. She told me that her neighbors were complaining about the smell of cooking beans from her flat. They said to her that they were sure she was not Irish. However, I would say that interaction between Irish and other cultures is more normal now and has changed the hegemony of native Irish with different ethnic groups. Now we see Koreans, Africans, Chinese, Polish, Brazilians, Italians, Spanish, Pakistanis, Slovakians, Romanians and so on. Sometimes, we can hear more than five different languages in just one journey by bus from the city centre to the airport or even in the usual places around the city.

It is difficult to think sometimes that Northern Ireland and Republic of Ireland are two different places/countries. This can be confusing. In sports such as rugby and boxing there is only one team, one country. I cannot understand and I suppose that when they are playing against other countries Irish people don't think about the team as composed of Irish from EIRE and from Northern Ireland; on those occasions, it is just one team and theoretically one nation. Maybe one day things will change. I see some advertisements in tourist buses in Dublin to visit the North of Ireland as if it was in Ireland as a whole.

When I leave Ireland at the end of this year (2008) or beginning of next year (2009), it is going to be for good. Perhaps one day I will be back here with my kids and maybe grandchildren and I hope to see Ireland in very good circumstances for all Irish. Maybe I will sing: Ring a ring a rosie, as the light declines, " I remember Dublin city in the rare auld times".

China

*Many Chinese have come to study English in Ireland over the last ten years and some have stayed. I met **Cheng** at the bank where he works in Dublin and I taught **Chu** English.*

Cheng

There have been tremendous changes in China in the past ten years. The economy is booming and more and more people are moving around. They want a taste of what the other life is like and they do not want to be confined in one place. That is the main reason I left China seven years ago.

I grew up in Shanghai, where my family home is. I studied and worked there for three years before coming here. I was more mature than some of the young people are who leave and I had an idea of what I wanted to do. I realised that I was not interested in the work I was doing in transportation and wanted to have a look outside and see how I could further my education. I applied to two countries but Ireland was the only place I was accepted. That is why I came here. I came first as a student and was in a language school for a year. Then I applied for a Master's course in DBS. My first degree was in Computer Science, which I do not really like now. I found I was much more interested in the Marketing side of Business. I set out to do a Master's in Business because I had been working in that field for a couple of years and needed the qualification. Though I was not from a business background, I was accepted to do the MBA because I had had three years experience working in business.

After I graduated, I got a job in one of the financial service companies working in the marketing department. That was a very interesting experience because it was different to my experience in

Shanghai. The business culture was different – the way people think, the way people talk, the way people make jokes – it was difficult for me in the beginning. I would not get what people were laughing at; I would have no clue about jokes. For a while, others would not joke with me because they knew I did not get it. Now since I am working in a place where I am dealing with customers and different clients I am learning. I would say that I have adapted very well.

I think Ireland seven years ago was very different to what it is now. It took me a while to get used to things at the beginning. The people were not very friendly and they saw you as different. That would be the first impression I had but as time has gone by things have changed and people have started to change their attitudes. There are more people coming from the new EU countries, from Eastern Europe, Poland and so on, and Irish people have started to realise that this is the way it is now.

From an economic point of view, China has changed tremendously. The government has opened the country economically to try to encourage foreign investment and many foreign companies have set up branches in China because the labour costs are so much cheaper. The government provides a package to attract these companies. About 500 foreign companies have branches in Shanghai. From a political point of view, there are changes also. The government realises that if it keeps doing things in the same way China cannot keep up with the pace of the world. Politicians cannot hide everything; they have to let people know what the truth is. People need to know when corruption is happening in the government. They have to open up and let people discuss things rather than trying to control everything. People are free to practise religion now. Obviously, there are still some restrictions here and there but I would say it is getting better and better. There is a revival in Christianity in China. There used to be only home churches but now there are churches that are more proper even though the government still has some rules for these in some areas. I would say it is much better than it was 20 years ago.

I am the only child in my family. The policy of having only one child was introduced over 25 years ago. The government did extreme things to people who had second children but now because we are all only children the government allows you have two if both parents come from a single child family. All these only children are very spoilt by their parents. My parents miss me a lot of course but at the same time, they think this is a great opportunity for me to develop and to realize my potential. So they see this as a very important development for me. They can come and visit me so it is not too bad for them.

Officially, there are 50,000 Chinese in Ireland. There is a Chinese cultural centre and a Chinese church. There are two Chinese newspapers and over 500 Chinese supermarkets and many restaurants. Parnell Street is going to be Dublin's Chinatown. You can see all the Chinese supermarkets and restaurants there. I have adapted very well to living in this society. I have made a lot of progress here from being a student to getting a job. My wife is Chinese; I met her at the Chinese Church. My son was born here two years ago. It is difficult for two working people away from family with little support to have more than one kid. Sometimes you have to take time off from work because you cannot take the baby to the crèche if he is sick. My wife is a doctor. She came here from Hong Kong twelve years ago, graduated from the Royal College of Surgeons and now she is a GP. Both of us have settled in well here. Buying a house is very expensive and the price has doubled over the last few years but compared to Hong Kong where my wife comes from it is not as expensive. Prices here are credible for her but for me it is very difficult. Luckily, because of my work in the bank and hers as a doctor, we are able to get a mortgage.

I heard about DBS in Shanghai because they went to China to market there. A guy came and left his business card in our university and that was how I got to know those people. After working for a couple of years I decided to apply to one of those schools and that is how I came here. I sent applications to a few different countries and DBS gave me an offer. They got me the visa and organized everything for me. I would like my child to learn Chinese and I am more worried about him learning Chinese than English. He was born here and he plays with the local people so English is not a problem. It will be interesting to see if a Chinese child who grows up in the West will see himself as Chinese or Irish. From a nationality point of view, he is Irish but at the same time, he was born into a Chinese family. We want him to know his Chinese identity so that is why we will encourage him to speak Chinese at home. Two schools now provide Chinese classes and the church I go to also has Chinese classes for the kids.

The question of Chinese integration into Irish society is mixed. Some of them are integrating quite well but some are struggling because when they arrived they did not have much English and they had not gone through much education. It is difficult for them to pick up whereas for those who have a good knowledge of English and a good educational standard, life is much easier and it is easier for them to adapt to a new society. Not everybody wants to settle down in a new country. After some of them finish their college education and work for a couple of years, they will then go home. For me, having lived here for seven years it would be difficult to settle down in China. The way I think now, the way I talk to people is different, and my friends say that I am different. I can say in a way that I have become more Irish than Chinese. But if you have not been here as long as I have and gone through different phases of your life here you may need to go back to China to develop more. There is plenty of work there now and in some ways, life is easier especially in terms of the cost of living. You also have friends, relatives and family to support you. Therefore, many people choose to go home when they finish their college study. Speaking on my own behalf, I think I have settled in very well into Western society.

Chu

Chu is my family name and Bo is my first name but in China, it is common to call people by the family name. I have the same name as my father but he is known as the equivalent to 'Old Chu' as he gets older. Chinese names are very short; the longest is no more than 4 syllables and therefore many people call you by your first and family name especially when you are 15 years and older.

I grew up in a big city in the north of China about an hour's flight south of Beijing. Like so many families and because of government regulations I am an only child. This was good for me as I got a lot of attention from my parents. My Dad is a film director who makes films and soaps for the TV. He works freelance but is always busy. You can say we are quite well off and would be in the upper levels of Chinese social class. My father studied film in college and my mother has a university education. Her first job was in a type of cooperative about which my father always teases her. She returned to university and did a Master's degree. She passed a special test and now works for the government as head of the labour division.

I studied for a BA degree in a Teacher Training College in China and graduated in 1999 with a specialization in Information Technology. I found that I did not want to be a teacher because I felt very nervous in front of the class. I want to be like my Dad; he can do so many things. He cooks, fixes things and makes all the decisions. I always wanted to travel and my family supported that desire. My Dad took care of the organisation and went to the agency to organize my trip abroad. I applied for a student visa first to Australia but they refused. Then I applied to Ireland they granted me a visa. I had studied English in China and knew a lot of words and grammar but could not communicate effectively. When I first arrived, life was difficult as it was a new environment and a new culture.

I went to a private language school for the first couple of years. At that time around the year 2000, the language schools were very strict and we had to study five to six hours a day five days a week. We had tests and homework every day and there were many activities for us. It cost a lot of money to get here. My family paid €6,000 to the Chinese agency for the flight and application though I know the flight only cost €800. I do not know who got the rest. When I arrived, I paid €3200 on tuition fees and €200 a week to an Irish family to live there. I stayed with the family for only 2 weeks and then I moved out into a flat with seven other students. A Chinese guy helped us find the flat but then we had to pay him money for doing this. It was only a two bedroom flat and there were eight of us living there with two people in a small bedroom, four in the large bedroom and two sleeping in the living room. The landlord thought there were only four of us in the flat and when he came and saw eight of us, he kicked us all out of the flat.

I slept one night in a park, one night in an overnight café and one night in a B and B. Then a friend called me and I was able to move into his house. I have lived in many places since that time. In my spare time, I tried to find a job. A Chinese guy I knew took me to work as a cleaner in a computer company but he wanted me to pay him €200 for introducing me to the job. I refused because I did not have the money and I could not work there. I went back to China for a visit in 2001 and stayed one month.

After I got back to Dublin, a Chinese friend helped me to find a job. I had bought a bicycle from a guy I met on the street. He had long hair and a beard and he offered me the bike for €5. I thought he needed the money for food so I bought the bike but then discovered the bike had been stolen. Anyway, my friend took me to the pub where he worked; it was about 20 minutes by bicycle. It was a bar mainly for old people and the work was easy. I just had to collect the empty glasses from the tables. I thought my friend would want money for introducing me to the job but he did not because he wanted to leave and had to find someone to replace him in the bar so he felt I had done him a favour. I was paid €4 an hour plus tips. The people there were very nice and working helped me a lot. I had my first pint of Guinness there. After a while, I got a better job in a petrol station and made some good Irish friends there.

I was advised to apply to the CAO so that I could attend one of the universities. I did and was accepted in DCU and offered a place on the Foundations Program. I went back to China in 2003 to visit my family and they were very happy that I had gotten a place in university in Ireland. However, I really struggled in my first semester and found that my confidence was shaken by the experience. I passed everything in the first semester but could not continue into the second. It was something like a mental collapse, a kind of phobia and I did not want to go out of the house. I went to the doctor but he could not find the cause of my distress. My immune system was very low and I started taking medication. I thought the reason I had lost my confidence was that my English was not good enough. I went back to Alpha College but my physical condition got worse. I felt very frustrated and angry and the year did not go well.

The following year I returned to DCU and repeated the Foundations Course. I was the oldest student on the course and many thoughts kept rolling around in my head. I found I could not continue coming to class so I studied at home and passed the course. I came back here in January and since then I have been OK. I think I have been under too much pressure. I am trying very hard to please my parents and maybe I am too competitive. I hope to be able to finish this BA in Communications. I need to prove I can do it, go on, and do a Master's degree. I have to renew my visa every year here. In general, I like Ireland and I have learned a lot. My problem is I think that I have been too harsh on myself and I am too competitive. In general, I think the Chinese do well in Ireland.

Colombia

*Ireland has had some real and surreal connections with Colombia. At one time DIT had an exchange program for student architects with Colombia. I met **Dolly** from Columbia in Dublin where she has lived for a number of years.*

I am from a very big family, 12 children of whom I am the second youngest. I grew up in a small town called California, so-called I think after California in the USA because of the gold found there. Recently some company found the biggest deposit of gold ever in that little town. Two companies, one American and one Canadian are currently digging for gold. For years, gold has been extracted but now the companies have made this big find.

My father was a civil servant and he moved to a bigger city in a county called Santander. We lived there for a few years and then moved to the capital of that county. This city was probably the size of Dublin population wise. When we moved there, it was a big change for us, as the city was very busy. I was the second youngest and some of my older brothers and sisters were already married with families. We were not wealthy; my father was the one who worked and my Mum took care of the house. My Mum used to make clothes for us and this was normal for me. We were not well off but we had food and a house.

We have had problems in Colombia for about 40 years now but it did not affect our growing up. Our house was normal and I did not notice anything but people were always talking about politics. I think the situation now is worse and more serious at all levels economically, socially and politically. There is no hope for change right now. I went to primary and secondary schools and when I wanted to go to third level, I had to work and try to study. It was difficult. At that time, more universities were public but now most of them have been privatized. In our town, there was only one public university and it was very hard to get a place there. It was also very difficult to find part time work in the city and if you had a job, you were expected to work from 8 in the morning to 5 in the evening. It was very difficult to work and study. I started a number of courses but I never finished any of them.

Then I met Thomas, my Irish husband, so I did not finish my course. I have two children and I have been busy minding them. He came to Colombia to do some exchange program as an architecture student. He studied in DIT and went to Colombia for 6 months. Then he met me and decided to stay for a year. We came back together with a 3-month-old child; we had another baby and Thomas started working. The plan was to go back to Colombia but the situation in the country got worse and we did not go back. We came to Ireland in 1993 and we are still here. We go to Colombia as often as we can, about every two years. All my family is there and I want my children to experience a little bit of my culture. They can speak Spanish and Thomas also speaks Spanish. I have four grown up nieces living in Dublin, but not with me. Three of them are working with Thomas. One is a graphic designer, one an industrial engineer and one a civil engineer. For them, as foreigners it would not be easy to find this kind of job but Thomas gave them this opportunity because he has his own office. He is doing very well now. I have another niece in Switzerland married to a Swiss guy.

In the big cities in Colombia, you do not feel the trouble, the violence but you feel the economic problems because there are not enough jobs. The jobs are also not very well paid and if you are not happy in a job, they will just tell you to go because there are 500 people waiting behind you for the job. Some employers take advantage of this situation and exploit workers. The Colombian economy is not in such a good shape so it is a risk to try to set up your own business. Multinationals do not want to invest there because of the violence.

For me, living in Ireland is like living in another world. There are good things about Colombia. We have tropical weather and we see the sun all the year round. When I came to Ireland, the weather here was very difficult. The change in language was also difficult because in Colombia, we learn a little bit of English but when I arrived here, I could not understand and could not speak English. I found Irish people quite friendly, and I never had any problems with them. However, I could not find friends as I had in Colombia, close friends - people you know well. I met people here but did not get to know them like my friends in Colombia but here I found the comforts I did not have in Colombia. Here I drive a car. In my family when I was young, we never had a car. Now my brothers and sisters have cars but my parents never had one. We did not have a washing machine; our present to our parents when they were 50 years married was a washing machine. Things are changing now. New couples have these things but when I was young, everything was done by hand.

Another thing that I love about being here in Europe is that it is so easy to travel. In Colombia, you never think about going to the next country because it is so expensive. The country is so big that you can spend your whole life trying to get to know everyplace. Here you can think about the continent and the cost of travel is unbelievable. My nieces are single and they love that too; they can travel. When you see another culture, you learn and you start to appreciate the things in your own culture. It is very educational to travel.

I never heard of negative happenings in Colombia to anyone in my family or friends but in the news you hear these things and the media are terrible. When you hear news of Colombia, it is always about terrible things happening there. When you go there, you do not notice these things. One of the reasons why people do not visit is probably because of what they hear in the media. There are very violent, cruel people in Colombia. We have guerrilla and para-military fighters. A small number of very rich people in Colombia controlled most of the wealth and the guerrillas came into existence to fight the injustices of those few rich people. This was about 40 years ago. Things have changed since then. The government never negotiated with these people and never let them come near power so they have been fighting all this time. The very rich people had these big farms and the guerrillas were threatening them for money. If you wanted to live in peace, you would have to pay a million pesos in Colombian money. The rich people created these para-military groups to fight the guerrillas so the owners of the farms did not have to pay the guerrillas any money.

I think the government is involved in all this. They say our current president is one of the founders of these para-military groups. He is supposed to be democratically elected but you know there is a lot of corruption in the country. You hear that people are afraid to travel around the country because the guerrilla groups may kidnap them and demand money but I never heard of this happening to anybody I know. The campaign of the current president was to stop this kind of kidnapping. He has put military lines on all the main roads and people are now happy because they can travel so they say he is doing great work. People have cars and they are not as afraid as they were before. The government is concentrating on security rather than the economy. We have a drug problem; we grow a lot of drugs so North America is helping the country to eradicate the drug problem. The Americans are investing a lot of money but Colombian money is also going into the war on drugs instead of into education and health so I do not like what the president is doing. At the time of Pablo Escobar, he and many like him paid youngsters to kill their enemies thus making the society more violent, but now there are fewer of these drug barons but the problem still exists.

My sons are 14 and 11 and they love it when they go to Colombia because here they have only two small cousins, girls who live quite far from them. In Colombia, they have cousins the same age with whom they play football. They do all the things that are harder here because of the weather. They love it but they say they prefer to live in Ireland. Perhaps this is because they grew up here and it is more comfortable here. They are fluent in Spanish and English and they are learning French and Irish. I am happy that they are learning more than one language because it is much more difficult to learn another language when you are an adult. Now I am studying at university also. I tried in Colombia but I did not finish anything for different reasons. When the children were small I did courses but then I decided I want a degree. I would love to have perfect English. After I finish the degree, I will see what I can do. They say the first year is easy but the second year is more difficult. By the end of the second year, we need to be writing as a native speaker.

Ireland has changed very much since I came here. People have more comforts and more money now than they had in the early 1990s. What surprised me a lot when I first came was to see so many girls with young babies. In Colombia, we know education is very important and so we try to study. I was shocked to see so many young girls with babies when I came. Perhaps they have the opportunity to study but they are not interested. I do not know the reason. Perhaps they prefer to have a family rather than study.

I missed my culture a lot when I first came. I missed the music and I love to read Latin American literature. When I am at home, I listen to my Latin music. I like music from everywhere and here the radio is not enough for me. It is not easy to get Latin music here. Every time I go to Colombia, I bring back a lot of music or when I travel to Spain, I get some. I was very happy when I found the Institute Cervantes, a Spanish library where you can read and borrow Spanish books; they only have Spanish and Latin American writers. They also have music and videos as well. It is not easy to find Latin American writers' books here in Dublin. Now that I am studying I do not have much time to read.

Another difference is the food; there is Mexican food now but when I first came, I could not find anything. In Colombia, breakfast is very important and we would have a big lunch, the main meal and then dinner. Before we used to have a two-hour break in the middle of the day but now it is only one so people do not have time to go to the house for lunch. My father still takes a siesta in the middle of the day because he has retired. Mexican food is not exactly the same as Colombian because the Mexicans use chili for everything even for sweets I believe. We put the chili sauce on the side and do not put it into everything. It is a tropical world so we have all kinds of vegetables and fruit that you do not see here. The flavour in food is very different as well because food does not have to travel for so long. We eat organic food straight from the garden. We have a lot of markets right in the cities. I remember my Mum going in the morning to buy things for the lunch, fresh food. I miss these things.

I have four grown up nieces living here in Dublin. They are young; they are single and they go out more often than I do. Every time they meet people from Latin America, they introduce them to me. I know people from every Latin American country from Chile, Brazil, Argentina and Mexico. We used to have an honorary consul here but we don't any more. We do not have any kind of club that would unite us all. We celebrate Independence Day on 20th of July and all the Colombians come together but it is up to ourselves to do it. There are few Colombians who stay here for a long time – mostly young people come here for a short time and there are few families because it is difficult for a whole family to get a visa. I am quite happy here. I can study and there are more chances. The trouble in Colombia is that unless you are very good or you have plenty of money you cannot get into a good University and if you are over 40, the chances of getting a job are very slight. Here it is amazing; there is something for everyone.

I tried teaching Spanish. I taught with the Irish Rugby Association whose members were going to Argentina. That was very stressful because they wanted to speak Spanish in two weeks. Now I am busy with University but we shall see in the future.

70

Congo

The Democratic Republic of the Congo, a country rich in natural resources, is also a country where people live impoverished lives in constant danger in many parts. Tim Butcher in his 2007 book 'Blood River' explains, "The humanitarian crisis in the Congo claims lives on a staggering scale. The most recent assessment, published in January 2006 by the eminent British medical journal, 'The Lancet', suggests that 1,200 people die each day in the Congo as a direct result of endemic violence and insecurity." I met **Junior** *in Dublin.*

I was born and brought up in Kinshasa. Growing up in the Congo for me was very privileged because my Dad was a general in Mobuto's army and my Mom was a business woman who worked for presidential private affairs. For most of my early life, I went to Belgium on holidays. In a sense, you might say I led two lives – one in the Belgian system and one in the African. As I grew up, I began to notice differences between how we lived and what was right outside our houses or from meeting the children of the people who used to work for us. That got me into wanting to know a bit more about Zaire (We called it Zaire at the time and for me personally calling it Zaire is somehow making a statement because we do not believe in the new Congo name).

My growing up was under a Belgian school system and it was quite peaceful until I got to around the age of 12. That was when I started having problems. We had soldiers guarding our house and I started selling weapons from our soldiers. When I say weapons, I do not mean big quantities or anything. As a child brought up in a military system, I saw weapons in a very different way to the average person. For me they were normal and I started stealing weapons from our soldiers and selling them to make some extra money. Some of our intelligence services caught me doing this but I could not go to prison because my Dad was a general. I sold the weapons to Lebanese people who sell diamonds. Those people will buy almost anything you have and they usually have ready cash. Our guards were from the presidential military unit and I would take weapons from them, sell them to the Lebanese, and get some money for myself. At the time that I was doing that, I was sort of under punishment for certain things I had done. Other friends of mine would go to the airport and when new Lebanese people came, they would help them get into the country without any documents because we had special presidential permits. When I was caught doing that I was not supposed to be arrested but my Dad said that I should go to military training because that would be a punishment for me. Therefore, I went to military training during the day and at night, I was in a prison. When I was 13, I spent about 4 months between military training during the day and military prison at night. My dad viewed it as a punishment but for me personally, I found it gave me a much better understanding of many things. It helped me understand how our so-called regime was and it made me see that many things did not make a lot of sense.

My Mum wanted to send me to a boarding school in Mobuto's village but one of my aunts thought it was not a good idea. She said the climate was not good and she asked what would happen if one day there was a coup and people wanted to remove Mobuto. Then we kids would be too far away from home and something might happen to us. The best solution for my Mum was to send me to boarding school in South Africa. This is what happened but I would go to the Congo every year for about a month. I would go through a short type of military recycling during the holiday at the same time. I first went to South Africa in 1994 and I came back in 1996 when the war started. I returned to the Congo in December 1996, stayed

72

there during January, February of 1997, and left there in March of
'97. In April 1997, Laurent Kabila took power. When I left, I went
back to South Africa but during those three months back in Congo,
we did not actually go to the front but we went very close. At that
time, there were very big trust problems among most of the units.
What would happen for example is if you were the child of a general
and had a bit of military training, you would be given a unit or a
certain type of command. Things were not organized in the way
that your armies are here. They would give you a command and let
you do whatever you wanted. That is when I got close to seeing
what was going on as Kabila's army got closer in their march
towards Kinshasa. We were in the very last place where we were
supposed to be, the last army post before the capital and we put in
every effort believing that we could stop them because we had
gotten aid from Angola. We realized after a couple of days that it
was not going to work and we had to pull out. Some soldiers were
left because there were not enough planes to take everyone. We got
out because we were the privileged ones.

In my view, the main problem in the Congo arises from the
importance we had during the Cold War. When that changed, many
things had to change. The second problem is, I believe, that
tribalism is destroying the place. You have to understand that my
generation is a different generation. Our parents were brought up in
villages. They came to cities, studied, and got to see a bit of the
western world. We have been brought up in the cities. We went on
holidays to Europe and we don't have any of those tribal notions that
destroy them. Another problem and probably a bigger one at the
moment is 'colza'. This is a mineral that is needed for computers and
mobile phones and in 1994 or 1995, the biggest reserves of colza in
the world were discovered in Congo. Though Congo is very rich in
minerals, the riches in a sense do not belong to us. They have been

mortgaged and even when we say the people in power today are corrupt they have hardly any money. Now when it comes to gold and colza, American companies mainly control them. When it comes to diamonds, they are usually shared between Lebanese and Jewish companies. Mobuto used to work with the Lebanese and when Kabila came he wanted to change things so he brought in the Jews.

The real difference between the Arab oil rich countries and ours is that when the Arabs get oil money, the money is deposited in banks in America and the Americans still have a certain power of investment. In the Congo, if I am a diamond merchant, I would allow you get diamonds from here and then I would put the money into a private bank account and I would not be able to be manipulated totally, because I would keep some of the money secret. You would not have enough power over the money and that is where the big difference is. When I look at it in a wider sense, I realize that colonization has not changed. We have a saying that goes: *'they first came in as explorers; the second time they came in as missionaries; then they came in as colonizers and now they are coming back as investors'.* I believe that if we are not strong enough to take care of our riches and our wealth, whoever is stronger can take it from us and in some ways they deserve it. This should make us wake up and want to hold on to it.

When you look at what we have done under true colonization, we have had certain institutions, for example, justice and so on and even if they don't work the concept of those institutions is there. But I think in Africa we have messed up what western society has. Here you have your institutions but I believe that behind these you have a kind of invisible system that keeps it all together. I believe that the western world has certain types of invisible governments, transnational, that have certain views. Since the time of Rhodes and the Rhodes conspiracy and all that kind of thing, I believe that there is a sort of underlying government that might be hereditary or superrich or whatever. When you look at certain things, they keep things going though they can create trouble too. This government does not have to sit anywhere – you have got the Rothschilds and you have different groups. Now if you can control five big companies in the world and you can have people on the boards you can control things. True control of the western world started with the banking system. The people who control that system are the people who truly control what has happened.

When the war started in the Congo in 1996, I was in South Africa. By March 1997, I realized nothing could be won. We had lost many soldiers and there was a lot of treason on our own side. Soldiers were not well paid, in fact they were hardly paid at all. When the President gave money for military equipment, they did not buy it and I know this from personal experience because even when my Dad was given money he did not buy the equipment. He took the money for himself. That is where the problem was and even the mercenaries that were brought with us to help were not doing their job. In the so-called Kabila army, there were no Zairians at all. The front was made up of Ugandan Special Forces, one or two South African mercenaries and Rwandans. The Ugandan forces were doing most of the attacking and the South Africans did the strategic work. They were all being paid directly by the Americans because in the old days Mobuto was the main CIA man in Central Africa. But things shifted. Take the Angolans – well they used to be Marxist and that is why you had a long war there while the Americans supported Savimbi. Then the Americans wanted to get rid of Savimbi and they started working with the ex- Communists guys. Right now, the main CIA guys in Africa are Musevveni of Uganda and Dos Santos of Angola.

My Dad went with Mobuto when he left Zaire. But instead of going to Morocco my Dad went to Belgium. My Mom stayed in hiding in the Congo. I went to South Africa. In the beginning when Kabila came, they just took our houses, our cars and our companies. They gave certain orders to freeze our bank accounts. At that time, they did not do anything wrong or harm anybody. They were a few months in power before things started to change. People who had worked for us like our military drivers, our security guards, and people like that, were killed because they had worked for us and they could not be trusted. They could not be taken to jail because at the time Kabila's army had a new doctrine which was that to take someone to jail and feed him would cost $3 – $4 a day but to kill a person would cost about 90 cents to $1 dollar for the bullet. If you belonged to the presidential division of the army and if you were caught, you were killed.

About my journey from South Africa to Europe, well you know legally you cannot say because you are supposed to seek asylum in the first country you go into. Before I came to Europe, I got involved in a small story in Ivory Coast. I got a few contacts of mercenaries who used to work back in the Congo. They had a new idea that something was about to happen in Ivory Coast. At that time, I was much younger and just emerging from that war and I had a great urge because I still believed that we could go back to Congo, as Mobuto was still alive. We believed that if we could help the guys from Ivory Coast, then that country would become our staging base to get back into the. Congo. One very powerful general and a very good friend of my Dad was in South Africa. He sort of financed us and asked me and another guy if we wanted to go on an adventure where there would not be much combat and where we could go and take power easily. He said it would not be very dangerous. I went to Ghana first and from there we were smuggled into Ivory Coast. I stayed in Ivory Coast for almost a year. I went there just before the military coup; we saw the coup through and then a few months later I got out of there. It was difficult because we did not get the money we were supposed to be getting and I had many problems. Then I decided that Africa was not for me. I could see how they would tell you that there would be a coup here or there and to try and go there. You would either end up getting killed or something would happen. I just thought to myself that I had quite enough. I would be better somewhere else.

From Ivory Coast, I went to Gabon because my uncle was an ambassador in Angola. My Mum is half Angolan and though I have never been to Angola, I know some families there. This uncle was the Angolan ambassador to Gabon and he said that from there he could organize a French visa for me. The condition was that because I had been involved in some of the military coups in Ivory Coast and had been involved with some of the South African mercenaries that I could not live in France. I could only stay there for one month. He had an argument with the French Ambassador in Gabon who said that he could let me in but only for one month. Then he said that I would have to get out of France or I would be arrested. When I got to France, I made my way to England and from there to Ireland.

I have been in Ireland three years now. To me personally, Ireland has been the loneliest place I have ever been in my life. It is the coldest place and when I say cold I do not mean weather wise; mainly it is the cold of human relations. I do not necessarily call it outright racism because it is not only racism. You see when people meet in pubs here they think that is closeness but it is not and this is just a big smoke screen that hides the true separateness of the Irish people. Maybe in your history people were much closer. I understand that when I see some things but today with the economic prosperity people are being driven apart. When I came into Ireland after living in England for a year, I had a bit of an English accent. That created many problems for me. I did not know about the animosity between the countries because outside Ireland, people think that England and Ireland are the best of buddies and that they are the same place. When I first came and I was talking with people, they would say to me 'you have a bit of an English accent'. Then I would say 'yeah I lived in the UK and I loved the place'. It took about a month for me to realize that it was not like this when someone explained things to me and I had to change my accent. I know many Nigerians here; in most European countries, there is a mixture of nationalities.

Ireland opened its doors and the first group that came was the Nigerians. I do not mean to say that every Nigerian is bad. Let us face it most Congolese guys are not criminals. They are soft on those things. If you go to South Africa, there is crime and if you go to Nigeria, people are into crime. But in the rest of Africa you find soft people. The Nigerians are real warriors and as a black person, I believe this has sort of traumatized Irish people. I also believe that most Irish people do not have any interest in approaching other people and finding out about them because it does not really change anything in their lives. If you look at the history of Ireland, you see that every foreigner who has come here has come as an invader. I believe there is a psychological, genetic in-built thing that even though they did not live through the invasions they are born with a kind of tiny resentment of whatever is foreign. A study says that the grandchildren of people who suffered through the Nazi holocaust have stress symptoms and even though they never lived through the holocaust, they are born with certain signs. So I believe that we can carry a certain psychological genetic tendency even though we never experienced the event.

When blacks were new in England, during the first ten years progress was very slow. When you compare it with the progress made here in the first ten years it is much better here. In England, it has been 50 – 100 years since the first blacks started to come and here it is just ten years. When you put it in that perspective, things are OK. For me personally I would not want my kids to be brought up in Ireland. We do not have any dignity here. If something happens to me when I walk out into the street, I am not going to report it and I am not going to ask for my rights. The other sad thing about integration is that until it becomes politically beneficial to your leaders to have a totally integrated society we will not see real changes. Now it is not politically beneficial for them. The fact that people are here is economically beneficial to the government but that is about it.

The other sad thing about people in Ireland is they are being manipulated by politicians. The greatest manipulation that I have seen was during the nationality referendum about children born in Ireland. The government tricked Irish people. When the referendum was held it was done with the European referendum. There were two things being voted on at the same time. If the government presented it only as a European referendum there would have been only a 40% turnout. Then they realized this is an issue that enrages people so they decided to put the two together on the same day. Then you had 80% turnout. Sadly, the average person did not understand that they were being used to show Europe that the Irish people are concerned about Irish issues. They did not tell Europe that there was a nationality referendum at the same time.

I have tried to study human psychology and wherever you go human motives are the same and power has the same effect even if the scale of power is different. Wherever, power usually does the same thing to people. If something is beneficial for people they do it and if not they don't do it. I myself would have liked to live the illusion of the cosy life in Europe but now I believe that I have to go back to Congo and if not Congo at least somewhere in Africa. You see I would like to have the protection of a European nationality first to give my life some kind of guarantee. If I got into any kind of difficulty and had that nationality, it could save my life. I do like material things, good economics and money as such but I believe that I could make a better life in Africa. You cannot really change too much of Africa but if you could make some effort here and there in certain things, I believe that my life would be more useful in Africa. It does not necessarily have to be the Congo it could be Gabon or somewhere else. I would like to go back and forth between Africa and Europe.

I am far from getting an Irish passport. It has been three years and I am still an asylum seeker. I don't have the right to work in Ireland. I do not have the right to study in Ireland. The first problem is that I give a military account of certain things and you have not had military people coming to seek asylum. You have mainly had civilians and you do not have anyone who understands the military reasons. On paper and according to all the regulations I should get asylum but the people who are the adjudicators do not know anything about the Congo. Even when you explain things to people here, they believe that things work in the Congo the same way they do here. You tell them that the army there was treated as if it was your own private company. We did things that they cannot understand here. That is where my main problem has been. Congolese people who come from a much lower social stratum have a much easier time here.

People who came earlier than 2002 had an easier time but when I came in 2002 things had started to change. When we go to the courts, the decision rests with one person and when we talk to them, we explain. I had another problem. I was advised not to tell them that I speak English and I had to have an interpreter whose English was much worse English than mine. Half way through the interview, I realized that his English was bad but he still has that job. I was refused asylum the first time and it was not about the story but about the translation. The second problem is the people who make those decisions know nothing. They read three or four pages of the UN report on the country and that is it. They know nothing about how things go on the ground and that is the sad thing about Ireland. If I tell my story in Belgium, they will know exactly what is true and what is not. There are things I could explain to them about how the government works and the army works and they would know. Maybe that is because we have had a long history with Belgium. I appealed the first time when I was turned down and through that appeal, I was given a judicial review. When the guy refused again my solicitor went and explained that we would take it to the High Court. They usually don't want these cases and have to pay for your fees if they find out that you are right. But when they took my papers there they refused them and told me to go back and have another try.

So I am on an appeal again. It can take over 5 – 6 years to get through this. They keep going on and on waiting for you to make a mistake. My Dad is back in Congo now and they reinstated him in

81

the army because they are trying to unite people but they have lowered his rank. It is like they are trying to keep him away from the rebellion. He is there as a token and whenever there is a bit of trouble he gets arrested. My Mom is in Angola. Things went bad for her at first. She was arrested and tortured because she was responsible for certain business endeavours of the presidential office. She was incarcerated for about a year – no trial – and when she got out, she had to go to Angola. The rest of my family are in Belgium, France, Germany and Canada – there is nobody back in the Congo. Without any status here, I cannot do anything. I cannot plan what I will do in five years and even in a year. I cannot get into education or do anything.

France

*Connections both religious and political between Ireland and France are centuries old. In recent years, we have learned to enjoy the social and cultural aspects of each others' countries. I met **Pascal** at the Language School where we both worked.*

I grew up in Versailles where I went to school. I went to university in Paris and I had to commute every day by train. It was quite a long trip. I studied about Ireland in university. There was a choice, to take something about Ireland including the Republic of Ireland, Northern Ireland and the military relations between Ireland and England in addition to studying American Literature.. So it was like a little bit of history of three English speaking countries – the economics, the history, the past – that is how my interest in Ireland started.

Thanks to all that, I went to the Irish Embassy in Paris to collect more material to write an essay and to make a presentation about the country. This was in the 1980s. When I went to the embassy, it was a kind of love at first sight. I met a cute little Irish lady who and very warm and friendly. She invited me to sit and relax and she came back with a lot of brochures and books. There was plenty for my research. I asked her how much I owed her and she said *'oh it is all free, take whatever you want'* and she produced a plastic bag for me. That was my first contact with Ireland. This really stuck in my mind. I read everything. It took me some time; I made a presentation. I was annoyed because the other students didn't know much about Ireland, the economy and all that and they didn't want to believe that it was a potential economy starting to grow and that there was something there. They were all surprised. It was a bit annoying because I was the only one to think in a positive way about the place.

But it happened; just a few years after my presentation there was a boom and the Celtic Tiger happened years later. Therefore, I thought I was right. I did not invent it, just from the statistics and from an analysis of the figures, I could predict that something was starting there. It was growing but maybe nobody was paying attention. Before coming to Ireland I went to the States. That was interesting but I decided that it was not for me. This was not because of anything other than it was a long way to go and if I settled there it would have taken me too much time to come back. It was also not the same mentality at all. It was interesting but it was very complicated. In my experience in America, they are keen on the family but they do not have real friends. They are very friendly, very practical, and very intelligent. However, they stick to their family, their tribe but they do not keep in touch with their friends. When they move from one state to another, they do not write; they don't keep in touch. Just the family, that was all. For a holiday, it's great but to settle I do not think so.

In Ireland, there is a difference between the countryside and Dublin. There is not the same mentality; there is not the same accent. But I observed and I learned here. Before arriving, I really wanted to settle. When I did my first trip, it was not to give it a try; it was to come, settle and stay. It was not too difficult to adjust. I came here to work, to live and to start a new life. The most important people, the key people in my family had died. Things were not great in my life and I needed a change of scenery, a radical change whatever it was. Leaving my country was the right decision for me. Many people are attached to their country; many French people are attached to their country as are many Irish people so it is not for everybody. It depends. I did not feel lost. I did not miss my family any more. I did not think of them a lot; just at weekends like that. So it was not a big thing for me.

I have been in Ireland for ten years now. Things have changed over the years. I live in County Wicklow and when I came, there was no Spar shop. Now there are a lot of renovations, new shops and novelty things. The roads have also changed and the roundabouts and some things you will hardly recognise. Some of the changes are for the better but on the other hand, I think people's attitudes to material things may have been affected. You feel people just want material things, an 07 car, a house and if people become like that maybe it is not so good. I suppose it is the same in every country. When I go back to France, which is not on a regular basis, there are many superficial people living there as well. Not everybody of course is like that here. I have my pets here and they are Irish. I rescued them in Co Cork and Co Wicklow. They are not French but I love them and they bring me a lot of pleasure as only people who love animals will understand. I have my harmony here but not everybody will have it in the same way. It all depends and not everybody will find harmony in the same way. I love the countryside, the fields, the trees. If you hate the countryside, it will be a problem. Some people can leave their country and live in hot countries and exotic places; these are different experiences and I can understand that need. I do not have any trouble with the weather here. It is fine with me but I can see the effects of global warming here. There are three big greenhouses in the property where I live. In 1996 there were no grapes. Ten years later, there are grapes everywhere. It is getting hotter here so global warming roll on in Ireland. I myself do not like the weather too hot but I can understand people who do like something hotter and drier.

My food preferences are not exclusively French. I like exotic food, Japanese, Indian food, Italian. I also like roasted Irish turkey and Irish potatoes, the red ones. I love the brown bread here. We do not have brown bread in France. This bread is exploding with vitamins and is beautiful to taste. The basic good healthy foods are here. I don't go for the cream and the butter. It does not matter. If you do not take it, you do not take it. You are free to choose what you want. With the food and on the road, I never feel like an outsider. I never go to the pub on a regular basis; that is not a problem. If you stay at home the French way that is OK. You can go to the pub occasionally but I do not go on a regular basis, that is not my style. I do not need that, it is not part of my personality. But I can understand why people go. It helps them to relax. I do not drink so I would not go for drink either. I don't need it but I can understand people doing it.

Germany

*Germans were some of the first Europeans to settle in rural Ireland in the 1970s attracted often by the unspoilt natural environment. I met **Ulrike** at the Language School where we worked.*

I am Ulrike and I came to Ireland in 1981 from Berlin where I was in college. I came to Dublin because I met an Irish man in Berlin. I came back here with him so he could finish his degree in Trinity College. I am still here and I am afraid I fought all my personal battles in Ireland. I have not contributed much to society because I came up against what I think are typical phenomena in Ireland, alcoholism and gambling. I didn't expect it and it took me years to come to terms with it and to find my way out. For me, in 1981, the experience of coming from Berlin, a city pulsating with life and lots of views and ideas to a Dublin at the other end of the continent was quite traumatic. I suffered from total culture shock even though it was within Europe and I fought hard to survive here. I had to come to terms with having children with a man who was an alcoholic and a gambler.

For me, Ireland was difficult. On a personal level, I found the Irish hypocritical from the beginning. They were not open. In terms of the educational system I did think that the Irish had a lot of knowledge but I felt that they did not think for themselves, did not come to their own conclusions about things and that there was a lot of hypocrisy and dishonesty. I have lost everything a couple of times round here. The problem is that there is no support because alcoholism is accepted by all the different classes. There is something I could not really comprehend. People can drink away their family wealth and if you disagree with it, you are seen as the black sheep. I came up against religious prejudices as well because

I was a Protestant though not even a practising Protestant. The only good thing was that when my children were small even though times were difficult there was a stronger connection to Irish people because there were other people with young children and that would tie or bind you together. Now I have a couple of good friends but for different reasons that have nothing to do with Irish society. I have found that you cannot get close or intimate with Irish people even when you are from the same cultural background as them. I thought it had to do with the Catholic Church and religious prejudice that forced them to remain private. There may also be private things within themselves. I think up to this day I feel like a blow-in. When I first came from Germany, I was definitely exotic which I could not understand because I considered myself just like the others. I could not understand why I should be seen as strange or different.

About the educational system here, I remember one of my children's teachers said once that there is a conspiracy to keep the Irish people from learning to think and that is my impression as well. This has not changed over the years and though my children went to the Irish German School, the most shocking thing was that they were never encouraged to think for themselves. They were given texts to learn off by heart for exams. Therefore, even though students get a lot of general knowledge there is not a lot of encouragement to think for themselves and to come up with choices that are outside the norm.

In general, I like individual Irish but I do not like Ireland as a society. It is better now than it used to be because in the past it was closed and very cautious of anybody who came from anywhere else. You were treated kindly but people were not particularly interested in you. My time in Ireland has been OK to some extent but I would prefer to have been in other places though not necessarily in Germany.

The new generation in Ireland is different and I think that politically the country is a little bit more transparent than it was before. People have woken up and you cannot get away with things as you did before. Things like tax evasion here are a national hobby and if you do not do it, you are considered crazy. I think when I first came there was a lot more poverty and people had to think about themselves. Time and people's sense of time have changed and people have learned to be more punctual.

What I found here in Ireland is that people did not acknowledge their prejudices against other nationalities. They thought that they were free of prejudices but I do not think that any country is free of prejudice. It is only now when foreigners have come that they realise they have prejudices and racial issues. I think the way Irish people try to see themselves is that they are fun, harmless and innocent and they don't do anything to harm anybody. By comparison with other countries, they may still have a victim mentality. When other national groups came into Ireland, the Irish began to realize that they may have some of the same issues that other nationalities have. The Irish like to see themselves as being 'cute' in the American sense. They believe themselves to be nice and that there is nothing nasty about them.

I think the younger generation in Ireland is more open and has more exposure to other nationalities. They make friendships and they probably deal with it quite well. The older generation I think are still stuck in the same groove. Personally, where I am coming from I think Ireland has a huge wound. The questions of gambling and alcoholism are very widespread but the whole of society tries to protect itself and deny it. As a result, a lot of damage has been done to family members and society. It really is a shame. Nowadays I think people are becoming more health conscious. But I think for generations families had to struggle because I don't think there is any family that has not been touched by alcoholism. This may explain why Ireland did not do well economically. I remember giving a dinner party in my first years in Ireland. I made dinner for our friends who were all Irish. I expected everyone to arrive by 8 o'clock. Nobody showed up until 11.30, and I wondered why. I was so disgusted that I threw a scene, which I shouldn't have done because I didn't know them that well. When I came, I found people didn't do anything except drink.

Denial of facts and an inability to face up to reality is also very prevalent. Irish people try to cover up some behaviour they cannot deal with by telling a funny story. In my case, when the relationship was just about over because of his drinking and gambling his mother suggested that I buy myself some more sexy underwear so he would not have to go to the pub. At that stage, I was only delighted to have him out of the house. There is this absolute inability to do something about the problem, except to cover it up.

There are good things as well. Irish are funny and for me it was an eye-opener as well coming from Germany. I am not an organized German, maybe disciplined but not organized. For me coming here was easy in that respect because I did not have to try to live up to the German standards of organization. I liked that attitude of if it does not happen today, it may happen tomorrow or the day after. For me that was a great relief. I embraced that easily. I know there are many negative aspects to that but for me it was definitely good.

Otherwise, I personally feel I have lost myself in Ireland and I feel that I have lost touch with a lot of what is going on in the world outside. I have been so tied up in my personal battles here that I am only starting to come out of it now. When I came to Ireland I was wide eyed and full of buzz but I feel I lost myself and I am only starting to come back to my old self. For me Ireland has been hard but I have learned a lot about myself. I would definitely have lived a very different life if I had stayed in Germany but maybe I would not have learned so much about myself. It has been very hard I have to say.

In the '80s, people used to try to excuse everything by saying *'well you know we are like this because of the British'* but I wanted to say *'well you know that was a long time ago.'* I understand all of this better now and I know that anyone with a bit of initiative would get up and go out of Ireland. Maybe what is lacking in the society is that those people who would be willing to think differently or out of the norm were not here to influence the society. I find it amazing how willing the Irish are to let themselves be put into a boxed society and to be what is required of them. I cannot understand it. When I came here, I was in my '20s and my in laws' family were smart well-educated people. However, when we talked about religion they would come out with remarks like *'Protestant people can be nice too'.*

People don't exercise their democratic rights here and cause change to happen. In Germany if something was not being done people would refuse to pay their taxes until something did get done. I remember a Canadian friend of mine came to study here and one day the bus was half an hour late and she said she would not pay. She expected the other people in the queue to do the same. The bus driver just said *'everybody pays; a half hour late is nothing'.* She couldn't understand how people would put up with it. I think if people united, things might get done. I think the only time something did happen was when people refused to pay road taxes because of the pot holes in the road and the holes did get filled in. There are initiatives such as people who form groups to work on social areas.

Another thing that is hard to comprehend is that 25% of the adult population is considered to be illiterate and four out of five people in the inner city area cannot read and write. I find that is dreadful and nothing is being done about it. I felt that this could not happen in any other European country. People would be inflamed if nothing was being done about it.

India

*The following four interviews illustrate the multi-cultural, and multi-religious nature of India in addition to the diversity of contributions made to Irish society and Irish culture by some of these new voices. I met **Sujada** on a bus in Dublin and we met later to talk about her time in Ireland.*

I was born into a family in Madras (Chennai) that was not very Catholic. My mother was a Protestant and my father a Catholic but my mother had to become a Catholic to marry him. My father was an army man so he was often out and only came back for about two months every year. He served in the Indian army all over the country. My mother brought us up as Catholics. She took us to Mass almost every day and reminded us of family prayer. I lived in a village and we only had five classes in the school so I had to go to boarding school. While studying there, somehow I decided I would like to become a nun. When I was a teenager, I did not bother going to church but once I reached the end of school my family started talking about marriage. However, I made up my mind that I wanted to go on studying. I began to study Mathematics. When I had finished two years in College, I decided I wanted to become a nun. My father never thought I would go through with it. He was anxious for me to marry but my mother encouraged him to let me go. I joined the International Congregation convent thinking I could go to Africa where people were poor and where I wanted to help.

The International Congregation is a German order. I did all my teacher training in Bangalore. I worked in remote villages helping children to read and write. We had school outside under the trees and I really enjoyed that. When it came to my third year, I had to take my final vows and we were asked where we wanted to go. I wrote Botswana in Africa. They sent me to Germany and I spent five years there in the motherhouse; I learned German where I worked with young people. The house is on the borders of Germany and Holland in a place called Style where our founder founded the congregation. There were a thousand sisters, all of whom were German except me living in a massive house.. In the beginning, I had a very hard time, a new language, a new culture, out of my home country. I stayed there for five years, after which, I was told I could go back to India if I wanted to. Before I left Germany, I was told to do a course here in Ireland, to prepare me to train young sisters in the convent, to become something like a novice mistress. That was when I came to Ireland. The congregation had two houses here at that time, one in Rathfarnham and the other in Maynooth. Both houses are closed now. At first, I went to stay in Rathfarnham and took the course in Blackrock College for one and a half years.

Then I went back to India where I was taking care of young sisters who wanted to become nuns. I spent two years in India before I was called back to Ireland, and asked to be director of three girls who had just joined the convent. Two of these were Irish and one British. I came back to Ireland to do this job but eventually two of the girls left the congregation but one Irish girl stayed. She is from Kilmacud near Kilkenny. Nobody joined the convent from 1992; there were no vocations at all. I asked my congregation if I could do something here with different religions. In Birmingham, there are many Indians and we have a play school. I asked if I could go and help people there since there were no vocations in Ireland.

I went to Birmingham where I spent time with many Indians, Hindus and Buddhists as well as Christians. I went to visit their families and got to know them. While there, I went to study in Birmingham University and I did a Master's in Inter-Religious

94

Dialogue. I worked for nine years in Birmingham. I did social work and there was the Birmingham Council of Faith of which I was secretary. We had many meetings to which we invited different faith groups so I learned a lot about different faiths.

After nine years in Birmingham, I was transferred back to Ireland. I went to Maynooth where we have sisters from all over the world especially from non-English speaking countries. They come to learn English and then go off to the missions somewhere usually in Africa. I am in charge of the sisters now. They also do other courses besides learning English. At the moment, there are two Indonesian sisters studying English in Harcourt Street. A Ukrainian sister is studying in Milltown; she was in Maynooth at first. Many sisters come here; they stay for a year or two and then go off to the missions. I take care of them, look after all their needs and organize visas and anything else they need. I help them to become part of the community. That is my main job. Usually they are funded by whatever country they come from but sometimes this is not possible. For example, when they come from a poor country like Indonesia that country is not able to pay for them and then we get money from the motherhouse in Rome. We are an international congregation and some countries are very rich while others are very poor. The rich countries put money together and distribute it wherever the need is. We have a very big congregation in India, at least 400 to 500 sisters working there. We have hospitals, schools; in Bombay, we have a very big hospital and we have boarding schools. We have leper colonies; we have orphanages; and we work with street children.

I have been coming and going to Ireland for the last 18 years. I have seen many changes during that time. When I came in 1988, there were not many foreigners here. I was younger at that time and people would look at me and say how gorgeous and beautiful I looked. I felt the warm welcome here and people were very friendly. But there have been very rapid changes over the 18 years and now there are a lot of foreigners here. When I first came, I felt a foreigner because there was no one else like me but now I see many of my own people here. I feel at home here; I feel really at home here. My neighbours are very friendly and I feel one with them, maybe it is because I have lived here for so long.

Every year missionaries go to different dioceses to speak about the missions. This year I am doing Cork; last year I was in Cavan. Wherever I go in the countryside people are really friendly and welcoming. Now and then, I hear people say that they don't like foreigners but honestly I have never experienced anything like that. I am an open person and I would talk to anyone. I would also look at the positive things about people. If someone speaks to me in an angry way, I would just think that she had had a bad day. That is how my thinking is so I do not see any negative things around me. People are very welcoming and hospitable. I have very good neighbours and if I am at the door, they call and ask how I am. I do not feel out of place here though of course when I look at the colour I do but that is just a superficial thing. I think human beings are the same all over the world. Whether you are in India or here, it is the same. I meet new people who have come from India and they all seem to be happy with things here. People say how happy they are to have Indian nurses and how good they are. But the warmth and welcoming that I found when I first came to Ireland is not here now. I think it is because there are so many foreigners and I am just one among them all.

I think also that the economic prosperity has changed life style and values. When I came in 1988, I used to love to go to the houses and they would often invite me for a cup of tea. We would sit and talk about things but that does not happen now. First, everyone is very busy now. Twenty years ago, it was not busy like today. Now it is rush, rush, rush and money talking. People talk about holidays; they go here and there, and they talk about the food and the holiday. When I first came they would ask me about India, the poor and the mission but they don't do that anymore. But I understand the other side. People themselves go out now more than in those days and they see everything including the poverty. People, for example, the middle class give to the poor but the very rich don't like to give. It is the same in India, the poor and the middle class give but not the rich and you see that also when there is a collection. But I think people are becoming a little selfish now.

When I go to Cork and places like that, I am really going to say thanks to people because they are very generous. When the tsunami hit, people gave generously and I saw that in India. I also want to say thanks to people for the missionaries they sent over the years, thousands of missionaries who went all over the world. For example, in Madras in India I was taught by Presentation Sisters and there were Loreto sisters and so many more. So I am basically telling the people thanks for all the missionaries who came to us and asking them for prayers. I also want to tell people how blessed we are in this country – we are so blessed because we have plenty rain and we always have food here. Even people who cannot work get some money on the dole but in India, it is not like that. So we should stand back and look at all the good things we have and share with people who are less fortunate than us. That is my message when I go to churches and I do not directly ask for money but I tell them where the money goes. Recently we opened a house in South Africa and an orphanage for the AIDS orphans. When we get money, we use it to support the sisters there. We send the money to Rome and then they distribute the money.

Now we are not many sisters here in Ireland and Rome helps us when we need help. We also have two sisters who get pensions. I go back to India once every four years. I went in 2004 and I will go again in 2008. My mother is still alive and I have two brothers and two sisters in India. They are all married. My elder brother joined a seminary. He wanted to become a priest but he could not because as the oldest one in the family it was his duty to take care of the rest of us. So my father put him in the army. He spent 25 years in the army but now he has left. He has started an orphanage and he works with orphans in Madras. He is not far from Pondicherry, a very beautiful place in India.

I sometimes go to schools and talk to children especially those who are preparing for first Holy Communion but now I am very busy. We have one sister who has cancer and I take her to chemotherapy and take care of her. I do find when I go to the schools now that it is hard to get the children to concentrate for very long. You must say everything in five minutes because they cannot concentrate for longer than this. In Birmingham, I was able to do a lot of things with different religious groups because most of the people in the Muslim community were from places like India and Bangladesh but here they are from Saudi Arabia and so on and they don't understand me. The problem here in Ireland is that communities like the Anglicans, Protestants and Catholics must learn to get along together before you even think about Hindus or Buddhists. Here people don't understand about other communities but in the UK there are thousands of them living together. Maybe in ten years or so it will be relevant but now it does not seem to be.

But you can see the changes in Ireland. When I went on the roads 18 years ago, they were full of potholes but look at them now they are amazing. I travelled the road from Dublin to Cork 32 times this year and it was very easy. Next year I will go to the diocese of Down and Connor; I drive to the place on Saturday afternoon for evening mass and sleep in a convent or whatever is organized for me. I speak at all the masses on Sunday and I come back to Dublin on Sunday evening. I know the country very well; I love the country and Ireland is blessed with so many good things. The land is wonderful, there are fields and forest, and it is all so green. People say there is too much rain but where I come from it is all dry, hot and humid. I really enjoy the weather here and there are seasons, which we don't have in India. It is beautiful and the leaves falling around – people have everything here.

*I met **Dr Puri** at the Interfaith Roundtable and later visited him at his home.*

My name is Jaber Singh Puri and I am a doctor by profession. I am working as a consultant anaesthetist in our Lady of Lourdes Hospital in Drogheda. I am a Sikh, born in New Delhi in 1951. I was brought up and educated in the Sikh way of life in India. I did my schooling in New Delhi, studied medicine and got a postgraduate certificate there. I worked for seven years in India.

In 1980, I went to Africa because I was looking for adventure, for greener pastures. When I arrived, I liked it very much. The lifestyle was very good; I stayed for seven to eight years but then I thought that professionally I was falling behind so I decided to move to Europe. I applied for registration with the medical council of Ireland because there was no need to do an examination here. Everything was based on my experience and my qualifications. I got temporary registration here in November of 1988 in the middle of winter and started working as a registrar. My first job was in St Luke's Hospital in Kilkenny, as locum for six weeks after which I got another six months in the same hospital. after which Then I left there in June of the following year and started working in Vincent's Hospital in Dublin. I worked also in the Eye and Ear Hospital in Blanchardstown. I have worked in about 18 hospitals around the country. I got the fellowship in 1993 and started working as a consultant here and there. I have worked from Dublin to Drogheda to Bantry, all over the country. Finally, I got the job in Drogheda.

I did not move my family around all the time. In 1989, I decided that my family should live in the one place even if I had to keep moving. I bought a house in Palmerstown and got involved with my neighbours who were very good. They are still in touch with me. There were not many Sikhs in Ireland at that time. I remember when I was in Kilkenny and I went to the store the children would gather around me and ask me if I were a genie or Aladdin. I used to tell them that I am a Sikh from India and I work in St Luke's. I would sit around with them on the floor or on a staircase and I would answer all their questions. I never felt bad about that because the children wanted to know and it is their nature to ask questions. They were not discriminating in any way; they were curious to know this man with the turban and beard. They gained in knowledge and I had the patience to tell them all that. My wife used to say when we went shopping – 'oh your friends have come'. I never forgot those kids. I felt I should impart the knowledge and I never felt offended by their questions. At that time there was no racism or discrimination in Ireland.

My children were brought up here and my daughter got married to a Sikh boy who came to Ireland to study. After 2001, many students came to Ireland instead of the USA. She met him in Dublin where she is working now.   Now I have a grandchild. I grew up in India but I gave India only seven years of service, more than that to Zambia and 18 years here, almost two decades of my life here. This is home away from home for us. We go to India very often to visit our families with whom we have good ties. We don't know where the children will finally settle so eventually we will spend half time with them and half time in India when I retire. I have been in Drogheda seven years and I have a permanent job there. I travel from Lucan every day because my son is studying here and the school is near our home. People were surprised when I bought the first house after just arriving in the country. It was very difficult at that time especially for foreigners to arrange a mortgage. But I got help and got the mortgage. I thought instead of paying rent it was better to pay for my own house. I worked hard and I still have that first house.

Things have changed here since I came. The economy has grown. From '94, '95, '96 onwards the economy really sprung up. The value of property has gone up. When I bought the first house, it was about £52,000 and now it is worth more than a half million. When we first came, the people were very friendly, they were inquisitive and wanted to know about us. They were lacking in certain points. They didn't know anything about us but they asked about the culture. But when a lot of people started to come that is when the bad words started. Before 1997, I never got a comment. After that we got comments regularly such as *'you asylum seeker, you this, you that'*. Everywhere you found the comments and I think it was because people felt threatened. After 9/11, it became more rampant. They started throwing stones at us and calling me 'Taliban' and 'Osama Bin Laden'. The children and adults shouted at us; even in the hotel foyer in the countryside. I was walking through a hotel foyer in Drogheda when someone insulted me and called me Osama Bin

101

Laden. So I asked them *'Do I look like him?'* I think their parents had never taught them manners. At the same time, in the same pub the husband of one of my patients came and thanked me for looking after his wife and said not to worry about these negative comments. You can see the contrast – both sides exist. There are people who are ignorant and uneducated. They may have a degree but they are missing the human education and life education that are important. You may have a PhD but if you do not know how to behave, you are illiterate.

I consider that education in common sense and common law is missing in many places. But you see in the examples I gave you there are both types of people here, and that is true of any society. You find people who are polite, who come and talk to you and that is the reason probably why we are still here. This is our home. It is important to get involved with the local people and in 1998 I went to St Patrick's Cathedral for the 50th anniversary of the Declaration of Human Rights; this was probably the first Interfaith gathering in the country. The Dean of the Cathedral arranged it all. Since that time, we have been working in Interfaith and we founded the Interfaith Round Table in Dublin. We were five to six people initially and this year we are holding our third conference on June 9th. Whenever they need a Sikh to attend any of these events I go; I have gone to one of the Church of Ireland Parishes in Bandon. I met a Minister of the Church in Bandon at a cultural week she had organized in the Rathgar Church. She invited me to go to Bandon and talk to the parishioners about Sikhism. I was surprised; about 70 -80 people came to listen at 8 p.m. at night. People really want to learn about other cultures and other faiths. At the end of the day if we say that God has created the world and the creation lies in the creator and God has created everybody then all human beings are the same. He was sitting in different designer modes when he made the different designs.

If God lives in you as a soul when you hurt yourself or another, you are hurting God. In Sikhism, we say God is one. He is omnipotent, omnipresent, and omniscient. He is timeless, eternal, not inimical and friendly to everyone. The most important thing is he is autonomous. Nobody created him and he has not taken birth. Anyone born cannot be God. Sikhism is also a monotheistic faith and we recognize the human race as one. Whether you go to a temple, a mosque or a church, God is one. Who is the generator, the operator and preserver? He is responsible for everything.

This is how it has always been done in our religion even in our guru's time. When Guru Nanak was born, there were two religions in India: Hinduism and Islam. Guru Nanak was born in 1469 and when he was five years old the teacher came to teach him and he wrote his own alphabet and then wrote poetry. When people came to give him a sacred cloth because he was born into a Hindu family he refused to put it on. He said this isn't for me. He said he did not want silk but cotton. He said let there be mercy and contentment and let there be hard work and sincerity. He contradicted the way of the others right from the time he was a child. He was lost in the river for three days and when he came out the first thing he said is: *'There is no Hindu; there is no Muslim; they are all human beings.'* From there the light went on from Guru Nanak who was the founder of the Sikh religion. The light went on to the 10 different gurus. The present guru is Guru Gransahib.

Most of the Holy Scripture is written and we treat that book as if it is a guru. We cannot assume any human being as guru; we say the book is our guru and we take all the comments from there. All the divine law is taken from the book. Most of the religious books are what people heard from memory and they were written after the prophets or founders of the religion had disappeared. These prophets had gone and we do not know to where so the writings are not correct. They are right in their own way but the books were written later on whereas our fifth guru wrote Guru Gransahib. It contains the teachings and sermons of all gurus before him. He wrote and signed the book while he was still alive. He said that the book was a divine revelation from a higher place. Sikhs believe in three things that Guru Nanak said: God is one; have an honest living; remember the name of the God and share your things. In these three things lies the ethos of Sikhism. Guru Nanak emphasised the following: you accept the truth; you follow the truth and live a truthful life that is much higher than the truth itself. It is very difficult to live a truthful life and he emphasised this. The Sikh code of living is very strict. We never cut our hair. I have never cut my hair. There are the five K's (Kakkar) of Sikhism: the long hair (kes), the comb (kangha), the steel bangle (kara), the boxer shorts for chastity (kachh) and the dagger (kirpan). The bangle shows your strong determination and you are handcuffed to God with this. Women also wear the bangle. When we comb our hair, we turn it up to infinity. God has given us this long hair. Nobody cuts their hair, neither the men nor the women.

Sikhs believe you have to have a temporal and spiritual life. You live in this world but you must also have a spiritual life not just for yourself but also for the whole community. Our gurus wrote 84% of our book and the rest comes from the thoughts of Muslim saints and from the outcaste, high caste and low caste Hindus, the thoughts of the Hindu saints through history. It is not a fusion; it is a collection of common thoughts. The Sikh religion is for the whole of humanity, for every member of creation and that is why it includes thoughts of the Muslim saints, the Brahmin caste and the Shastriya caste. You can say our holy book is like a Parliament of the Faiths. We have many principles to live by. We do not cut our hair; we do not smoke; we do not drink; Sikh men are not supposed to womanize. The woman has equal rights; why should be consider the woman bad or inferior? She has given birth to the man, the king and the saint. When the wife dies, we marry another. We enjoy the woman's company so why should we consider her inferior. We include these thoughts in our daily prayers.

We do not believe in any rituals. We just believe in accepting the will of God. We believe that God is doing his thing and we should not interfere. You live honestly; you share your earnings with others and at the same time remember and thank God. It is like when you take a loan from a banker and you pay instalments every month. Then you receive a letter from the bank telling you that your loan is finished and asking how much more you would like to borrow. He will give you more and more and if you are regular in your loan payments, you can top up your loan. God is like this. You keep thanking him and he will keep giving. We do the same with our children and we keep giving them more and more when they perform well. We believe that we are all the children of one God and everybody is our brother.

We are allowed only one wife and we do not have a word equal to divorce in our language. We have borrowed a word from Persian. Divorce is not allowed according to the religion but a widow can marry again. We are the only religion that has banned smoking. We live a very healthy life because we are supposed to live like saints. We put on the kirpan, the dagger. We see it as justice and by the mercy of God I can keep things just. It is a symbol of the defence of faith.

105

If you go back to the 15th century when the Golden Temple was first built you have the first interfaith gathering of humanity. Our fifth guru picked up a Muslim saint who was a co-disciple of his and he used to go visit him. When he wanted to choose a person of divine nature to lay the foundation stone for the temple, he chose this Muslim saint. Here you see a Muslim Sufi saint putting the foundation stone of the Sikh temple. You will not find such an example of humility in any other religion in the world. Every Sikh has to become like that. We do not believe that you work for salvation for yourself; it is salvation for the whole community, the whole world. We don't believe in heaven or hell as such. We don't know about an afterlife. We say that we started from God and we have to return to God. We want to be liberated while living. We feel there are contradictions in the teachings about heaven and hell and we do not believe in that. We know there is no place. Some people say that there are seven floors, seven skies, seven seas but we do not believe in those. We believe that you have to be part of society and work for the good of humanity. Only in that way can you get salvation. Whether or not there is life after death we don't know. We call it transmigration of the soul. Whether it goes in animal form or back to the God where it started, we don't know. Our aim is to go back to where we started and that is what the saints believe.

Our language is Punjabi but we call it Gurmuki. Our fifth guru was executed by the Mogul forces of the time. He was put on a hot plate and hot sand was poured over him. Then he was taken and put in a boiling water cauldron; oil was put on him but all the time he was in a trance and he did not feel anything. Eventually he died and we don't know what happened about his cremation. They wanted to drop the body in the river after they took it out of the cauldron but his body was never found in the river. At that time, you had to pay tax to the Muslim government if you were a Sikh or a Hindu. He refused because he said this is against humanity. He could have saved his life by agreeing with them and he had followers who would have paid the money. But he did not because he was laying down the principles for the foundation of humanity that we are the creation of one Lord, one God and everybody is equal. His son carried on and then he and the seventh, eighth and ninth gurus were executed by the Mogul emperors of the time. The Muslims were trying to force everybody to convert to Islam.

At the time of the 10th guru, women were given the right to serve in the army as soldiers. In 1699 at a huge gathering of the Sikhs, Guru Gobind selected a group of five from the ordinary workers and gave them the right of leadership over the group. The caste system was no longer recognized and everybody was considered equal. We had a democracy that was higher than today's democracy. Everybody was given the name of Singh signifying 'king'. These five baptised the Guru and they had full authority. They could challenge him and he could challenge them. It was a type of corporate authority. In 1702 or 1703 there was a fight going on with the Muslim soldiers and one fellow was giving water to every wounded soldier. Then another soldier said *'Look we are wounding these people and this other fellow is saving them'*. They made a complaint against the man giving the water. When the guru asked him why he was giving water to everyone, he answered that the guru had taught him to recognize the whole human race as one and we are all the children of God. He said that when he saw them in distress he gave them water. The guru went inside, came out with a bandage and ointment, and told him to take those and help. This was a mission higher than the present Red Cross because it was the one side helping the enemy whereas with the Red Cross it is a neutral country helping. So what we had in 1702 was much higher than anywhere else. Women were in the army and could be army generals and do work greater than that of the Red Cross.

Sikhism is quite a modern religion and we recognize all others. Many people fight in the name of religion but there is no need. We should not tolerate the oppressors or tyrants. The Sikhs are like inert gas; we move and stay quiet but if there is a problem we will come and fight and settle it. First, we will try to talk and if this does not work, we will fight. We say Sikhs are sane soldiers – they will fight only if there is oppression or insults to somebody's dignity or if the dignity of the woman or humanity is hurt. We act as a defender of justice and equality.

In 1984, the Indian forces stormed the Golden Temple in Amritsar and after that Indira Ghandi was assassinated. The state of Punjab had been asking for autonomy because the central government had not done anything for the Punjab. Then the politicians twisted the issue and said that the state was independent. In 1984, accusations and counter accusations were in the air everywhere. A lot has been written on this so I do not want to go into detail on it. We say that the government should have acted wisely instead of storming the temple. The government said there were arms and ammunition in the temple. There had been a cordon all around the temple for three years so how could the arms have been taken in. It means that the army allowed the weapons to be taken inside. Even if they had weapons was it necessary to storm the fulcrum of a nation. It was not necessary because it is possible to solve everything through talk. Indira Ghandi acted impulsively and said *'Let's storm the temple.'* Then she was assassinated but we still do not know the answer to who shot her. The Indian soldiers shot the two people who were involved. I think there is more to it but we do not know. The Sikh nation has been harmed by this because the Sikhs are not violent.

There was also the Indian flight that blew up over the Atlantic in 1985 you will see another example of uncertainty about who did this and why it happened. The book 'Soft Target' is an eye opener. The person accused was acquitted last year and the book says that it was some agency that planted the bomb. The plane was delayed in Montréal because they had to put a Rolls Royce engine into the plane. The aim, it is claimed, was to discredit the Sikhs of Toronto and London by showing after the plane landed that there was a bomb on board. The Sikhs would be discredited and no lives lost. The plane was delayed by 2 hours and that is why this happened. I have been to the site of the crash many times and we say prayers there. I do not think the Sikhs would do that. Reading 'Soft Target' will amaze you. Whether it was intelligence agencies or another group doing it to discredit Sikhs we do not know and the author of 'Soft Target' poses the question of conspiracy. Whatever the cause, we lost 350 people. More than 60% of the people on the plane were Sikhs and many were Canadian Sikhs.

In India right now, the Prime Minister is a Sikh; the army general is a Sikh and about 6% -7 % of all professionals are Sikhs. About 10% of the Indian army are Sikhs. We are hardworking people in the Punjab. Sikhs do everything. They run factories; they farm; they work in industry, transport, in fact, they work in every field. You will find them working all over India. They work hard and they buy a house. We don't think any work is beneath us as long as it is honest. We give 10% of our income to community causes; it is like a tax. It is not just for the Sikhs; you have to look after the human community, whatever his religion or beliefs. The Irish people do the same; they help people from different nations and religions. Look at the Pakistani Earthquake fund here; the Irish people contributed so much to that. What we do, we do for humanity.

*I met **Sudanash** through Dr Puri and later visited him at his home in Tallaght to hear his story.*

My name is Sudanash Shorma and I come from the very north of India, very close to the Nepalese border. I grew up in a small village where my father was a farmer. At that time, India was not a growing economy and things were not as good as they are now. There were not many chances to go to a good school but my father insisted on sending us to a good boarding school. I am the eldest in the family and I have another brother and a younger sister. My father was an only son and because my grandfather had a huge amount of land and there was nobody else to look after it my grandfather asked my father to stay in farming. My father got a very good education and did a Master's degree, which was unusual for that time. He could have gotten a very good job but he decided to stay at home with the family and keep the family together.

As we grew up, he decided to send us to boarding school. The one I went to was a military school the aim of which was to train people for the defence forces. There was huge competition for places in this school but I was very good in school and was always top of the class so I could make it. There were only 32 seats each year out of about 200,000 applications. I learned many things about the army and air force and many defence tactics. The many extracurricular activities were associated with defence. My brother joined the same school later.

After I did my leaving certificate I was not able to join the defence forces for medical reasons because I had had an operation on my stomach for a hernia. I was considered medically unfit for flying because there is always a chance of such a thing recurring. I was a bit disappointed because that was the reason I had gone to that school. I then went to university in another town and did a Bachelor's degree in Arts. I did English Literature, Political Science and Ancient History. I spent 3 years getting my degree and after graduation I decided to go into management. I did my Master's degree in Business Management in 1996 – 1997 and started working in Mumbai. That was a big change for me; I had gone from village to town to city and now to a major city. I ended up working in Sales and Marketing and the strategies for these areas because of my MBA studies.

Things went well for me but I also always had a very soft feeling for people and wanted to do something to help. I had wanted to serve my country by being a soldier but that did not work out so I thought I could do something else. I had done a lot of work in the students' union when I was in university and did a lot of work for different charities. I did start my own charity in India in 1996. When I was going to do my MBA course I used to pass through an area that was not as well off as other places. I found the only thing missing was that these people did not get a chance to get a better education. I have always thought that education could make a very big difference. I went to the parents, explained things to them, and found the children spent the whole day doing nothing and never went to school. The parents were poor labourers. They made just enought for their daily bread. They thought the family was a gift from God but they really lacked education. I did not know how much I could do for them but I went to them one day. At first, they thought I was a government employee who had come to give them money. I explained to them that I was a student myself but that I wanted to teach their children for two hours a day. I thought I could teach them some numbers and things like that. The first two days nobody showed any interest but on the third day I took some gifts and they all ran over to me. So they came to expect gifts every day and that was their reward to come to me and sit down and learn for an hour or two. After a couple of months, I had about 35 students in front of me. It was a very good experience but I never told any of the people around me. One fellow who shared with me used to ask me where I went every day after class and I just said that I was going to visit a friend. One day he followed me and he found out what I was doing. He thought it was very good and he asked to join me as well. The number of children grew but after about 9 months I had to move to another city for work. He took over the whole thing from me but the government decided to move all the people from that area because they wanted the land. My friend rang and said all the children had gone. It happened over night and we could not find out where they had gone.

I did whatever I could and I have since moved on but could not cope with social work and professional work. I was travelling a lot because of the nature of the job. I travelled around India and I could see that people in the north and south of India were very different. The languages are very different as well as the skin, hair colour and people's physical features. There is a common language in India, Hindi, and English is also used but this is restricted to the educated class and society. Travelling gave me a chance to see how different people can live together peacefully in a multicultural society. This was a great learning experience for me because I came from a different part of India, a different culture and a different race. I was working with people who were very different to me. I never felt anything wrong. You can come across some odd things but the main thing is that you think positively and realize that every human being is different.

I finished my job in Mumbai and got a job in the city where I had been to boarding school in Lucknow, the capital city of Uttar

112

Pradesh. This was one of the main centres of the Mughal Empire. It was ruled by Muslim dynasties for a very long time. It is a very calm and peaceful city so I decided to move back. It is my home and I got a better job. Then my company decided to send me on a project to Singapore because I had done very well with them. When I got back to India from Singapore, I thought that I should get some more international experience and exposure. I had heard about Ireland a long time before when I was in boarding school. The principal of the military school had a wife from Galway and we always called her 'Mrs Daniel'. She is still alive; I think that this year she will be 102. She is all alone; her husband died back in 1986. She had no kids and still lives in Lucknow. She left Ireland in the 1960s or before and she used to talk about what a nice country Ireland was. I only came to know more about her after I left the school and formed the Alumni for people who had passed out of the school. We called it 'The Old Boys' Association'. We invited her for our first inaugural function and I had a chance to speak to her. We did that every year after that and we used to talk a lot about Ireland. When I came back from Singapore, I was thinking of Europe and then I thought I should try Ireland. I was working in the oil industry so I came here and joined Shell. Before I came, I finished another Master's degree. I worked for Shell for a year and a half and then they decided to wind up the project here. I came here on 30th September 2001 – the month of the crisis in the USA. Everybody was seen as suspicious at that time. I never faced any problem though.

When I came to Ireland, I started living in Shankill. I was a paying guest staying in a house with a woman called Doris and she was very welcoming. For dinner she boiled up carrots, potatoes, parsnips, and she put ketchup and salt beside that and said *'that is your dinner'*. You know Indian food – we have many spices. That was my first day of work and I was so hungry. I could not find any taste in the food. I literally cried and it was night so I could not ask for anything else. She went off to bed because it was 10.30 – 11 and I did not know where I could find anything else to eat. I did not know where anything was in her house. I ate one carrot with salt and drank two glasses of water. The next morning I had breakfast and everything was fine. But I decided I had to tell her that I couldn't eat the dinner. So I asked her if there were any spices that she used and she said 'black pepper'. That is not a spice for us and I needed something else. She said there were a few shops around and she would try to buy some things. I am vegetarian and my family also and we never had anything to do with meat. She asked me if I would eat chicken but I do not. I said I also do not eat egg or fish. She thought then that we do not take milk because we are vegetarian. I did not get any milk for breakfast so I asked her and she said *'But you are vegetarian, are you changing your mind?'* But I said *'No, I do drink milk and eat dairy products, it's just the meat.'*

I also found the climate cold, windy, and rainy every day. In India, we have monsoons. When it is winter, it is winter and then it does not rain. It rains during the monsoon season. It is all predictable. You can also have harsh winters when it is -3 or -4 in the north. Slowly I found my way here and got used to the dialect and the accent. It was a learning experience. Shankill is on the DART line. I went to the station to buy a ticket and I told this man I wanted to go to Dun Lukhaire and he said that there is no Dun Lukhaire. I said there was Dun Lukhaire on the DART route and he said that there was no such place. I was not in a hurry so I let other people go and when everyone had gone I asked him if he had a map of the DART so I could show him where the station is. He took out the map and I counted through the stations and then he started laughing. He said that the station was called Dun Laoghaire. I said OK but why do you call it Dun Laoghaire with the 'gh' there in the middle. In India, we would pronounce this 'kh' and this gives Lukhaire. So he told me the 'gh' is silent. We used to call this place Tallat when we did not know that the last sounds are silent and that Tallaght is pronounced Talla. That is the way it goes with language.

When I first came to Ireland, there was not a big community of Indians here. I remember when I first arrived I looked for some Indian functions or festivals that were being celebrated here and I could not find anything. There was no religious activity at all here and as a Hindu, I could see no temples or any religious signs. Even though your prayers are personal, you still want to meet people who share the same beliefs. In 2002, I organized one Hindu festival here. We had a big Hindu prayer celebration in a hall and I invited a few Indians from the UK, as there is a very big community over there. This was the first Hindu celebration in Ireland. Many people came and it was a huge success. That was the beginning and the following year in 2003, we had 600 people at the festival. Some Hindu priests came from India for that festival. They were here for about 10 days and they conducted a number of programs like house warming parties and so on. I organise it every year now. We have a lot of different programs, discourses and talks. We do not have a temple but we have started a project to get our own temple. A few people decided to form a company and get charity status. We thought it should be close to Dublin because most of the population is here. We decided to buy a place in Tallaght, in the Business Park. We applied for planning permission and it was refused so we decided to try somewhere else in the countryside. We bought a place in Clane in County Kildare and we are still waiting for planning permission. We need a change of view for the building to convert it to a temple and we need a lot of funding to develop it as a temple. We depend on donations and we have set up direct debit for people to contribute. The cost of construction is very high here but in the next few years, we should be able to do something.

Another project involving Indian people is a cultural centre which we want to act as an interfaith centre also. It is all about giving, sharing, and relationships. We think we can do something with this centre to accommodate other communities and cultures. We are working on that project now and we will be able to register it by the end of the month. That idea has come from the membership because they want to see something happening for the youth. They can come together and relate to each other because if not they will become very confused. They learn one thing from their parents and they see other things in the society around them. We want to have a set of events that will accommodate as many people as possible and allow them to come together because when you come together and share your children get a sense of community.

I believe that the more things you do the more time you have. It all depends on how you see it. The community feels that we should do something here in Ireland because wherever you live it should feel like your home. You are in a different country and of course when you are in Rome you should live like the Romans and you can't expect everything to be the same as in your own country. If you look back at the civilization of the world, anybody who migrated to other parts of the world had to follow the laws and ways of the other country. But at the same time we are very fortunate people to live in a democratic world so the chances are we have more choices and are able to live a better life than people in other parts of the world. I thank God for these democratic values. The value of life is appreciated in democratic systems but this does not happen in some parts of the world. Things are changing rapidly everywhere. Here in Ireland I have seen many changes over the last five years. In India, also every time I go back I see changes. Huge buildings are appearing; people have more money now and there are more cars on the road. The sad side of that is that the families are breaking up. There are many pressures – buying a house, educating the children and keeping the job. It is a challenge but that is reality and just like in India, some things have changed for the better and some for the worse.

The issues are both global and local but I see it from a marketing perspective and the global companies that come and act local are more successful than others. I am very interested in the issue of social engineering and this plays a very big role in both developed and developing countries. Social engineering is a fancy term but it involves the number of people you have on your data base, how many you need to talk to and how many you share opinions with. You have your peer group; you have your friends and then your society. You have to look at how you react to all of them and how you react to changes. I feel on the broader level things have changed for the better. I am running a charity school in India and funding it from here. I send money; the school has about 535 students. Some other people also support it; it has been ongoing for the last couple of years. I believe that education has to play a major role. That is the only way to eradicate the poverty around the world. Creating awareness is very important and good quality education is the key. The problem is that most societies do not concentrate on real education. They have a kind of trade education and this is no good. My school is in the village that I come from. It is not that people are poor there. People have farms and have a reasonable life but they are putting their kids into a poor form of education. Until recently, this area had an agricultural way of life and when a farmer had sons he divided the land among them. So after years of division the piece of land a son got was very small and there was no other source of

117

income so your standard of living went down and you couldn't send your kids to school. What we are trying to do is bring 15 students to Leaving Cert level every year and then they can decide what they want to do. These people are from the deprived part of society. The government is also working in this area, as are some of the NGOs.

I see many people here in Ireland who do not go to school. It seems some of the children are not very focused. The parents groom them for school but the parents are also very busy in their lives and the children are not very interested. Children get what they want without putting too much effort in so they do not think of the long term consequences of a poor education. This happens when people are born into a society with a silver spoon and they get the wrong signal. They don't see the challenges in life and don't understand what their parents have faced. But we can only do our best and then leave the rest to God.

I got married in June 2004 to a girl who is also from Lucknow. She did her M.Sc. in Biotechnology. She wanted to do a PhD but her parents decided that she should get married. Marriage in India is a very important institution and getting married is a major step in any family for a son or daughter. She came to Ireland in September 2004 and then we were together for about 6 months when I suffered a major health blow. I got chicken pox that went to my brain and damaged my nervous system. It happened all of a sudden. It was a very complicated case and I was in a coma for 45 days and was in hospital for nine months. I was very lucky to survive. These cases are very rare in medical history so doctors were not sure how to handle the case. Worldwide it is one case in 10 million. I was paralysed with no sensation at all. My eyesight was gone completely. I do not remember anything that happened in the hospital. When I came out of the coma I found myself completely paralysed – no eyesight and no voice. I always had the belief though that God was there. This was a belief from my childhood and my parents and I always believed that there was someone there looking after me. The doctors told me that I am the miracle of Ireland. That pushed everything in my life back because I could not work for some time. You can see the traces of the paralysis still in my face. It is getting better every day. This was all a huge shock for my family and me. My brother is a doctor in India so he came over to Ireland. My wife was very new here and she suffered a lot. All this happened on the 4th or 5th day of getting chicken pox. It happened suddenly and I had not told anybody that I had chicken pox because it is a contagious disease so thank God my wife was with me. She called the doctor and he sent me straight to the hospital. I was in St Vincent's for five months and then I was moved to Dun Laoghaire rehabilitation centre. Finally, I started to walk and got some movement. Now I am fine and back to running, walking, talking, and doing everything. I still have to visit the hospital every now and then.

The good thing in my life is that I see many good things happening on the social side – setting up things for the kids and trying to be part of the interfaith community. I try to be part of the things that are happening in Ireland to gain some more experience and to see how I can contribute. I go to a lot of schools and explain things to the children. Children bring their food and celebrate their own culture together with others. I go in and say Hindu prayers with them. If we focus on 20 years ahead, we have to plan it now. Ireland has changed a lot in the last five years. In terms of Indians, you could name the people on one hand who have been here for the last 30 years. Most Indians only came very recently. Most of these people are young, newly married or with one child. There are no official figures on the number of Indians here but I think there are 30,000 –

119

60,000. Most of them are working in IT or as doctors and nurses. They are all very well educated. They have not come just for the sake of coming. They have skills and they want to improve those skills and do better in life. 99% of the Indians I know here are working in very good jobs. Those doctors and businessmen who have been here for a long time have made a very good living also. The good thing about Indians is that they are ambitious; they want to do good and they are open minded. They want to mix with the communities they come to. That is one of the best things about Hinduism – we do not see fundamentalism in the religion and that is good. They feel everyone is a human being and religion is a very personal thing. Hinduism does not have any particular day so we all do whenever we want. Every day in the morning before we go to work, we pray and in every Hindu house, you will little pictures of the gods and goddesses in a corner. These are like little temples in every household. The community temple is just to bring people together.

When I came, there was only one shop in Camden St with Indian food but now there are many shops even in Tallaght. I think there are over 30 shops and you can get every food you can think of. We get everything we need now – we live as we live in India, socialise with Indians; the community has grown a lot over the last five years. I think I will eventually go back to India because we still look to our roots. That is another time in the future and maybe we all want to retire to our homeland. But I think for now I can contribute more to Ireland than to India. You should live where you are. I do not know how it will be when you have kids because things change then. You have to see life from their shoes. It is hard to decide from here, as you have to wait and see it from the family's view. Now I can contribute more to education in India because I do not understand how to do it here and it is not possible because it is too structured.

But I can get involved in other projects here and I think I should do as much as I can because it should not be all take – we have to give also. I believe very strongly in Mahatma Ghandi and his ability to bring people together through peaceful means. However, his view of how India should develop has not happened. He did not believe in large universities. He believed in small-scale industries and in developing from there and as the purchasing power goes up you can build bigger and bigger. People should get the basic education first and then they can carry on. But what happened after independence is that Nehru opened big universities and did not focus on the small. Some people who were educated got the jobs and could afford to send their children to school. The gap widened between the rich and poor.

*I met **Siraj** at his home in Dublin where he told me about his contribution to Irish drama and film.*

I was born in the 1962 in a city called Lucknow, the capital of Uttar Pradesh (UP), a northern state in India. That was post independence India, a secular India with a constitution according to which all religious communities were given an opportunity to express their culture and their religion. India got its independence in 1947 and some Indian Muslims believing ideologically that they needed a nation created a separate Muslim country, Pakistan. However, the majority of Indian Muslims did not go to Pakistan at the time of partition and migration from India to Pakistan has been gradual over the years. Our parents and particularly my father did not believe in this newly born nation called Pakistan. He felt this was a country built on a very shaky foundation. He was a member of Indian Congress Party and believed in Congress values and ideology. He

121

was also a senior civil servant working with British people who were his senior officers. They had intellectual discussions every now and then; I remember serving them tea, coffee, and cold drinks at home when they came to our house. They were Dad's friends and these intellectual discussions used to go on late at night. The point I want to make is that India in my experience has always been a country that embraced and promoted a lot of different ideologies, religions and cultures including the Muslim, Hindu, Christian and Sikh cultures. Four major religions co-exist and I grew up in this multi faith system. I really valued this when I left India because most people I met did not have the rich experience of growing up in a society which is a mixture of all cultures, all religions, multi-faith and multicultural. I went to a school called Christian College, a very famous college in Lucknow with branches all over India. I graduated from Lucknow University- Christian college, an institution run by Christians with Hindu, and Muslim staff; at the same time Christian values were being taught at primary and secondary level. We were told about Christmas, and Jesus. At home, I grew up in a Shii'ah Muslim family. Outside the home, the majority of my friends were Hindu and a few Christian friends, friendships I cherish. Automatically, when a child is growing up in this kind of environment, you learn about other religions and you are comfortable and easy about it all. You learn to respect all other religious values. That was my upbringing.

I left India in 1982 after I graduated with a degree in Biology. I very quickly made up my mind at the time that I was not going to continue the family tradition of doctors, engineers, teachers, biologists. I come from a large family, nine children, six brothers and three sisters and I am the youngest in the family. My father made sure that all of us got at least an education to graduate level but most of us went on to postgraduate and professional qualification level and went on to careers such as doctors and one even became a banker. I was the one who was inclined towards something other than these professions. India is a place where the culture of the world outside the home dominates. I was attracted by the cinematic culture of India, now universally known as Bollywood. I had to make a conscious decision about whether or not to go the cinema /theatre route after my graduation, a decision that had to be made against the wishes of my elder brothers and sisters. My parents were getting old at this stage and they were least concerned as long as I did alright in life and as long as the elders were making the right decision for you.

I went to Delhi to study theatre and from there I went to London to study drama at a professional school called the London Academy of Music and Dramatic Art (LAMDA). The plan was that I would finish a two – three year course, then go back to India, and join the film industry. However, when I stayed in London and lived independently for the first time I realized that I had to learn and absorb some things that the city of London and Europe at large have to offer. To travel to Europe you have to learn a bit about the place. You see India is a very complete country and it has its own world culture in it. It has a bit of French culture, some English culture; in fact, you can say the whole world exists in India, in a very Indian way. However, when you live outside of India and you develop a bird's eye view of India, you realize the real picture. The BBC World Services offered me a job while I was a drama student. I was asked to do a couple of programmes and translations for BBC radio scripts and then broadcast them for Hindi and Urdu services. So I used to do that three times a week as an outside broadcaster. The World Service had a department called the Indian subcontinent department and they had a huge listening public. Many Indians in India would listen to BBC World Service for more reliable news than their own local radio stations – The All India Radio. Perhaps the colonial past was the reason for the reliability of news coming from BBC.

Anyway, when I got this opportunity I telephoned my father. He was by that time retired and he advised me to grab the opportunity. He thought BBC was a lovely institution and he told me to stay there, work and try to be a broadcaster. He thought I should get into media and forget about this acting dream. To him acting was not a respectable profession but broadcasting certainly was. I was, however, much more interested in acting and the entertainment aspect of the business than broadcasting. I did it because it was handsome pocket money. At that time, I was getting £9 per minute for a 30-minute programme so you can imagine as a student, how much I was earning. That was very good money. It was great to stay in London, enjoy that city, go to a lot of theatre, galleries, and bookshops, and absorb all that the city of London has to offer. That was purely for personal development reasons, to develop myself because as an actor, we were told that acting is not something that someone can teach you – you do not act from your body or voice. Of course, these are your vital instruments, but the real instrument is the brain, the most important part of acting. The more intelligent you are the more capable you are of playing a part in a very convincing and intelligent way. When you are offered parts, you have to do proper research. So knowledge was seen as very important.

I continued all that and then one day I met a very old friend of mine called Mervin Row, a Welsh guy, a theatre and film scenic designer, who asked me if I had been to Dublin. He said it was a cultural city, a very literary city. He said it was easy to take a flight or boat to Dublin and Ryanair was just about to start. He explained that there was a lot of movement between Ireland and England and that Ireland had a good society and good people. I was doing nothing during the summer holidays so I decided to take a boat and come to have a holiday in Ireland. I came to Dublin.

My first experience was when I got off the boat and took a bus from Dun Laoghaire harbour. I stayed in a place in Glasnevin on the north side with a lady called Maureen who used to run a bar in the Olympia Theatre – a bartender with a very powerful personality and a good friend of Mervin. Before that when I went to get on the bus the bus driver got out from his seat took my case and said 'thank you very much and welcome to Dublin'. That struck me immediately. In my four or five year stay in London, never ever had a bus driver done anything like that for me. I realize now that this is an indication of the intrinsic goodness of the Irish people. So that was my very first experience in Dublin. I had not yet put my foot into the city. I realized that it was a different kind of place. I stayed about two months in Dublin and met some people. At that time, Bertie Ahearn was the Minister of Labour and there was a scheme to train people in theatre studies. There was a department called ANCO, which later became FAS. On the north side of the city, there was a group of people who wanted to be trained in the theatre. At that time, Fintan O'Toole used to write for the Sunday Tribune as a theatre critic. I read one of his articles in which he said that theatre was very exclusive in Ireland and geared towards the middle classes and people from the inner city areas particularly the disadvantaged areas were excluded from the Irish theatre scene. The idea had emerged to take people and train them in the theatre and introduce them to the culture of theatre. That appealed to me and I decided it was definitely something I would like to do. I met a guy called Andrew Clark, an English guy from Cambridge, and Myles Kennedy, a Dublin guy, very Republican, very strong and very interested in promoting a theatre for everybody. This strange trio, an Indian, an Englishman and an Irishman, set up this theatre training program at the north inner city constituency of Tony Gregory at the top of Rutland Street, at a community centre there locally know as Dog Box. My experience of mingling with the ordinary people was extraordinary. I felt very comfortable and immediately compared it with London. I realized that London is a big city with an awful lot of things but I felt Dublin was a place to which I could really relate.

Dublin of the early '80s was not a very attractive city economically while the '80s England, Maggie Thatcher's England, was prosperous. Richard Branson was up and coming and it was a strong economic era. In England you were judged not by who are you but how much you earn. My cousins used to ask me if I drove in Dublin. My reply used to be I am driven by nice bus drivers. England and that kind of environment did not go down very well with me. I needed a city where I could actually enjoy my artistic freedom. Therefore, Dublin was a god given city to me. I realized that perhaps I did not enjoy the commercial pressure. I had good family connections in England; my brother was a GP and I stayed with him when I first came to England. I was introduced to an upper middle class, who drove expensive cars and they would expect me to do the same. My people, aunts, uncles, all came to the UK in the 1950s as professionals, as doctors and they carried that baggage with them. They had to achieve a certain level and compete with the English upper classes. You might call this an immigrant understanding that you have to make yourself a good life, educate your children and prove to society that you have made it. Those things did not matter to me at all. I decided that I would probably go back to Bombay after one to two years and start acting in films and would have my own stardom status, so it didn't really matter to me. I did not plan to stay for too long in Europe. I never saw myself as an immigrant in the sense that I have to make myself a successful person in order to climb up the social and economic ladder. My priority was artistic expression, work and learning as much as I could learn.

In Dublin, we finished that year successfully. It was not easy to carry through that project – all three of us were trying to set it up but the bureaucrats of ANCO were humming and hawing about whether to give them another year or not. It came under the Department of Labour and the Minister was, I discovered, a guy called Bertie Ahearn who had his office above Finnegan's Pub in Drumcondra. So we went there and I met Mr. Bertie Ahearn and I explained that we were trying to set up the project and that it had been put on the long finger for quite some time. He immediately took out his note pad and pen and said 'go to the Department of Labour tomorrow morning (at that time it was where the Mespil Hotel is now) and your request will be approved'. The others could not believe that it was all done in a jiffy and immediately it was approved because we had Mr. Bertie Ahearn's signature. Things were done that way in the 80's . That project was very successful. We did four plays and we travelled to communities around Dublin. We had 16 youngsters aged 16 – 21 and we were in our late 20s and 30s so there was not a huge age difference between us. I thoroughly enjoyed that experience and it gave us great access to the community centres.

After a year, this project ended. It was a shame that it did not continue.

I moved on after the year and went back to London. I did a bit of filming for a feature film and television work. Somehow, however, Dublin called me back. I think it was love and the slow and easy pace of life. I came back again to Dublin. At that time, I moved to Rathgar and ever since for the last 19 years I haven't actually moved too far. When I came, I set up a film and television production company. Initially, I thought of doing theatre but theatre work turned out to be extremely difficult. Major theatres like the Abbey, Gate and Gaiety at the time and even the Project, which was very 'hot, hot' because of Jim Sheridan, Alan Stanford and all those guys could not place me anywhere in their repertoire perhaps because my name was Siraj Zaidi and not Michael O'Connor. Their reaction was 'How can this guy be in Irish theatre; there is no work for him'. There are no parts for him. So I did a lot of independent work and created work for myself. I did two productions, independently produced and directed, one based on a piece of work by the Indian writer, a noble Laureate Rabindernath Tagore in which I ended up drawing a parallel with W.B Yeats. There was a connection because Tagore was a friend of Yeats. When I did the play, Yeats' daughter, Ann, was around. She came and we presented a manuscript to her. It was a literary play that I directed and acted in and created work for myself with the help of the Indian Embassy.

I wondered how long I could continue creating work for myself when the established theatres, radio, and television were not going to give me work, as far as RTE was concerned. I knocked on many doors. I came from a radio background where at BBC world services I used to do regular radio features but the radio play repertoire was a closed shop in Dublin's Radio 1. I met many people. I used to hang around in the RTE canteen to see if they would give me work. But even if the work came in it was too little – £60 - £150 per play – this was not really enough to survive in a city like Dublin. At that time, I was very independent and did not get any support from my family. That was the way I wanted it. My older brother had been to Ireland in the 1960s for seminars and training to Dublin, Cork and Galway and his image of Ireland was not very good. He asked me why I was wasting my life in a poor country like Ireland which had nothing to offer me career wise particularly in the theatre and he thought I would be better off going to New York or somewhere even Los Angeles. He said 'you are a trained actor, what are you doing in Dublin?' perhaps he was right but intellectually, I think he and I differed. But I had been reading the Irish Times and local news and views and I could see the possibility of an economic turn about. Ireland had joined the EU and many good things were being talked about. I felt that Ireland would prosper and the economic tide was going to turn. So I thought I should put in another couple of years and see what would happen.

I liked the city of Dublin. On a nice summer morning, coffee at 11 11 in Bewleys, followed by reading the Sunday papers in St. Stephen's Green - I was enjoying the city. I walked around attending free public talks in Trinity College and going to the different philosophical societies – the tradition was that even the old Bewleys used to have talks, lunchtime theatre that appealed to me. Those are some of the reasons why I stayed in Dublin. The city was relaxing and amazingly hospitable. I could not tell my brother that I was not interested in making a financial mark. He had paid for my acting course and he had spent a lot on me. Being my guardian and older brother, he had expectations that I would become a successful film star, seen and known out there in a world of glam and glitz. I disappointed him in a way in that sense. Then, a bit of work came in from Glenroe, the television soap opera. I was being recognized by some people from the artistic world. I was surviving. Being an Indian citizen at that time, I was not entitled to any state support. This did not bother me as I was creating work for myself. I have been lucky in that I have never had to do any menial / labour type work, the struggling kind of thing. I always created artistic work for myself. It was fine because I was free and I was doing the kind of thing that satisfied me. Then in 1989, I set up a film production company, Media Entertainment Endeavour Management (MEEM) and that turned out to be an interesting adventure because I became a writer in the sense that I co-wrote a film script that I wanted to make. Again at the back of my mind was the idea of creating a work for myself that I could act in. I co-wrote with two other writers, one called John Ardel McCardely who had done some work for RTE television. It was not easy to find the money to make the film, as there was no film industry in Ireland at that time. In the late 80s there was no film board, just a generous tax incentive recently introduced and known as section 35 of the finance act. But no one knew how it worked and only the established Irish film producers had access to this fort of money.

My real struggle started as a filmmaker because I wanted to make a feature film. RTE was pushing me to make a TV movie and looking back perhaps I should have taken their offer because that film never got made. It is still in the making and perhaps it will be finished in the future. That film developed to the ninth draft. I always knew that the script was very powerful. I was exploring a relationship between an Irish Catholic girl and a British born Muslim boy based on a true story that I had come to know about. I was mingling in the society of Indian and Pakistani communities that included a number of Asian doctors. I thought this was a powerful universal concept. I wanted to direct the film. I showed it to Jim Sheridan who was riding high on the success of 'My Left Foot' in 1992. I became an acquaintance of Jim Sheridan and he offered me some work in the films that he was doing. I worked with him twice, in small parts as special extras but it was an experience to work on big budget Hollywood financed feature films.

Gradually I began to pick up more film work with Ardmore Studios and all that because of the film company I had set up. It grew from there and I continued to develop the project. I travelled a lot because I was going through European film markets and festivals as an Irish Producer. My first experience of the Cannes Film Festival was in 1992 when I was officially supported and assisted by Coras Trachtala, the Irish Export Board. There was a seminar in Cannes Cannes for the five English-speaking countries, Ireland, UK, Australia, Canada and New Zealand, who all wanted to set up a group for five English-speaking nations to co-produce quality feature film of English language in opposition to the USA. There was nobody in Cannes who was officially representing Ireland that year. I got a call from Derry O'Brien in Coras Tractala who asked me to go in and attend this Canadian colloquium. So, I thought about what to do. How could I look Irish? I went through the back streets of Cannes and bought a green tie so I could officially represent Ireland. I sat in front of the tricolour and spoke about the Irish film and Television industry when my turn came to talk. I spoke about the success of 'My Left Foot' and all that and a bit about television. This kind of experience made me feel that I was more comfortable in Ireland and much more recognized, helped and assisted by people who said 'you are one of us'. This was enough to make me continue to live and work and be part of Irish life and society.

Then I became a member of the Irish Film Producers Association, worked as an Irish producer attending film festivals and markets in Germany, Luxembourg, Italy, and London, and met the international film community and producers. My script gave me the opportunity to travel to Europe, to meet other filmmakers and talk with them. I came close to making that film. I had over half the budget, about 1.6 million pounds and I needed 2 million. I created two seminars through the Dublin Chamber of Commerce in 1992. I encouraged local business me to put money into film - that seminar was repeated twice and a working group was set up to rejuvenate the Irish Film Board which had been abolished by Mr. Haughey who never paid any attention to the culture industry especially the Film Industry. Filmmakers like Jim Sheridan and Neil Jordan were all abroad making films. At the same time, I was knocking on the doors of bankers, solicitors and accountants to know if they could help. Looking back now, I feel that I was not being pushed as I deserved particularly in the world of TV, which would have helped me, a lot. I was funding that project myself and I started teaching media studies at a private college in Dublin. I lectured two shifts, one in the morning and one in the evening. I made good money and I put all that money into the development of my project. I continued and I had a star cast organized but somehow the shortfall of 400,000 was too little from one point of view but too much from another if you do not have it.

I had to ask myself how long I was going to live on nothing and continue to struggle as a producer. I ended up doing two television series. First, I did a series 'Away and Home' about returned Irish emigrants. You are talking here about the early '90s when the tide was beginning to turn, when the money the famous eight Billion Albert Reynolds got from the EU was coming into the Government Government Coffers. There was euphoria and the gravy train was starting to run. The television documentary was about indigenous Irish who had left Ireland/ My experience in 1986, 1987 was that the entire class of Trinity College left the country to look for work in Boston. People went away from Ireland, following the traditional pattern of emigration. They were all going out of the country and I was coming in so there was a very interesting juxtaposition and contrast in our situations. Irish people were graduating, qualifying and leaving the country. Here I was a qualified graduate coming into the country. Madness you can say but maybe people did recognize the genius in the madness later on when I pioneered in certain areas. Then in the '90s, these people started to come back. Youngsters began to ask why they should struggle in America when there were job opportunities back in Ireland. I found that subject matter very interesting and I interviewed 32 people nationwide from Donegal to Kerry. I travelled with a cameraman, John Daly, and we made this documentary on a shoe string budget. The first two episodes were shot; we sent them to RTE and they agreed to buy them. When we got the green light, we went ahead and completed the project. I did six episodes. We covered the stories of Irish people who went abroad, why they went, where they went, what kind of experience they had and why they came back to Ireland. That series was very well received; RTE One broadcast the programme.

I was also interested in knowing more about Northern Ireland. The north was topical in India and people heard many IRA stories. I always wanted to go to Northern Ireland and experience this Great War. Movies were coming out like 'Some Mother's Son', 'The Crying Game' In the name of My Father. I wanted to experience the place first hand. We decided to work on a second project. At the same time, the peace process was proclaimed and there were positive speeches from both sides. So I thought 'the iron is hot, strike it' and go and make a television documentary there. I went there and started planning a series called 'Our View'. The pal was to illustrate the views of minority communities who had been sandwiched between the two major communities. There were groups such as Pakistanis and Chinese there and I wondered how they could survive. I interviewed an Indian businessman who rented a house to IRA bombers. He told me that when he went to collect the rent, some of the boys were enjoying a beer and watching TV. They were in arrears with their rent. So when he met them, he saw the gun on the table, he said, " it did not scare me, I told them, I do not care what you do as long as my rent is paid on time."

They really tried to tell their stories. The planned four part series series would try to give the views of the various international communities. The first interview I got was with the SDLP leader, Mr. Seamus Smith, the Sinn Fein person Mary Nalus in Derry city and a Unionist MP Rev. Martin Smith. We interviewed these people and we were just doing those interviews when the Omagh bombings happened. We were shocked. The crew was a bit nervous but I thought we had two options, one of which was to pack up and go back to Dublin, and the other to go to Omagh and do some work. We decided to head off to Omagh and we photographed original images of the carnage at the actual site of the Omagh bombings. I twisted the whole series and decided to open it with the Omagh bombings and show how people had reacted. I wanted to show people's views and let them explain how long they felt the trouble would continue and if it would end the peace process. In fact, I found the opposite and discovered that the bombings united people more whereas the bombers hoped it would push them apart. It did not work and it was clear the Peace Process and the Good Friday agreement was here to stay.

My idea was to record the first year of the peace process in the light of these new communities. All the multicultural communities and the stories they had to tell were amazing. We interviewed a doctor who treated a patient who had been involved in a shooting; we interviewed a lady who had been caught in cross fire as she went to the shop. She saw two Indian ladies killed. They had nothing to do with the conflict. There are people who become victims just because they happen to be in the war zone at the wrong time. That was fantastic material for me. I know it is horrible to say that but being a documentary filmmaker that was what I was looking for and I got it. The series had not been commissioned by RTE. They turned down my project and told me that I knew nothing about Northern Ireland. Those kinds of comments were annoying but they did not know that I had been in Ireland 15 - 17 years at that time and listening to news on Northern Ireland every day in some shape or form. I had done a lot of research for that project but they showed no respect for that. The independent Production Unit IPU turned down that project.

I went ahead and completed the project and UTV took it straight away. They thought it was a great project and agreed to buy it. That gave me the courage to finish the project. There was not a great deal of money because there is less money given for acquisition than for commission. TG4 also bought the documentary to broadcast late at night around 10 p.m. That was a relief for me coming out of a 5-6 year struggle of trying to make feature films and then these documentaries. Two good television projects were made, completed and broadcast. This gave me status as a producer. People began asking about my next project.

My next project was a personal one – marriage. I had neglected my personal life and I thought it was high time that I get married. I was now in a position to do that. I had set up a distribution company of Bollywood Ireland to release Indian films in Dublin. That really took off in 1997 and continued on from there and in 1999 we started screening popular feature films from India in the Irish Film Centre now the IFI. We continued releasing a film every month at 12 o'clock in the morning slot. The Irish Indian community was growing and the IT industry was expanding. A lot of young Indian IT people were coming to work and live in Ireland, forming a handsome Indian diaspora community. They felt at home watching Indian films. At the same time, the press picked up on this phenomenon. The main established film critics never actually thought it would happen. They saw Indian films as B grade movies – you know people running around the trees, all singing all dancing – not worth reviewing. But some film journals like Film Ireland gave huge coverage, thanks to Ann Sheridan who wrote a three page story on Indian films. That was taken seriously. Then the other papers began to present an occasional review on Bollywood. At the same time, I was sending regular press releases and explaining about Indian cinema. Bollywood got established in the year 2000 and 2001. That was something I really enjoyed because I then became a main distributor for Indian films in Ireland. I learned how distribution works. In Ireland, filmmakers make films through subsidies, tax money, handouts but they don't know anything about distribution. Great films are being made but they are not distributed. They go straight to television without the cinema window. Hollywood Junk films still dominate our film screens in Ireland. During the first years of the establishment of the Film Board, the aim was to produce films. Now they are finally beginning to learn about distribution so this area was an interesting learning curve for me. I am still releasing these pictures. I have just renewed my contract with the Irish Film Institute for another year. I don't know what will happen after the year as they have their own view about Indian films. I want to distribute Indian films nationwide to go to Cork, Galway. I have already screened in both of those cities.

In the last year, I have been pushing Ireland as a location for making Indian films. I have been trying to convince producers who traditionally go to Switzerland, Australia to come and shoot here in Ireland and this would benefit our own local economy. There should be some kind of relationship between the Irish film industry and the Indian film industry. The recent trip of the Taoiseach to India is part of this initiative and there was a lot of encouragement on the part of the Indian Ambassador and my part to push for Bollywood. There has also been a lot of work over the years, which I think should now pay off. Indian producers are coming into Ireland and shooting films here. Tourism Ireland has wanted Indian films to come here. I have done a lot of groundwork. I went to Mumbai and Delhi, met different people, and talked to a lot of people. But then something else happened and some producers were not issued visas to come to Ireland because the officials in the Department of Justice felt these are optional immigrants coming in and will try to stay here not knowing anything about Indian films and the Indian film industry. These people are stars and can hop on a plane and go anywhere in the world. They have absolutely no intention whatsoever of staying in Ireland. I suppose it was lack of education on the part of the officers who know little about Indian cinema. That was one of the reasons that I pushed the Ambassador to undertake this major campaign and trade delegation with the Taoiseach's visit and see what the industry is like. The current India Ambassador Mr. Kumar is very committed to developing relations between the two countries. Thanks to his efforts, 130 people travelled to India recently in this delegation. This was the first Irish Indian trade delegation.

In terms of the social side of things, I have always been interested in doing social and community work. A few years ago, Dublin City Council introduced something called Dublin City Community forum. I was invited to the opening, went, and explained what I do and ended up being elected to the culture chairperson position of the Dublin City Council's Community Forum. I have been acting as a culture chairperson for the last four years. This is a twelve year project to make the city an all-embracing centre for everybody but it is a slow process. My grand vision was to get a document done outlining the building of a multicultural centre in Dublin, a centre where all multicultural activities happen 365 days of the year. I got this document done and now it needs implantation. This centre will provide information on places from Timbuktu to India to China, wherever local Irish people wander in the darkness. At the same time, we could have talks on the issues of each particular country. Performances could happen, documentaries, films and a fantastic international food restaurant – a kind of centre Dublin Intercultural Centre. That project is now at a paper level and we have started the document that has to be presented to some state bodies that have responsibility to cater to the multi ethnic societies who are here now.

What I have experienced is that people are setting up their own shops. A huge international community is coming into Ireland. They are not getting the jobs they are looking for, and they are saying 'hey that is an interesting thing – let us set it up.' They get grants of a few thousand euro and that pays their bills. If you pick up any brochure, you will find hundreds of refugee centres, hundreds of this and hundreds of that. They do some work but a grand vision is missing. That is what I would like now, for the government to see the bigger picture, and cater for it. We like talking about the issues – look at all the radio programs – but doing the real work with a place where there is a dedicated exposure to international culture where people can learn languages, this is more difficult. Embassies are not interested in these kinds of things so there must be a centre. It is our responsibility; it is the Irish citizens' responsibility. I say ours because ten years ago I became an Irish citizen I feel that I can now live and work in Ireland while at the same time not losing touch with the fastest growing economy in the world, India. It has 8.5% economic growth now. I want to work and enhance both societies, the Irish and Indian. I have knowledge, expertise and contacts. Film distribution is my business but culturally speaking I am involved in the Indian society. I am vice president of the India Club of Ireland and we do three or four functions a year. That is something that I cherish, the fact that I can work with both groups.

In terms of film production, I would really like to produce my own film. The irony is that the World Cinema in their annual cinema book accepted it. I really would like to make that film because I feel that it is more pertinent now than ever. The whole Iraqi war happened, the twin towers, the London bombing and now the cartoon business of Prophet Mohammad has made the whole issue of Islam more topical. Many people including the ex-director of the Irish Film Board, whom I knew from his days in Channel 4, used to tell me that I was ahead of my time when he read my film script. Some members of Enterprise Ireland, IDA also mentioned this. Perhaps they were right. Ten years ago, when I wanted to make my film it was too early. Maybe the things that you feel and sense are right to do may not be right for the country where you are at the time. Now I believe is the time, particularly with recent developments.

Another multicultural programme that I proposed to the then director, Mr. Joe Mulholland, was a programme that would have regular multicultural stories. Again, that programme did not happen. Later there was a knee jerk reaction to things that were happening and people in RTE said 'let's do a multicultural programme with the people on the street'. I was not part of that programme but I was glad to see that something was happening at the multicultural level. There were eight or nine episodes of about half hour length where the countries of some of the people are visited. It was promoted on radio quite well. It was an attempt to look at the local stories of some of the people in South Africa and Mongolia. Now I think it is the responsibility of the public broadcast network to provide that service, to create regular programmes, and to make people reflect on what is happening. What form this would take we do not know yet. One thing is for sure I am here to make films, distribute films and do some real creative work.

Iran

*Iran, known as Persia until 1935, has had troubled relations with the outside world since 1979. I met **Mohammed Ahmadi** in Dublin where he is trying to adjust to a new way of life.*

I am from Iran. The country changed completely at the time of the Revolution in 1978 – '79. Before the Revolution, Teheran was a normal place. It was like any other city; some parts were expensive and some cheap. In the 1960s and up to 1978, money from petroleum was used to improve the country. The roads improved and so did the educational system and the Shah gave money to the people. Iran was a rich country and was industrialized and developed. Most of the farmland around Teheran disappeared. When the Revolution happened, I was a child but I remember everybody was happy, but they did not really know what was happening. People were excited because change was in the air but they did not understand the real meaning of the revolution. Just after the Revolution, the Iran/ Iraq war began. The Mullahs talk well but they don't act. They make many promises but they do nothing. After the Revolution, they had power but they did nothing. Everything changed. During the Shah's time, travel was very easy but after 1979, everything was forbidden.

I come from a Shii'ah family but I decided to become a Christian. There are not many Christians in Iran; about 2 -3% of the population no more and there are also some foreign Christians. It is difficult to practice as a Christian but now it is a little better than right after the Revolution. I had a shop and a restaurant in Teheran but it is difficult to live there. Anybody with an open mind has two choices. They can stay and have a very hard time or get out of the country. I had to leave Teheran. I went to the border with Turkey and met

141

some people there. I had no idea where I was going but at the border, people told me that Ireland was a good place. I paid $12,000 in total to some lorry drivers and I spent about 16 days in lorries travelling across Europe. I had only biscuits to eat. When I arrived in Ireland, I did not know much English but when I went to the Ministry of Justice for an interview, there was an interpreter who translated from Farsi to English for me.. After five months, I was granted refugee status in Ireland. Now I live on social welfare. I have been in Ireland for two years and I would like to work but the problem is that my English is not very good. I did a test for a college and I am going to take English classes. I would like to work as a welder.

I do not know how many Iranians are living in Ireland. I do not find any difficulties in living here. Sometimes some teenagers can be rude but mostly people leave you alone. I think Irish people are very interested in material things but it is definitely more comfortable living in Ireland than in Iran. I used to care a lot about politics but I do not anymore. I hope that life improves for people in Iran. You know Iranians are very intelligent, cultivated people with a high standard of education but now there is no freedom especially for women. Women are clever and there are actually more of them in university than boys.

Before the Iran /Iraq war, Iran was a wealthy country with plenty of money but the war caused many problems. Now Teheran is very crowded with two to three million cars. You have to remember that there is a difference between the people of Iran and the government. The people are good but the government is not organized. The mullahs want everything for themselves. They do not show their wealth outside and they pretend that they just want to serve the people but they often have lots of money and some of them live in very expensive houses. They have everything now they did not have under the Shah but power has changed them. Khomeini was a very simple man but then he wanted power for himself and he wanted rid of the Shah. Perhaps he wanted to help people but he had no knowledge of politics.

I do not think Iranian people hate the West. A minority may but not in general. I know the government will change but the question is when. Things are changing gradually. At the beginning of the revolution, music was not allowed but now it is. Now you can even hear music in the cars.

In the past, I believed that talking could change things but now I know it cannot. You just have to get on with life because politics cannot be changed. I was interested in many things – history and geography – but now I just want to get on with life.

Iraq

*We are all aware of Iraq's recent history and the suffering of its people both during and after Sadaam Hussein's reign. Iraq has had a long and complex history and **Mustafa**'s story helps to illustrate some of these complexities.*

I was born in Baghdad, the capital of Iraq. My family moved to Kerbala, which is about 110 kilometres from Baghdad. The reason for this move was because my father refused to join the Baath Party at that time so he was punished and the government sent him to Kerbala, a big Shii'ah city. My family is Shii'ah. We stayed in Kerbala and I went to school there. After finishing secondary school, I moved to Baghdad in 1984 where I joined university. I stayed in Baghdad until I left Iraq in 1994. In 1984, I joined the university and worked toward my Bachelor's Degree, completing it in 1989. I took Science and studied in the Physics Department. After graduation, I joined the army for a year and worked in the Ministry of Defence. The Iran /Iraq War had finished by that time. I was supposed to finish college in 1988 but I tried to delay it to avoid joining the army so I missed one year. I joined the army because everybody had to go to the army at that time but the Iran Iraq war was over by that time.

I was appointed to the Ministry of Defence in the Computer Department. In that department, I had a lot of records, files and records of army officers. I read some very important documents during my work there. I was supervisor of about 18 people and our task was to transfer all files and records from hardware to software. We were aware of everything that happened during that period. I used to read about people who were kicked out of the army or people who were executed by the regime and the reason why. The

144

Ministry trusted us. People in the government at that time thought that I was Sunni because of the family name, the tribal name that sounds like a Sunni name. It was not common to have Shii'ah in the Ministry of Defence as they selected people whom they believed would be loyal. They believed that they could not trust the Shii'ah. They trusted their people, the Sunni people, from the tribes of Tikrit City or Ramadi City or Falujah.

I was in the top two in my college. We were sent for training for two months and then some people came from the Ministry of Defence to that camp to select people. The most favoured people at the same time were from the Sunni people and the Sunni area. At that time, they needed about 19 people and they asked who had gotten a good mark in the college. I was the top at that time with a first class honours degree. When the government people talked to us, they asked which city we came from. If a guy said that he came from the south of Iraq or from Kerbala or Najaf they would just tell him to stay there. But if he said from Baghdad, for example, they cannot tell if he is Shii'ah or Sunni so they would ask 'What is your tribal name?' They would ask about the tribe. Then they would see if the tribal name is Shii'ah or Sunni. If the name is Shii'ah, they would tell him to stay away. So when they asked my name, my tribal name I told them 'Al Obaidi'. This is a very well known name in Iraq and they thought that I was Sunni. Then they asked me where I lived. At that time, I told them in Baghdad but I did not tell them that my family lived in Kerbala. Then they asked for an address and I gave them the address of a friend of mine. He had an ice cream factory. My friends were worried about that and they told me not to do it. I told them *'No I will just go there'*. They warned us that if we gave any wrong information we would be in trouble. Anyway, they took us to work and after a while, I became a supervisor but we were still soldiers.

Our job was to transfer records from hardware to software and we used to read about people who were executed by the government and reasons for the executions. Most, about 98%, of the people who were executed, were Shii'ah. We also had a system in Iraq that if any Shii'ah was promoted to the position of colonel what they usually did was give him the stripes and at the same time retire him. They did not give any Shii'ah a chance to act in his new position. They promoted him to the new position and at the same time, two decisions were made together – he was made colonel and you will see on the same day another decision where they retired him. They did this because he was Shii'ah, as they did not want anyone from this group in a high position.

They were against Shii'ah and they used to hunt them down. Most Shii'ah were against the government and the government didn't want them. You could see this racism everywhere even at the university. The difference between the Sunni and Shii'ah goes back a very long way. The prophet Mohammed assigned Ali to be a leader. Then you know the story and from that time, there were two sections. Some Muslims followed Ali's group and we called them Ahl Beit, Mohammed's family. Mohamed's family were against this dispute but all the governments at that time were very corrupt. Some people supported the government and some people supported those who were against the government. It was very complicated and all happened centuries ago.

People around the world think that Muslims are Muslims but in reality, there are differences. We believe in Allah, God; we believe in the same book, the Qur'an, and we believe in Mohammed as the prophet. But at the same time they, the Sunnis, have a double mind. They convince their people through the books that the Shii'ah have a different holy book and do not believe in Mohammed as a prophet.

146

With those ideas, the Sunni people say that the Shii'ah are Kafir (hypocrites or non-believers) and they should be killed. So their leaders cheat their people because they do not tell the truth and that is why the Sunni people believe that the Shii'ah are not Muslims. They say the Christians and Jewish people should be killed. In the Qur'an, we have no problem with Christians and Jews; we believe in Moses and we believe in Jesus. We call Jesus 'Eisa'.

In the 1980s, the regime in Iraq was strongly against religion. They appeared to the media to accept religion but they were against all religions even the Sunnis because religious people could see the corruption. They had to make jihad (holy war) against this corruption and that did not please the government. There were some Sunni people who were against the government and who were punished but compared with the Shii'ah the ratio was very low. The government was against all religions because they were against morality.

While we were doing this job at the Ministry of Defence, I saw many important records for one of the ministers who was killed by another minister because he planned to topple the government. He wanted to kill Sadaam and Ahmed Hassan. Sadaam at that time was the vice President. The plan did not succeed and this man was killed but he was not very good either. There were many plots and these are just a few small examples. Most of the Sunnis were high party supporters. The situation is different now. The problem is that Iraqi people are not very well educated. It was as if Sadaam put them in a camp and closed the border. We had the war with Iran from 1980 to 1988, followed by the Gulf War after which the situation became very difficult in the country.

Sunni people do not like to see the Shii'ah in power and they do not accept Shii'ah rule in the country. Unfortunately, they are getting support from other Arab countries for various reasons. Because of those countries, we now have hell. I think we are not going to forgive these Arab countries. In general, people support those people with the same ethnic background as themselves except the Arabs. They are the worst nation in the world because they are racist against their own people. For example, they do not accept Shii'ah as Arab. They say we are Safavid, for example, and this means from Iran. We are one of the groups of people who will ask to be separated from the Arab countries. In Iraq, we have Kurdish people, and other races like Turkmen all of whom have the right to live in Iraq. At the same time, most of the Shii'ah people do not want to be part of this Arab nation because of the problems they create for us.

After a year with the Ministry of Defence, I joined a postgraduate course in Al Moustamceria University from where I had graduated. Then I left Iraq and went to Libya. I finished my postgraduate and did a Masters in Physics. One problem was that Sadaam did not encourage people in the right direction. He used to send his own Sunni people to do post graduate degrees in Britain and America. Many Sunnis but very few people from Kurdish groups or from Shii'ah groups went abroad to do their postgraduate degrees. So if you are intelligent and smart but you are Shii'ah you will not get the chance to study. This was not 100%. You might find 2% - 4% of Shii'ah and 96% of Sunni. The selection was not based on the worth of the person but on racism. Many people came to teach in the college but not all were good. Not all had the same ability. If I were Minister of Education, I would select people who have the ability to make progress but what Sadaam did is he held back science and education in Iraq. For example, in my college, some people were Sunni with a PhD but they were poor as lecturers. They had no ability. They were not lecturers and we suffered because of them. We were sick of them and it was easy even for the Sunni students to recognize that.

I believed in Ahmed Hassan Bakir. He was racist as well but not as bad as Sadaam. At that time, he really created a good system in Iraq in general but Sadaam destroyed everything including education. He did not even know how to use his money. He had a lot of money. He paid out a lot of money, and gave people a lot of money for example for nuclear knowledge. I used to go to an organisation that was related to my project and I saw people that were not in the right position but because they were from the right area and were Sunni and members of the Baath Party they were there.

I went to Libya in 1994. During the Gulf War, it was horrible in Iraq. I do not like to talk a lot about that time. I left Baghdad because it was dangerous. The Americans were going to attack so people moved from Baghdad one or two days before the start of the war. I went to Najaf where my family had a house. We moved from Kerbala to Najaf just for two years and then we went back again. It was a terrible time. We were attacked by the Iraqi army and shown no mercy. I remember I used to walk and see many children and women dead on the street.

I went to Libya to a place about 160 kilometres from Tripoli and worked at a university there. Then I moved to another city but it was not a comfortable place and it was very difficult to deal with the people and the government as well. People were generally racist against foreigners, any foreigners including Arabs. The government itself is a racist government. Here if you have a car – you do not know if you are a foreigner or not from the registration plates. In

Libya, there is a plate for Libyans and another for non-Libyans. You usually get worse treatment and are treated badly on the road if you are a foreigner. It is a shame and sometimes I feel embarrassed to talk about such things. In general, Libya is a backward place. People are strongly related to or attached to their tribes. If we could get rid of all the tribes and the religion as well, countries would be fine.

In Iraq, people are attached to religion and to tribes as well. That makes people backward and we will never make any progress in this way. All religions, I believe, are the same, Christianity, Judaism and Islam. They support morality and that is good. Take what Jesus and Mohammed did - it was to help society to make people more comfortable. The negative point in a religion like Shii'ism, something that makes many educated Iraqi Shii'ah unhappy is the Festival of Ashura, which is very backward. People hit and beat themselves and waste time and money on something that happened centuries ago. Every year they give the same useless speech. They should give a good speech to help people understand the world. Give them something useful instead of beating themselves in this way. These are backward things. The people at the top are not helping people; they are helping themselves. The Sunnis believe that they should kill those who have different beliefs. This is their general solution. I am not thinking about all Sunnis here because you can find some who are sensible but they are in the minority unfortunately.

When the media in Europe want to get anyone to talk about Islam or they want a description about something they usually interview Sunni people. That is why people think that Muslims think in this way. There are many Muslims here and they are Irish. When the media talk especially the Independent they never say Irish Muslims;

they say a Muslim in Ireland. That is very clear. I am not Irish but I know many Irish Muslims. My friend wrote a report in which she made a comparison between the media in Ireland and Australia and she found the media in Australia talked about Australian Muslims 100% while the Independent newspaper never mentioned anything like Irish Muslims. The Irish Times referred to Irish Muslims only about 5% of the time. The Independent never refers to Irish Muslims; they always say Muslims in Ireland.

Irish people in general do not accept foreigners. I think this is because they just opened to the outside world in the last few years. About ten years ago, there were not many foreigners here. We are facing problems here in Ireland; there are two types of Irish people: those who have education and the uneducated people. The uneducated people are a problem because they are racist against foreigners. It is much better to deal with the educated people. In general, you find that people who are aged 35 and above are not very honest like people under 35. That means that the new generation is much better than the older generation. This has been the experience of some people. I may not be right on this point but that is what I see. When I deal with educated people in the college, they are good. I have no problem with them and they have no problem with me.

I am doing more than one job now. I have done my MSc and got honours and I have changed my major from Physics to Computer Science. I have started a PhD with Trinity College but I also have a chance to do it with DIT. I am waiting for funding. I am doing security work and at the same time, I have got part time work in IT. This job is not for money but for experience in computers and in my field. In the IT Company, people are nice because they are educated. In the security job, it is hard to deal with the people. For example, in the roster we are two people doing the same kind of job. I usually get bad shifts and if they need to close down a section, they take it from my shift and not his. I get less hours and I need to cover my costs here, my rent and other things. They take the shifts from me and never from him. I gave them a ring last week; I talked to one of the managers, and I asked about fair treatment. I hate unfair treatment; that was my main problem in Iraq. I am a better worker than he is. Whenever they do a check on us, he is missing. He is very old, over 65 years old and I never miss any of the checks in my job. I look after my job, I respect my job, and the employers know that. I have been there for three years and I have never missed a check yet. I am always awake during the night. These small things can show you other things that lie behind.

My family is in Iraq but everything is not OK. Two years ago, one of my brothers was injured. Fortunately, he survived but five splinters entered his body. One of the splinters went very close to his lung. Another brother was injured two months ago. It can happen at any time; we don't know when and we don't know where. It is not safe but the government is working very hard to solve the situation.

I support what Bush is doing in Iraq. If America leaves Iraq, there will be civil war. We need the American troops to stay there. We need their support. We were very happy that Bush won the election not because of his personality but because we need the Americans there. We know that Bush will help with the project in Iraq. We were worried about the other guy, John Kerry, because he is a bit soft. We may lose some rights because of him. We do not like to take the rights of other people but we do not like our rights to be taken. So Bush in this respect is good for the Shii'ah. We need America there. We have to accept that it takes time for people to learn to live together. I believe we can do that and we can learn to live together. We are looking forward to going to vote and electing whomever we want. We are happy the Americans are there even though we know they are not there for the sake of Iraqis. Every single Iraqi person is aware of that but the Americans have their benefit for us. They are pushing democracy in the country whatever is behind this. It does not matter if the result is good for Iraq because it is better to have an educated leader for your country. I do not care who the ruler is but I care that the ruler is fair and that he makes progress in the country. I do not mind whether it is Sunni or Shii'ah as long as the person is fair. It all takes time for people to understand democracy in a proper way.

Israel

*The state of Israel based on a concept that dates back to the prophets Abraham, Jacob and Isaac, came into physical existence in 1948. The country's right to exist and the right of the Palestinian to a state and homeland are ongoing battles. I met **Joseph** through a colleague at the language school where I worked.*

I was born in Palestine so I am what you would call a Palestinian Jew. I did my military service and fought in all the wars with the Israeli army. I came to Ireland because I married someone whose parents were Irish. She did not want to live in Israel during the Yom Kippur war she got the fright of her life. So we came here, first for a year and we found it was not too bad so we stayed another year. We arrived in Ireland in 1977 and our children were born here. During the first few years, I thought the Irish were great, lovely people. However, after three or four years I realized that this was not the case. I got an Irish passport after five years in the country and continued living here. Eventually I suppose I became more Irish than the Irish, whatever that means.

Economically, we did very well during the first few years. I played a lot of tennis as well. I was probably born with a tennis brain, a fact I did not realise before coming to Ireland. I was chosen to represent Ireland all over the world in the veterans. They went according to age group and the veteran group was from age 35 up. We were involved in the property business but then after a few years the recession hit. Things went very bad. My ex-wife and her family were living just for money. When things went wrong with money everything went wrong.

My wife at the time had nothing to do so she decided to go back to UCC and study law. When she finished we had to go to Dublin for six months so she could practise at the Law Society before fully qualifying. We arrived in Dublin and things began to deteriorate. She was now a solicitor and she took me to court. I knew nothing about family law in Ireland. I was wiped out because the whole thing depended on bribery. Those were the good old days of Charlie Haughey – you know the time of the brown envelopes. It took me six or seven years to learn and then I knew all about the law but everything was gone. I decided to stay here for the kids' sake. I tried to start again with the property business but every time I started, I would get another brown envelope from the court saying it is not your property and you cannot touch it nor touch the rent. This happened every time I tried to start a new venture. Finally, I decided to teach Hebrew. The Israeli Embassy was established in Dublin about ten years ago and I began working for them. I became very friendly with the first ambassador, an avid tennis player also we became tennis partners. He became a very good friend. I started to work in a few institutes and here I am. In my undertakings in Ireland, I have been involved with the top people. I knew Jack Lynch, a very friendly man. When I first arrived in Cork, he was the leader of the opposition. Then there was a guy called Joe Goldberg who was the Lord Mayor of Cork. I also happened to know Brian Lenihan, the late Foreign Minister. I got involved with all those people and at that stage I was very wealthy.

You know with family law in this country everything was 'in camera'. You are not allowed to talk about any of it, give interviews or talk to reporters. This would be considered contempt of court and this would weaken the case for you. Talking about the court cases, I and a few other friends established an organization called 'Dads for Fathers' because we wanted to deliver the message to the court that fathers love their children and want to be involved in their upbringing. The Irish notion is that the mother is the head of the family and she has everything to do with the children unlike the Jewish tradition or the Middle East where the father is seen as head of the household. Here people could not get it. Once at one of the court cases the judge said to *'why are you so worried about the kids – they have a mother?'* His attitude was *'just go and do your business and leave the children to the mother.'* One of the guys I knew committed suicide. We decided to help those people and we used to meet once a week. Should that happen to me today I would know the law and things would be different. I had a student, a female judge – I won't go into names – who wanted to read the bible in Hebrew. There are a lot of born again people in this country and some of them like to read the bible in its original language. I used to teach her Hebrew and after we finished the lesson, we talked a bit about family law. She realized what was going on and after that, I heard about a few cases that she was presiding over in which the father won.

I liked Ireland very much at the beginning and got involved with the top people here. Along with the Israeli Ambassador, I used to play tennis against other ambassadors. I was the only one who was not an ambassador though I was the best tennis player. When all my money was gone, I had to go and work on building sites. I got involved with working class Irish. When you work with them every day on the building sites you get to know them. Normally what happens here in Ireland is that if an Irish person is middle class he gets involved only with the middle class. I went from the higher class to the working class all the way through. I happen to know all of them. Then I realized what type of society you really have here e.g. the hypocrisy. There are good people here but now I am speaking in general, if generalization is the right word. My view of the Irish is that they are hypocrites. They are not very honest because if you know in the normal conversation you will hear the words *'to be honest'* a thousand times and that to me means that they are not honest. They are also very unreliable. I found many similar qualities between the Irish and the Arabs. I have developed the theory that the Irish are the Arabs of Europe. Part of the hypocrisy results from the desire to try to please everybody. Apparently, they do not like to be rude. The culture that I come from in Israel likes the direct approach. In Israel, they tell you what they think and if they think you are an idiot they tell you that. There is no beating about the bush. Let me give you an example from tennis. When I played tennis if the ball is out you scream *'out'* but here they say *'I don't think it is in'*. I realized that I am a foreigner and that they do not like to take things from me. If I tell them how to say it, they may think they are stupid or they don't know.

Then there is the whole notion of the British oppression and they say *'we were oppressed'*. They really do not like to hear things from foreigners. During the last few year things have changed completely. People like the Poles and Nigerians will not tell the Irish what to do because they are looking for work. I did not realize this at the beginning and adopted the direct approach. It took me some time to realize that people do not like this. Some people became hostile towards me because they thought I felt superior to them. That was not my intention at all. That was what I was used to. It took me a few years to realize that and I modified my approach. Years ago I would just say *'don't do this, do that'* but I don't say that anymore. For that reason, I say I have become more Irish than the Irish. I try to blend in with society here. You know what they say *'when in Rome do as the Romans do'* because otherwise you are outside all the time. Anyway, you are outside here even if you have an Irish passport or have lived here for many years. They never accept you as an Irish person. You know what they used to say in Cork, *'The Dubliners are not really Irish people*!

157

We don't trust them.' I realize that I will never be accepted as an Irish person and I am not sure that I want to be. I have talked to many foreigners about this, including foreigners who have been here a number of years, and I have not heard even one say that he likes Ireland. I am not talking about the climate here but the people and the way of life here.

There are good sides here if you have plenty of money. You can get out every few months and go on holiday to a warm place. I found that I needed to leave the country every six months or so to clear out my head. You feel like you are under pressure because of the narrow-mindedness. Things are slightly better now. After Ireland joined the EU 25 years or so ago, things started to improve because there were more foreigners and people began to travel more. It is different now. You know I had friends in the country and when I went to visit, they used to say *'the Jew man is here'*. Many people had never seen a Jew – perhaps they thought they had horns or something. I never felt any anti-Semitism here. On the contrary, people say they like the Jews and that they are intelligent and they usually become scientists. The Jewish community here in Ireland is not very wealthy and they do not stand out. They blend in with the average society. There may be extreme people of course and there may be some connection between the IRA and the PLO and sympathy for the Palestinians. This is because the British oppressed the Irish and now the Israelis oppress the Palestinians. In general, the Irish would identify with the Palestinians.

There is a lot of ignorance here. People do not know the facts. I saw a guy once near St Stephen's Green; he appeared to be a Palestinian in Ireland. I tried to talk to him but he did not seem to know what it was all about even though he had some pamphlets about *'Help the Palestinians'*. The Israeli Embassy gives a party every Independence Day usually in a big hotel. Generally, the Socialist Workers' Party demonstrate and they shout *'Don't Oppress the Palestinians'*. Funny enough, they start at 7 p.m. and continue until 9 p.m. and at 9 the majority disappears. I asked one of the guys once why this was so and he told me they got paid for the demonstration from 7 to 9 but after 9 they are not paid any more so they leave.

Things are getting better but years ago, it was very bad. People are more interested in going to the pub and having a few pints. If you have a few bob on you, this is not a bad place to come and live. There is not too pressure here – people say 'manyana' is too fast for the Irish. Things changed a little bit after the arrival of the Celtic Tiger but it is an economic and financial miracle as to why the Irish are doing so well. Some people say they are living on borrowed money. People in the property business and real estate are making a lot of money. For a few years now, people have been talking about the bursting of the bubble but it has not happened. Since Ireland joined the EU, the economy has changed a lot. It is no longer the economy of 'Bust and Boom' but since they are dependent on other countries, it could go badly wrong. But who knows?

For me things have not improved. I was wiped out by the courts and I am sure that the judge was bribed. Things have improved a little since they appointed a few new young judges. In my case, the judge was an experienced person but had never married and had a family so he did not know about the feelings of fathers. I changed my barristers because I thought they were not good enough. Michael McDowell was the last one who helped me see the kids. You see it does not have to do with justice and the courts. I did not realize this; I was very naïve and asked *'why do you have a judge?'* It really depends on how the barrister plays the game. I got to know Michael

159

McDowell quite well during that period and now he is involved with the Holocaust Memorial. Michael gave a lecture to the Jewish community in the synagogue. After the lecture, I went to him and asked him if he remembered me and he said *'Yes of course'* and it had been about 15 years before that I had dealings with him. My kids are OK now. My daughter has qualified as a doctor and my son is doing a PhD. They are comfortable living in Ireland and I think the young generation here from 30 down are lovely. They have travelled a lot; they watch a lot of TV. To some extent, there is more transparency but it is hard to tell. The question is how do you measure it? I guess it is like most of the other European countries where politics is a dirty business.

In terms of young people even as parents, things have changed. You can see young fathers with their children and the children, boys and girls, may be running around naked. You can see the father washing, giving them a shower. I think this is something you would never have seen in the past. Certainly, there is an improvement. The ignorance may result from the fact that Ireland is an island and people in general used to be very narrow-minded. They are not interested in very much – mainly just the pub. This pub culture is still the predominant one. I do not drink and I do not like pubs but when I go there I am amazed.

Irish people know nothing about each other personally. They mainly talk about sport and other nonsense. There is no real friendship here. It is very hard for an Irish person to discuss things in an intimate way. In Israel if you meet someone after half an hour you know everything about that person – their life story, how much they earn but here you can live with someone for years and you know nothing about them. In Israel if you meet someone, you say *'come on home for dinner'* but here the Irish never invite you for dinner or anything. People don't care about other people and you can see this in the way that people drive – they really don't care about the others. People were not like that 30 years ago. There was a much greater sense of responsibility. Now you do not know what the person in front of you or behind is going to do. This is all creating huge problems because everybody wants to satisfy himself and does not care about the others. There are good laws and regulations here but nobody gives a damn.

I think the heavy drinking that people get involved here is an attempt to release themselves from their inhibitions. Once you drink a little you behave in a very different way. People cannot relate to each other naturally and there is a huge difference in people before and after drinking. That is part of the problem. Unfortunately, even among the young people the pub culture is very strong. For them the weekend is going to get drunk – they like it. I do not know what the solution is.

Generally, relationships are superficial. Something will not let people go deep. They never go past things like 'How are you, are you well?' and that is it. The friendliness seems nice when you do not know the full story. Then you realize that the whole thing is very superficial. It is like the Bedouin in Arab culture. He takes you to his tent, but the moment you leave the tent the knife gets stuck in your back. You know the joke they tell about the people at a party where nobody leaves because they know the others will talk about them as soon as they go.

There are good things and bad things. Ireland is a very expensive country and there are certainly many people making money on the backs of other people. It happens sometimes that if they think you are a tourist and you give someone €20 they give you change for

€10 only as if you are not sure how much you gave them. This happened to me a few times – the first few times I felt too embarrassed and then I said *'sorry I gave you €20 and you gave me the change for 10'*. Then they apologized but they had been trying to take advantage of me. There is a lot of dishonesty and that is part of the country. People who are in the right position are definitely making a lot of money on the backs of people who are not in this position. There are many articles that talk about 'rip off Ireland' but you do not feel that anything is being done about it. People do not complain here.

Japan

*Japan has an educational connection with Ireland through the schools and universities that goes back several years. Many young Japanese come on education programs to the schools and pay quite a bit of money for this privilege. Others come on exchange programs to the universities. I taught English to **Sena** and **Shin** both of whom were in secondary school in a Dublin suburb.*

Sena

I am from Sinalo in Tokyo, not a very big area in the city. The national company, Sony, is located there. I really like my hometown very much. My friends are studying for their Japanese exams right now back in Japan but I am only studying English here in Dublin. I am afraid that when I go back to Japan they will be much further ahead than I am.   If I want to go to university, I have to do the same exams as my friends in Japan. I am not ready to do that exam because the program of study is much harder in Japan than in Ireland. The system of studying in Japan is mostly different to Ireland so I have to prepare to take that Japanese exam in six months. If the exam were only in English, it would be no problem but I have to take five subjects: English, Maths, Science with Biology and Chemistry. I also have to study Social Sciences that include Geography, Business, and Economics and finally there is Japanese.

When we think of going abroad to study, we have four choices: Australia, China, USA and Ireland. Most students go abroad for one year but some go for three years. I did not want to go to America because it is dangerous. I did not want to go to China because I do not think I can learn English in China. Australia is very expensive so that is probably the reason why I chose Ireland. My mother found information about Ireland but I decided myself to come here. All the Japanese students come through an agency that we call ISI. This is a language school where we studied from the time we came in April 2006 until we started regular school in September. We studied English there but I think that it was not enough to prepare us for the school. Most of the students in the language school are Japanese and they speak Japanese to each other.

I went to live with an Irish family when I arrived. They are very nice people. Coming to school here has helped me a lot because I have to speak English all of the time except when I speak to other Japanese students. The Irish students are very friendly. I heard some Japanese students say they have a hard time in school but some do not. We are very lucky to be here in this school. I heard yesterday that Portmarnock is one of the most peaceful places in Ireland. I hope to come back next year because I like it very much. I love the school and I love my host family. The main reason I want to stay is that I like it so much. If I stay to do my leaving certificate, it might be difficult to enter a Japanese university because they do not know about the Irish Leaving Cert. They know about the French, German and British exams but not the Irish. You can get into university but it is through a different way. I'll have to wait and see and maybe study in Japan for 6 months after the Leaving Cert so I can apply.

I miss my family sometimes but not very much because I am used to living here now. The host family is very good but sometimes Ireland can be boring. There are beautiful natural places and good people but I want to do things that are more exciting. I want to go to the city and hang out with my friends. I would like to do some of the things I do in Tokyo. It is difficult to do these things in Ireland because if I want to go into town to hang out with my friends it takes a very long time. Transport is a problem and it is very expensive. I am looking forward to going back to Japan for the holidays but I am afraid that my English will get worse. I bought many books that my host brother chose for me. In these books, I will find proper English and even though they are difficult to read, I will learn from them. In the future, I want to work for world peace. My host brother has told me about world peace and he has a lot of knowledge about this. He helps me with my English too. I am very grateful to my host family, friends and teachers for my time in Ireland.

Shin

I am from Japan, from a place near Tokyo but it is still countryside. It is about the size of Portmarnock or Malahide and is surrounded by mountains. I like it in Ireland because I have lots of free time for myself. In Japan, we went to school from 7.40 in the morning until 4.30 and here we have a half-day on Wednesday and lots of breaks. Here summer vacation is 3 months but in Japan, there is only one-month's holiday. In Japan, I also have lots of homework.

I have one sister. She is living in Tokyo now. I decided to come to Ireland because first, I wanted to be able to speak English., We had four options. My sister was in Australia for 3 years so that is why I did not choose Australia. I do not like America. I thought Britain would be very expensive. My father likes Ireland; he has a great interest in the country. I knew that it was a historical country. At the beginning when I came here, I missed my family and friends very much. Now it is OK and I am enjoying it. My friends in Dublin are very helpful and we play a lot of football. At first, I faced some difficulties such as the weather and I did not understand anything. I had no idea what was going on. But it's OK now. My host family is

165

very nice – very kind people. They do not deny me anything. They have grown up kids but they run a kind of hotel so there are many foreigners there all the time. Tourists come from France, England and Brazil and stay for 2 – 3 days and I talk with them in English. We went to France at Easter time to visit some French friends we had met here and we stayed in their house.

My host mother is a very good cook. Every morning and at lunch, we have the same kind of food but the dinner is very good. She makes Irish stew or chicken curry. I don't miss Japanese food a lot. If I want Japanese food, I can go to a restaurant. Ireland is very expensive, maybe twice as much as Japan. Coming here costs a lot. For example, we pay €165 a week to the Irish family for staying with them . That includes our food. We pay about €2,000 for each student for the year to our agent. The agency is Japanese and so is the boss. It is expensive but I can experience many things that I would not if I were in Japan.

There are about 100 Japanese students in Dublin. Our English has improved and I feel that I have grown a lot here. When I went on trips with my family in Japan I used to feel very nervous if I was alone. However, when we went to France I went off alone one day and I wasn't nervous at all. I realised that I have grown. I feel more comfortable in myself.

In Japan, most people are indifferent to religion. They go to the church or the temple for the wedding. We celebrate Christmas – parents give their children presents. Some families celebrate New Year. Japanese people can accept anything. They are willing to accept most things and we copy other cultures and other countries. I thought I might go to university when I finish but I haven't decided yet whether or not I will go to college. That is one reason I wanted to travel.

Irish students are nice; they don't discriminate against others who are not Irish. However, they waste food a lot and throw it on the floor. They don't put it in the garbage. They are a bit childish but they are very friendly and they always say 'Hi'. They often shout, scream, and make noise in the class. I hope they will grow up.

Korea (South)

*According to recent Irish trade figures, South Korea is one of the fastest growing markets for Irish goods. Additionally, Ireland attracts a large number of South Korean students to study English. I met **Penny** through a friend who taught her in a Dublin language school.*

I was born in 1984, in the countryside in Korea where my father was a farmer. I have one sister who is two years older than I am and a younger brother. I lived in the country until I was nine. Twenty years ago, my father and grandmother's generation in Korea was very traditional. My father was the oldest in his family and my mother was the oldest in her family. It was very important to have a son and my grandmother was not happy at all when I the second daughter was born. Then my mother got pregnant again and when she realised she was carrying a daughter she had an abortion. She became pregnant again and she was very worried for the nine months. Finally, she gave birth to a boy who is four years younger than I am. I still remember the day she came home from the hospital with my brother. I still see my father's face; he looked so happy and she looked as if she had finally gotten rid of the guilt.

My mother and brother's relationship is very close and as a result, my sister and I have a very close relationship. When I was nine we moved to the city. My father sold his farm. He converted to some religion, Protestantism I think; before that he had had no religion. The church was in the city and he wanted to be near it so we moved. In Korea, education is very important and parents will give up everything to educate their children. My father set up a business but he was not very successful. My mother was worried about our future. At that time my father's father died. He was the oldest of five brothers and the tradition in Korea is that the oldest son must look after the rest of the family when the father dies. Even though my father got about 80% of his property, we were still poor. In fact what I remember from those days is being very poor.

I was very ambitious but we were very poor and that was a problem. There are many private institutes in Korea to further your study and it is very common for people to attend these institutes to further their opportunities. My mother in particular is aware of the importance of education and I was always complaining about the lack of opportunity because of money. My sister is not very interested in studying and they found the money for my brother when he wanted to go to a College of Fine Art. In Korea, Fine Art is not very useful but my mother gives my brother whatever he wants. In Korea, you go to high school for three years and then you do an examination for university and there is a lot of pressure on students. Every year many students commit suicide because of the pressure. Some people go abroad to study to escape the pressure of these final examinations. This is similar to what happens in Japan as Korea imported the Japanese education system when it was a colony of Japan. There is a kind of pre-examination before the exams and you take all the examinations in one day. How you do, all depends on that one day. I was very lucky and I did well and got a scholarship.

I studied history at university even though my mother did not want me to choose this subject. In Korea, if you study subjects like history and literature it is very hard to get a job. My mother wanted me to become a doctor or teacher because for a woman in Korea being a doctor, teacher or civil servant are considered very stable professions for females. I just wanted to study what I wanted. The other thing in Korea is that if you cannot speak English very well you cannot get a good job. After the first year many students go abroad to other countries to learn English. This is very common and then they return to Korea and finish their studies. When I was in my freshman year China became a very popular place for Koreans. Everybody was talking about the Chinese economy. It is so near Korea and everybody said we should learn Chinese. My sister studied Chinese and went to live in China. I went to visit her. I decided to stay in China for one year and study Chinese at an institute. The Chinese are crazy about everything foreign. They want to be the friend of anybody who looks Western even if his first language is not English, though he may speak English. They will do anything for you just to be your friend and learn English from you.

Learning Chinese was not so difficult for me because I had already learned Chinese characters in school in Korea. There are many similarities between Korean, Japanese and Chinese but the Chinese only respect you if you speak English. Most of the Chinese do not want to become friends with Koreans. They want European friends and English is very important in China. We could not work there but it is not expensive to live and study in China. I made some Japanese friends while I was there but the Chinese do not like the Japanese very much because of their history. I remember there were some demonstrations against Japan when I was in Shanghai. My Japanese friend and I were in a taxi and when the taxi driver asked where we were from she was afraid to say anything and I just said Korea. Korean and Japanese people look similar. I find that when Japanese and Chinese come to Korea to learn Korean their relationship is good but in China the relationship between the Korean and Japanese is good but not between the Japanese and Chinese. Chinese in China tell you they hate the Japanese but they love all Japanese things and after the Chinese have learned English if they want to learn another language they study Japanese. Japan is after all a very important country. I saw China developing very quickly but in my opinion, the European fear of Chinese hegemony over American is not true – maybe in 20 years time but not now. There are many problems in China especially with human rights and they do not really have a developed civil society.

I went back to Korea after a year in China and my life was study and work. In Korea, the parents have a duty to pay for the education of their children but it was difficult for my parents because there was my sister, my brother and me. My father's financial situation got steadily worse and I wanted to go back to China again but students cannot work there. This meant that I had to try to save a lot of money. At that time, my parents also divorced. My father's financial situation was getting worse and worse and I had to work and work. They still stayed together in the same house but my mother wanted to keep the rest of the fortune. In Korea, education is very important and even if you go into debt you must educate your children. My friends were able to go abroad to Australia, UK; learn English and every day they got money from their parents. But for me there was nothing just work, study and hard work. Fortunately, I got different kinds of scholarships. Every semester I managed to get a scholarship and working part time meant that eventually I made it. I managed to go back to China for half a year but my parents' problems and my money problems made my life depressing. I realized that after living abroad, I had changed a lot; I had appreciated the freedom and I was different with my family and friends in Korea when I went back. My personality had changed and I really did not find it easy as a woman to go back to Korea. I also wanted to learn English as all my friends had done. If you cannot speak English very well in Korea, you cannot find work.

There had also been a crash in the Asian area in 1988 and everything had changed. Competition for jobs was very high and difficult to find if you had no experience or had not lived abroad. The pressure was very great even for civil service jobs. In the past when people graduated from high school, they could join the civil service but that had all changed. Everybody wants to join the civil service because of the stability and if you get sick, you are taken care of. Many of my friends started to prepare for the civil service examinations or to work to get promotion if they were already working there. The typical Korean thing was to graduate from university, get a good job and after three years get married. I could not understand why it had to be like this. All my friends chose a major that would lead them to a good job. I chose history because I like this subject but the first reaction when people ask you what you have studied is that it is hard to get a job with this major. I observed my friends going to a private institute in Seoul to prepare for the examinations and as far as the society is concerned if you can't get a good job you are a loser. Even if you have to borrow money to go abroad and learn English, you must because it is so important to get a job. You must have an English certificate. For me I have no regrets about studying history.

The way it is in Korea even if you are very intelligent and you cannot speak English it does not matter. English is a tool that is necessary to get a job. In Korea the year ends in February and I had been working and studying but had no money to go abroad to learn English. So I went to my mother and told her that it was my last chance to go abroad to study English. I borrowed enough money to pay the school fees here, accommodation for two months and the airfare. This was about €10,000 because if you want to come to Ireland you need this much money. As far as Koreans are concerned if you come to Ireland you are not coming to work – you are coming to study and that is it. You come here to study, gain experience and prepare for the English examinations – that is all. But in my case my parents couldn't afford to send me and I had no idea how it would be when I got here. I just came. I had no idea what would happen after I ran out of money.

I paid two months' accommodation in advance – this included all my meals and was €185 per week. After two months, I had to phone my mother and ask for more money. I could not get a job. My mother sent me another €2,000 and then it was Christmas and I was very depressed. I had no money, no job and no way to borrow any more money. It was dark here at 3 o'clock and raining all the time. I had no friends, no family and I kept getting colds. Then January came and I stated to drop my CV off from shop to shop and tried on the internet for jobs. I did not care what I did. I felt I had to start from the bottom in this country and swallow my pride. Finally, I got a job in a coffee shop and now I am living in a flat with Chinese people. In Dublin, the Chinese community is very strong and help each other. They have their own newspapers, their own shops and they introduce each other to jobs. I can speak and read Chinese and that is how I found this flat – from the Chinese newspaper. I live with five Chinese students and speak Chinese at home with them. It is good because it means I will not forget the Chinese that I learned in China. In school and at work I speak English. Sometimes I get confused and mix my English, Chinese and Korean together. A lot of Chinese help me because I can speak Chinese. This is great especially when I have to go to the immigration office or buy something or need to know something about Ireland.

I realized when I was looking for a job that it was a disadvantage being Asian. If I were Chinese, I could work in a Chinese place but I am not Chinese. There is a lot of competition for jobs in Dublin especially from Chinese. But the funny thing is a lot of Irish people think that I am Chinese. One of my hobbies is going to the museums or galleries and everybody working in the galleries thinks that I am Japanese and when I am working in the coffee shop, everybody thinks that I am Chinese. Nobody recognizes me as Korean. Usually Korean students come here for a year, study, stay at home and then go back to Korea. Chinese people stay a very long time; there are very few Japanese here, and they do not need to work. For Chinese people work comes first and study later.

I have been working in the same coffee shop for five months and it is difficult. In the beginning I worked every day 8 – 9 hours – average 48 hours a week with one day off. I am supposed to work from 12 – 8 but the reality is I finish at 9. Chinese people prefer working under an Irish boss because they pay you for all the hours that you work. If your boss is not Irish, there is no holiday and no overtime pay. It is very different but I cannot complain about it because I need to pay my rent and all that. According to the law, students should work 20 hours a week but I work as much as possible if the work is there. I am supposed to come to school for four hours but usually I can manage only 2 -3 hours. I go to school from 9 – 11 and then go to work until 8 or 9 at night. That is still my life: study and work.

I love this school. I had experience of learning a language in China and I can compare the two. In China, I was a number and money but here the school is very good. I love Europe because I am respected as a human being. Korea is a very small country but it is very crowded. When you go to China, you really see population. In school in Korea or China, there are 50 people in a class but here there are about 12. When you go to a museum in Korea, there are many people but in Dublin there is a guide and no more than 20 people at a time.

I love this country. A few months ago, I was very sick but I had to work because my boss did not care. I felt very bad because I had no family here and had no one to help. I had to leave work and on the way home, I fell down. I could not stand up and had a very bad pain in my stomach. I was crying but I said to myself that I was the one who made the choice to come here and I must do it by myself. Then an Irish girl who was just passing by stopped and asked me if I was alright. She talked to me and comforted me and then I felt alright. I thought that Ireland was a very good country. It is very demanding working and studying but if I don't work I won't be able to pay my school fees and my rent. I do not want to go to my mother again for money. Finally, I am independent of my mother and I have enough money to pay the next school fees. I make €300 a week and this is OK because I am a foreigner here. If you are a foreigner in Korea, you will not get a job. You can work as an English teacher but apart from this, there is nothing. Ireland has given me a great opportunity to work and study here. I understand that some people may feel nervous about all the foreigners that are here – I do understand this. I think Irish people are very good in their attitude towards foreigners compared with Korean and Chinese. We prefer the Irish customers in the café where I work. The Irish are more middle class and educated and they are more generous.

I also love the cultural things in the city and I love going to visit these places. I love going to the cinema, theatre and galleries. You can walk to most places here. You do not need to go abroad or out of the city. You can just walk to places here.

Kurdistan

*Kurdistan is a country in name but without a state. The suffix –stan found in many place names is an ancient Persian word meaning 'land of'. The name 'Kurdistan', therefore, means 'land of the Kurds', an area that covers around 750 thousand square kilometres across large parts of eastern Turkey, northern Iraq, northwest Iran and small areas of Syria and Armenia, from the Zagros Mountains in the east to the Mediterranean in the west. Iraqi Kurdistan is the only part of the country that has gained recognition as an autonomous region. I met **Zhyan** in Dublin where she has lived for years.*

I arrived in Ireland in 1988. I come from Kurdistan in the North of Iraq where I grew up near Howliar City, a town about one hour from the city. I come from a big family; I am the fourth in a family of 12. My father worked in the post and in some ways I had a normal life. However, as a Kurd in Iraq, we were always disturbed and life was never fully normal. As you get to know the situation for Kurds in Northern Iraq, you know we never really felt safe. Sadaam took over in the late 1970s and during the Iran Iraq war, many Kurds were forced to fight in the Iraqi army against the Iranians. Our town was mainly Kurdish but Iraqi Baath Party officials ran it.

When I finished my school education, all the family moved to the city where I went to a commercial college. My education was in Arabic but I did two subjects, Business and English Language, in English: . When I finished college, I got a job in a university and Baath Party members tried to force me and all Kurds to join the Baath party. One year after the examinations, the security arrested some students who never came out again of the security room into

176

which they had been taken. I will never forget their faces; some of my friends died under their persecution. I remember I wore black because I was very close to one person. He was picked on because he had a beard, and they thought he was Ikhwan Muslim (Muslim Brother) but beards were just fashionable at that time (1980s). He was not religious at all. They forced us to go on demonstrations in support of the Party.

My father got the job in the postal service before Sadaam's time. He used to do different jobs on buildings to support the family. We were a large family. He would get a contract and build some houses. I got the job in the university but they (security) never left us alone. Sometimes they would call us into an office saying they wanted to talk to us and ask *'what do you think of the situation in the university?' 'can you tell us if any student did anything?'* or *'did they say anything against Iraq?'* I was very afraid as a girl you know and I would say *'OK I will listen and let you know'*. Then I would go and tell my friends to be careful. I used to help the students by giving them letters anytime they wanted to travel. I would create letters for them if they did not have IDs and they were able to travel with that letter.

Howliar was mainly Kurdish and Turkish with Iraqi administrators. We did not have any problems with each other; our problems were only with the Baath Party. We also lived with the Christians, Catholics and we all got along together. There are many Kurdish Christians. All the students in the University would work together irrespective of their backgrounds. As Kurds and as Iraqis, we never had any problems about religion and lived together peacefully. Sadaam was the only one creating problems. There are Kurdish Shii'ah but they all live in peace with people from other religious groups.

I was working in the University as an accountant and I met a lecturer in Sociology. We met a couple of times during the breaks and he asked me to marry him but I said 'no way'. I was not in love with him at that time but he was in love with me. Then he left and went to Europe to study for a Ph.D. in Sociology. When he came back after two years, I was still there. He asked me again to marry him and I really did not want to go live in a foreign country. I loved him so we went to talk to my family and we agreed to get married.

He studied English in London from 1986 to 1988 and then came to UCD to do his Ph.D. in Sociology and Criminology. The Iraqi Government sponsored him even though he was not a member of the Baath Party. He graduated in 1993 with his Ph.D. During the time that he was studying, the Iraq War with Kuwait happened. By that time, we had two sons. Now we have three, 17, 15 and 13, all of whom were born in Ireland. They all have Irish nationality and passports but the parents do not. They turned me down three times in my application for citizenship; the first time was in 1994, the next time in 1998 and the last on the 17th of October 2005. The last reason they gave me was that I am on Social Welfare; they give us dole but they do not give us citizenship. It is crazy you know. The other two times they turned me down in 1994 and 1998, they did not give any reason for doing so. I am dying to find out why they are turning us down. They make rules; they are wasting our time.

When my husband graduated in 1993, the Irish Government was not granting people asylum in this country. They said there was not anything like that in Ireland and that they don't take refugees here. My Iraqi passport had expired; my father had died but I could not go to Iraq. I had no passport and there is no embassy in Ireland. As a Kurd, it was very difficult. We could not contact the Iraqi Embassy in London because we were trying to hide from the Iraqi

Government at that time to protect ourselves. Eleven months later, my mother died and I could not go for the funeral. I got Irish Travel Documents in 1995 but my children were babies and there were no Kurdish people to travel with and I could not travel on my own. In 2000, I went back with some Kurdish family. My family is still there. I asked for my sister when I went and they told me she had travelled to another part of the country and that she couldn't come and see me until the morning. In the morning, they told me that my sister was dead. They, the Iraqi police, killed my brother too. The Irish Government never gave me a chance to go to my place to see my family. My brother was tortured and killed and I could not go. My sister died and I could not go to her funeral. The Irish Ministry of Justice is aware of all of this.

I do a lot of community work here in area one and area twelve with community groups and women's groups and I have done some translation. I do lots of volunteer work for example in Cairde with the immigrant groups. It is not enough to be so involved in Irish society here and to have Irish children. They don't give us a chance to do any work because of our nationality. They don't respect you in this country; they don't help you. My husband has a PhD and they won't give him a job. We can work but we can't find a job. When you apply and they see your name and your nationality, they do not give you any work. When you don't have an Irish passport they look at your nationality and they don't employ you. So we are stuck and we can't do anything. My husband also applied for Irish citizenship. He applied last year; he never applied before that because he said if they don't give you the mother of three Irish boys citizenship they won't give it to me. They did not want him. I was on their list. I waited three and a half years for their decision. Just two weeks ago, they sent me the letter. I received the letter on 17th of October 2005; the letter was dated July 2004.

We are in great pain because of all this. As parents, we have never taken our children to visit their family in Iraq. My children are now aged 17, 15 and 12; we have never taken them on holiday. We are 17 years in this country and it is like a prison. I did everything on my part; I am very involved in societies; everybody knows me. I am running helping different people and then it is so ridiculous that they refuse me because I am on Social Welfare. What can we do? I applied for a number of jobs but I got nothing. I do volunteer work. I work in a community office one day a week. Tell me what else I can do to improve myself. They do not even interview you for jobs. In one group where I did volunteer work there was a job. I applied and I had so many hopes for that job. They sent me a refusal letter before they even interviewed people. They did not give me a chance to do the interview even though I was a link between the women's group and the community. I was very disappointed. They gave the job to an Irish person to work with a Muslim minority group. I am sorry to speak like that. I am here over 16 years and I like Irish people; I have so many Irish friends but we are so disappointed with the situation and the Ministry of Justice.

I got so much advice from the barristers and lawyers that if I did not get it the third time that they would help me and take the case to the court of appeals. I get the refusal and I do not hear from them anymore. They lied to me all the way. I have a lawyer because legal aid is only for refugees. I am really fed up now. I really thought I would get the citizenship the third time because I work as a volunteer with ethnic groups, and the community. My husband is very upset too. You see the problem is that in this country they don't like honest people. There are people here who rely on lies but my husband and I are honest people. We don't lie and people don't like that. So many people take advantage of the country. I know because I have done some work as a translator and there are many people coming here who give false stories. They give them the citizenship; they give them passports and they give them jobs. Why when you tell your true story, do they not help you? Iraq is not the same country it was when we left especially for me because I have three Irish born children. They have never seen anywhere outside of Dublin, Ireland. They were born here in this country. They are pure Irish. They speak only English and Irish; they do not even speak my language. They have nothing to do with my culture. They have never seen my country, my family, my home. There is no way I can go back there until my children get married and they settle and have their families here. There is no hope now and still Iraq is getting worse day by day. Every day there is killing you know. Some Kurdish people are in the same situation as me and for some people it works well. But for me I have been treated unfairly.

Ireland has changed a lot over the years. When we came in 1988, people were friendly and they would talk to you and look at the babies. Now people shout at us and tell us to go back to our homes. My husband tried to get work but his name is very Muslim and they will not hire him. We are trapped without documents. When I went to Iraq in 2000 with Irish travel documents, it was very humiliating. I had to wait five hours at the border while people with European passports could go quickly. People just laughed at the documents and they did not take them seriously.

Howre: *I met Howre, from Iranian Kurdistan through some Kurdish friends who run the Laundromat near my house. Zhyan has been refused citizenship in Ireland three times but she is asked to interpret for other Kurds such as Howre when the government needs such services.*

I was born in 1975 in East Kurdistan that is occupied by Iran. The Kurds are a different people to the Iranians. We have a different history, culture, religion and dress. Kurdistan was originally colonized by the English and the French and was then divided up among Iraq, Syria, Iran, the Soviet Union and the biggest part went to Turkey. Now we can talk about East Kurdistan (Iran), West Kurdistan (Turkey), North Kurdistan (Iraq), and South Kurdistan (Syria). South Kurdistan (Syria) is much worse than the other parts because there are about 150,000 people living there without any identity and the government does not even allow them to change their nationality if they want. Many Kurds have been executed for looking for freedom. Usually, Kurdish people have big families for reasons of power and protection but I am an only child and there is a particular reason why this happened. When my Mom was pregnant with me there was an Iranian bomb attack on Kurdistan. My mother was 7 months pregnant and she ran to escape from the bombs into the mountain. She was injured as she ran and when she got to the cave a volunteer doctor did an operation and my Mom gave birth to me in the seventh month of her pregnancy. They put me in a box in the cave; I do not remember any of this but my parents told me about it later. My Mom's legs and stomach were injured and she could not have any more children. She also lost one eye.

My parents had a big garden in Kurdistan and they grew pears, peaches, apricots and lots of flowers. I lived with my parents until I left to come to Ireland in 2003. When I was young, I did not go to the local Iranian school because in those schools it was forbidden to use Kurdish as the language of instruction. Teachers and students had to use Persian. We did not learn about our history or culture. Iran wants to change everything in Kurdistan. My parents taught me the Kurdish language, grammar and reading, writing and maths at home. My father loved books; he had lots of illegal books from which he taught me. I never learned any English until I came to Ireland. If the Iranians found any books they confiscated and burned them. Most of the time they executed people if they had books that they thought were against Iran. There was no chance at all for people to have freedom if the Iranian government was suspicious of them.

Students who went to the Iranian schools could only learn about Iran. The Iranian government removed all reference to Kurdistan and Kurdish history from textbooks. If the Kurdish students wanted to go to university, they had to sign a paper promising to spy for the Iranians against other Kurds. Iranians know they cannot trust the Kurds. It is difficult for Kurds from the different regions such as Iraq, Iran, Syria and Turkey to communicate with each other and to create an integrated Kurdish society because the different Kurdish dialects are very different to each other. Kurdish is taught mainly in revolutionary areas such as you find in border areas but in some places like Turkey, some Kurds do not know Kurdish.

Iran does not view Kurds like themselves and they do not care if they go to school or not. Iran does not treat them as equals and does not give them any freedom. They would kill people if they disagreed in any way. For example if any Kurdish person said we have been colonized by the Iranians or if they try to put up a flag they might be arrested, put in prison, tortured and sometimes even killed. Genocide is on the Iranian agenda. I did not do Iranian military service. Military service is compulsory and everybody must do two years service when they reach 18. I was an only child and so my family could buy my way out. They paid a lot of money to the Iranian government and so I did not have to do military service.

Kurdish people follow a number of religions. You can find Muslims, Christians and Yazidis among them. My family was Yazidi whose prophet is Zerdash and predates Islam but I really do not know much about it. If Kurds living under Iranian rule do not follow government regulations, the Persian police would take our property. I joined a Kurdish political party seeking freedom for all Kurds and the Kurdish homeland. We discussed tactics, what to do next and how to improve our lives. When I joined the party, I was first put on six months probation before being allowed to become a full member. I designed leaflets, worked on a magazine and newspaper. We were able to cross the border illegally into Iraqi Kurdistan. In 1988 when 180,000 Iraqi Kurds were killed by Sadaam Hussein's army and thrown into a mass grave, we informed people of this atrocity. The Iraqis raped women and took photos to humiliate them before their families. Atrocities were worse in Iraq because Sadaam's desire was to kill all Kurds while the Iranian government wants to change all Kurdish people into Persian.

The reason I ended up leaving my home was because of an incident that happened. One of my friends and I prepared leaflets and we set out to distribute them one night after dark. I was walking on one side of a street and he was on the other. Usually if the Iranian police came, we could tell because of the sign on the car. That night a car came with no sign but it was a police car. Someone shouted stop in Persian. I heard my friend shout and then they shot him. He screamed and I ran away to the mountains to my uncle's house. This was a two and a half hour walk. I don't know what happened to my friend because I just kept running and never went back.

My uncle hid me in a room and gave me food. The police went to my parents' home. They took documents from my house as proof. During the past year, many Kurds have been killed there. I heard also that my mother had a heart attack and died. My uncle paid someone to help me out. I had no passport or papers. Someone took me to Turkey at night. We walked across the extremely high, snow-covered mountains that are always covered in snow and ice both winter and summer. I travelled in April and May when it was not too cold. During the day, we hid in caves and moved at night. The journey through the mountains took five days and nights. Occasionally we rode in a truck or van. When refugees reach Turkey, they have to deal with the Turkish mafia that arrange travel to Europe. Some refugees travel by sea to Greece and Italy. People who can be high on drugs drive some of these boats and so the death rate from accidents at sea is very high. About 30% of refugees die on these ships; three of my friends died in this way. I did not get on a ship but travelled overland. In Turkey, I was put in a truck full of boxes. I was passed from truck to truck. For this journey, I think my uncle paid about $12,000, which he probably raised through the sale of some of our land. These Mafia people took anything we had from us. They took my watch but I kept my money hidden, sewn inside my clothes. Sometimes these people raped the women along the way. It seems that many of these Mafia people had the support of the different governments. Sometimes they took money from people and then did not transport them to any destination. They arranged the trip by truck for me but I had no idea where I was going. Sometimes there were other people in the trucks. In the first truck, we were sometimes three people and sometimes I was alone. I don't know the nationality of the others because I couldn't speak their language. We were given no food and there was no toilet. We had to bring a container with us to use as our own toilet. I had some chocolate with me and that was all I ate.

In June 2003, I arrived in Dublin. The truck I was on stopped near a river. I did not know where I was or what country I was in. I thought I was in Greece because my uncle said he would try to send me to Greece because the Greeks are sympathetic towards the Kurds. When I got out of the truck, I sat looking at the river. I knew no English and I could not communicate with anyone. I had some dollars so I went and got some food but after eating, I felt very sick and vomited. I tried to stop a police car but it did not stop. Finally, I stopped a taxi and the driver took me to a house. I found it was an asylum centre. The driver took $50 from me. Some people in the asylum centre checked me and gave me some forms to fill out but of course, I could not read them and then I gave them back. They sent me to a hostel in Gardiner Place where I had a shower and some food. The first day was very difficult for me. I felt very depressed and even thought about suicide. We were eight people in a room and this was very difficult for me.

In the morning, they brought an interpreter, a woman who could speak Kurdish. I applied for asylum. I had an interview for four and a half hours that was very difficult but after one year and a half, I became a refugee in Ireland. I was depressed about the way I was questioned and I told the people from the Ministry of Justice that I did not choose to come here and that I wanted political asylum. I now have Irish Travel Documents and I have the right to work here. I have tried to get work but I am turned down all the time. One of my problems is language. I did not know any English when I came but I started classes in Parnell Square and I learned quickly. I also have some health problems with my kidneys. I have done volunteer work with Oxfam and some other organizations that work with refugees. I live in a studio. I get €102 per week for rent and €130 to live on. This is very difficult because the rent money does not cover the rent and so I have to use the food money. There are many difficulties here because sometimes other Kurds put religion before nationalism and I am not a Muslim. Some Kurds have become too Arab. It is very important to put nationalism before religion.

I went to a psychologist when I came but psychologists here have no understanding of our problems and what we have suffered before coming here. I watch TV a lot and this helps my language. My Irish neighbours help me with my English and so does a Malaysian friend. Many of my Kurdish colleagues suffer also from depression and recently we had to send one of them back to Kurdistan (north of Iraq) because he was in a very bad state in Ireland. He had been in Ireland for almost three years and he was still an asylum seeker with no status in the country. He became crazy, lost his mind and was unable to speak or walk. Another colleague is now in a mental hospital in Dublin and is unable to communicate or recognize anybody. Some of them face terrible worries and stress because they have no idea what has happened to the families they left behind. This is also my situation. I am happy to have this opportunity to tell people about the Kurdish situation because it is a very serious situation that is not receiving any help from any government or group. I beg you to think and support our situation.

Lebanon

*Lebanon suffered a long civil war and like many other war torn regions its citizens have travelled far and can be found on every continent. . I met **Dr Abdullah** through the anti-war movement in Ireland.*

I am probably an exception amongst Lebanese. I am a Shii'ah who was born in the holy city of Najaf in Iraq. My lineage is mostly clergy, mullahs, ayatollahs and it was expected that I would also be a cleric. The tradition in Shii'ah families is that the oldest son becomes a cleric and follows the father and grandfather's path. I joined the seminary when I was 15 but I always felt that I was missing something very important. For me that was a sense of equality. In the Shii'ah community, the mullah is always the leader and people follow him. If he does not have the quality of leadership, he will never achieve anything.

In the seminary, I was not the most brilliant student and was not always the top of the class, as I wanted to be. I finished my baccalaureate at 16 and was one of the youngest ever to graduate. I really wanted to study veterinary medicine but you have to realize that at that time in the Middle East veterinary science was not the most illustrious profession to be involved in. My family looked on it as being a doctor for donkeys and they would prefer me to study human medicine. My uncle (who was more secular than my father was) said that if I went to the College of Science first he would help me to go and study human medicine in Spain. I was supposed to learn Spanish and start to apply to different colleges in Spain.

Unfortunately, in 1966 when I graduated from school; many changes within Iraq affected my uncle's business. He went bankrupt and had to leave Iraq and go to the Ivory Coast. That year there was probably the only attempt at free elections in the modern history of Iraq. I was a member of an underground Shii'ah party while at the same time a candidate in a Muslim Brother Sunni Party. At that time, the Sunni/ Shii'ah conflict did not exist. The conflict is a recent thing and is a tool rather than something real. However, because of my financial situation, I had to finish my degree in Iraq. I studied microbiology, zoology and medical microbiology.

I found I had to leave Iraq and the reason was that Sadaam Hussein had begun his tribal rather than sectarian policies. Najaf has always been the centre of opposition to all Iraqi governments in modern Iraqi history because the most enlightened people live there. Although it does not look so, you can compare Najaf with the new Catholic Theology in Latin America where they are more sensitive to oppression; they have a conscience and they are always raising their voices. The Lebanese community though three generations in Iraq and therefore entitled to Iraqi citizenship had never lost contact with Lebanon. We read Lebanese newspapers and stayed in close contact with Lebanese people. This made it extra difficult for us to take out Iraqi citizenship. We might get a job but only if we joined the Baath party. I still had a Lebanese passport when I left Iraq. I worked in Lebanon for one year, then a year in Morocco and finally got a job in Libya. This was a very cheap country to live in and the salary at the time was very good particularly given the exchange rate against their currency. But living there was not the kind of future I envisaged for myself so I tried to set up a business in Ivory Coast with my brother.

I found living in Libya very difficult because I love to read and enjoy cultural things. I decided to go to the UK to study and started a Master's degree in Genetics which gave me a new direction in an area that was just developing. After that, I joined the Carter International Research Centre in Syria in 1982. Very soon, I found myself at the end of the salary scale in an International Research Centre. There was no further advancement for me. I was getting a very good salary and when I checked out the possibilities of more study, I found that one-year's salary was enough for me to study for three to four years in Ireland. Of course, Ireland at that time was very cheap. I got a scholarship from the Carter Centre to go for a PhD in India but when I went there, I discovered that India is created especially for the Indians. When you see them outside of India they are very tolerant, very hard-working but I didn't find it so when I was there. I went to one of the best research centres in India, Hyderabad, but I found it was not for me. I was able to transfer the support to a UK university in Kent. At the same time, I was corresponding with a professor in University College Cork but I decided to go to Wye College in the UK. My mother's relatives in Iraq were business people and they used to export scrap lead to Ireland. When I was a kid, I used to collect stamps and I would read the story of the stamps. I remember those dull stamps from Ireland with the map on them. I still have a good collection of those stamps; I do not know if any of them are valuable.

When I was doing my Master's in the early 80's, I visited Ireland and I was very impressed with the laid back easy lives of the people. I tried at that time to move here to do a PhD but I did not find a suitable subject. That was my early exposure to Ireland and I enjoyed the week I spent here. I remember at the time being amazed also watching the drunken people coming out of the nightclubs. No one believes me now when I say Ireland was like that in the 1980s.

After I had been two weeks in Wye College, I asked myself if I was going to spend all my life with these snobby people. I found it very hard. Then three or four days before St Patrick's Day I decided to come to Ireland to visit a friend who was in UCD. I met a professor who had a nice project that suited my interests. The only problem was I had to pay rather than be paid for my research. I sent a letter to the registrar and he was very generous and supplemented the money I had. The professor made the decision immediately and so I stayed in Ireland. The people I worked with and my supervisor all said they were lucky to have someone like myself join them. I got my PhD in 1988. It was very important that I finish then because I wanted to go back to Lebanon and join the civil service. There is a law in Lebanon that if you join the civil service before you turn 40 you are entitled to a pension. You can also join the civil service after 40 but you will not get a pension.

Things went well in my study but the years 1988 and 1989 were the most severe in the conflict in Lebanon. Muslims fought with Christians but by then it was Shii'ah fighting Shii'ah and Christian fighting Christian. My wife was very anxious that we settle down and so I sat down with a friend in Ireland and looked at the future of genetic engineering. We looked at the new ideas and the support for these ideas. In 1990, a big commercial company was developed and I was available to join. I was still temporary here because I had never thought that I would be staying permanently. I thought that if my wife joined me, we would not move for the next three to four years. I had to think of my daughters. I could find work because of my scientific expertise although at that time everyone was leaving Ireland.

In 1990, I moved to Wexford and my wife loved it. I still looked on it all as temporary. Then in 1993 – 1994, the company ran into financial difficulties because their ambition was much bigger than their reality. The big company went into liquidation and we scaled the original small company down to 28. We began to think again about what to do. My wife has always been a very active woman and she decided there was a gap in the market for fresh herbs. She set up a good herb production business. When we first started and we applied for a marketing grant. We were told that we were too optimistic when we anticipated a market of £400,000. Actually, that year the market was 2 million. We were the first ones to introduce herbs to the supermarket. We are out of that business and there are much bigger companies involved in it. My wife does decorative herbs at the moment.

By 1997, when I considered moving the technology company to Europe, I thought of taking out Irish citizenship. I had a very difficult time around this time and someone said to me that I was entitled to some kind of social benefits because I had been contributing all the time that I was here. I went to the doctor and she said this was so. I cried for the first time in my life. She gave me a medical report but I signed on for less than three months. I went to check about taking out citizenship in Enniscorthy and I met an old man; I am sure he is retired now and he said to me' *Do you think that giving you the citizenship is the key to getting handouts.'* I have to say that I do not blame him. At that time there were very few foreigners in Ireland, mainly students in the Royal College in Dublin and a few studying aviation. Anyway, from that time, things went OK for me and I employed between 20 and 28 people in my company.

Then in 2004, I had some difficulties again. The cost of labour had become very difficult. I wanted to buy the lab from our liquidator and scale it down for one of our customers, the biggest customer in Ireland. I started a small business for myself, which would employ my wife and me and I am also working as a consultant with the other guy. We are mainly producing ornamental plants through some form of genetic modification. In the past, we had no control over the type of plant but now we have good control. I still have the small business with my family. My daughters have finished university. One is a doctor and the other is a chartered accountant. The second one got a job even before she finished.

I do not think I regret any of my days in Ireland. I do not think the time was wasted. My wife feels the same. We have not any plans and we do not have any pension except the state pension. I ask myself how we are going to live here on that because it is not enough. We think about buying a house in Lebanon and if they pay the state pension, we can live more cheaply in Lebanon. If they do not pay us, you know the system in the Arab world where the children will help the family but we do not want to be a burden on them. My wife finds it very hard to move out even out of Enniscorthy where we are part of the society. We are involved in the local clubs and societies and I do not think we are going to find the stability we have in our lives here anywhere else. I do not know if this will continue with the advance of life and property but we are settled here.

I am part of the Irish anti war steering committee and we are not isolated but at the same time, we do not go to the pub to meet up with people. I used to look on this as part of the Irish culture but now unfortunately it is moving towards the binge culture. When we were students, we used to go with everybody to the pub. I did not like the idea of the rounds because everybody had to buy a round and I ended up with five or six cokes which were killing me. I do not do it anymore. Still I see Ireland as a good place even though we came here by mistake. When my oldest daughter started medical school, she could not understand why they did not treat her as Irish because she truly feels Irish. My younger daughter was always top of the class in Irish language and is always proud when she goes anywhere to say she is Irish. Both of them are practising Muslims; my elder daughter even wears the hijab but they look on themselves as Irish.

Libya

*Libya's contacts with Ireland began in the 1980s with meat export deals between Ireland and Libya. Many Libyan students also came to study in Ireland and some stayed. I met **Ibrahim** at the South Circular Road mosque. He has been in Ireland since the early 1980s.*

My name is Ibrahim Buwisir. I come from Libya originally, from a very well established political tribe in Ben Ghazi. My Dad was a businessman and my uncle was a foreign minister for Libya. My grandfather was one of the resistance leaders, 'mujahideen', who fought against the Italians. I have two brothers and three sisters. Both brothers are businessmen. Two of my sisters are married, one in Manchester and the other in Dublin. The oldest one is married to a lawyer in Libya. I have a few relatives around the world, cousins in America and cousins in Egypt.

I have been here since 1981. I studied English and my plan was to go to the States but I changed my mind. I did my Leaving Certificate and then studied in the Regional Technical College. I was involved in the meat business for four or five years and then worked for myself for three or four years. After that, I was involved in a charity called The Islamic Relief Agency and now I work for myself as a journalist. I have Libyan and Irish citizenship. I am involved in the Muslim Community and I am one of the founders of the IFI. I am also involved with the Muslim National Schools where my children go to school and where my wife teaches. My children also go to the Libyan National School on Saturdays where my wife also teaches. My children learn Arabic and English and research some knowledge through Arabic. We do not like the children to be left behind. We like a balance so they will be fluent in Arabic and English.

I think I have gotten used to living in Dublin. Dublin has become very big, noisy and hectic with a lot of traffic. I came to Dublin when there were very few cars and it was very open. I have noticed many changes in the Irish, some positive and some negative. The positive things are that they have more money now. The negative things are that they have become very racist compared with a few years ago. What I like about the Irish is they are kind, generous, not paranoid, very good supporters of causes against injustice including the Palestinian cause. I do not like the policy of the government. If I blame them, it is because they do not tackle the problem of racism and I think it is because they do not know how to do it. For Ireland all this is very new. Ireland actually does not expect people to come in. Ireland is used to people going out and working in Australia, America and England. Anyone who wanted to make a bit of money had to go to England, Australia or USA in the past. You could witness a queue of people, about 200 or more, outside the American Embassy in the past in Ballsbridge, all trying to get a visa to go to America. Now things are different. If I had the choice, I would prefer the country to the city. I find country people are more genuine, kinder. Another thing is the Irish are religious people when compared with other nations; they believe in God. If you speak about God generally to the Irish, they are believers and they respect anybody who has some values and principles in the religion.

I have been involved in the anti-war movement here. Over 100,000 people went on a demonstration against the war and that is a very positive sign in the Irish. They are against the foreign policy of the American Government. There are two or three reasons why I think Ireland has become racist. I think the media have played a big part.

The media create an image of the Arabs, the refugees, the asylum seekers as people who have come to suck the system. They portray them as people who take and give nothing. The ordinary man cannot sort himself out and he sees these people getting rent allowance, getting this, getting that and that makes him feel that he is not treated well in his own country. This has created ill feeling. I think the media play up this aspect of the situation and the policy of the government as well.

Take the Irish market; I know for sure that they need many skilled people to work on the buildings. In fact, there are only 15,000 refugees or something like that here in the country. If the Irish Government can provide an amnesty giving all those people green papers or giving them visas to stay, all these problems will be over in a week or two. But I don't think the government tackles the problem. Another thing is there are not enough programs to introduce the minorities and people who come to the country need transition time. When people come from state to state or from poor to rich they need a transitional social time to accept things and to realise who they are. This does not happen in a year or two. It takes decades, up to a generation. I think it is through education, awareness and mixing with people that integration happens.

I have noticed a very good start with one of the Nigerian refugees in Athlone; the whole community came out and was against the minister's decision to deport this person. These people are living among us; they have not caused any problems. Why should they be deported? The Irish people should remember that they were poor; they were emigrants and they went and made a living in America. They made a living in Australia, in England and in Libya. In the 1980s, there were more than 6,000 Irish people working in the oilfields. They were getting more money than the Libyans were. It is logical for me as a business man that somebody who leaves his own country, his own people, takes a risk and comes by himself should be given what the man who lives here gets; there must be some advantage for him. He must be attracted or else he will never make the effort to come.

It was much more comfortable living here in the 1980s, much nicer, much safer. Even though it was poorer, I was much happier. There is a lot of speculation now about the Muslims here. There is a lot of Islamophobia. I think it is the media. As a media man, as a journalist, and as an activist in the 80s, I notice many things. There is negative feedback. Now people have started to know about Islam, to ask, to enquire. In my case, after September 11th, I saw three mature people who became Muslim between September and December. One of them was a consultant, a very well established man, 65 years of age. Another man is a doctor and another fellow is about 20 years of age, a printer and a graphic designer. I know another fellow who was 16 and became a Muslim. So people are aware of Islam. But all these things are in the hands of Allah because he is the one who changes people and who converts them and makes them enter Islam. In my case, I have come under a lot of pressure from the media. This is a negative point. Whatever happens to you, you should see it from the other angle as well and we should walk over it and continue.

The Muslims here are not doing a good job to inform people about Islam. The Irish are a believing society and as I told you, they believe in God. As a Muslim, I believe that Islam is a religion and a way of life that is very close to nature and it accommodates the human soul, the human being. When people start their research, they find the reality. I remember at one time they ran out of copies of the Qur'an because everybody came and asked for the Qur'an.

Many racist tabloids here run very negative campaigns against the Muslims. They are unfair and biased. We, all Muslims, are under suspicion and we know the intelligence is watching us. In the end, come, get me, take me to the court, and charge me. Thank God, we are not in America because in America there are about 3,000 people locked up without any charge. I can tell you to be fair that though things have changed compared to France and compared to the UK and other European countries Ireland is still the best.

As a father and a family person, I have many concerns for my family. I see a lot of what you might call international traditions that I don't agree with. These are very different to our traditions and I am very concerned about them. As a Muslim, my way is to respect others and I expect others to respect me. We have our own beliefs, our own religion, our own ethics, our own values and our own standards. I devote myself to those. In the end, it is in the hands of Allah. He is the greatest protector. I choose where my children go; I choose who they mix with and what they do. I am trying to be a good example. Sometimes I fail and sometimes I am a success.

Finally, on the question of establishing a Muslim Khalifah or Muslim State, it should be in the Muslim countries. If the Muslims can do it fair play to them. Everybody has his own desire. Who is ruling Germany now? It is a Christian Party. If the Muslims want to have a Khalifah let them have it but I don't think it will happen. This system is not even happening in Muslim lands; in the Muslim lands, the Shari'a is not even being implemented. The governments there are puppet governments. They are not democratic. They are not elected. They are inherited. They are backward and they don't respect anybody's rights. Even if the people have a choice to vote for Islam, they will be demolished. That is what happened in Algeria.

I would not take all this as Islam. I think it is more Islamophobia, another series of conspiracies against the Muslims to show them *'Look we are taking over these countries'.* As for Muslims, we were a superpower before and if we have these ambitions now we are entitled to them. I mean America controls the world and why not the Muslims. In the end we are a fifth of the population of the whole world. We were a superpower for centuries. What we did for the world was a great justice. If you look at Andalusia and you look at Spain, we didn't kill people. The others, the Christians, killed. Look at the ridiculous crusaders. Look what they did to us. Who created the Second World War? Christians. Where did they fight it? They fought it in our lands. In Libya, there are 20 million mines left behind. In Egypt, there are 55 million. We are still suffering from these. Our countries have been occupied. There is not one Muslim country that has not been occupied. Before they were occupied by armed forces and by the army and now they are occupied by systems, thoughts and people who have no loyalty to our countries. I do not know if you agree with me or not.

To be honest, I have never met anyone who lived in the Muslim world who did not like it. Many people who lived with and mixed with Muslims, people who had no agenda, individuals like you, know and like the Muslims. But people who had an agenda who were spying who were doing this or that could be different. Individuals with no agenda who come to live in the Muslim world like it. I know a valley between Pakistan and Afghanistan and among them, there are a lot of converted Muslims, Irish and English. Many people through the 70s you know about it, from the hippy movement, went through Pakistan and Afghanistan and took drugs. Many people from those hippy movements went to that valley just to live in the wilds and have some free marijuana and hashish which was available then at that time. Everybody who went to that valley became Muslim. I know I talked to some of those people and they told me that when they came to the valley they found a quality of life, peace and love of human beings. I know some of those people; they worked for some of the charities and one South African talked with me. He said that when they came to those people they showed them love and tranquillity and respect for human beings. Those people are involved in farming; they pray five times a day; they share their food, bread and naan; they took us as guests for three or four days. They don't ask for anything and we saw they are happy. They live on a little but they are happy. We found Islam is the secret.

I think debating is a way to improve understanding between people. The media, the policy makers, should not be left behind. Those people have their agenda. I am not talking about the Irish, I am talking in general about what is going on in the West. Maybe the Irish government is more neutral than the others are. So those people have their agenda and this agenda is connected to the policy makers to George Bush to the multi-nationals, to people who have money, to people who want to control the world. Some people are fair and just like Robert Fisk, for example, but in the end, he is just one voice in one of the independent newspapers. Those people who have money and power are more numerous and they have an agenda of conflict between Islam and others. Their policies are clear; you are either with me or not.

The Muslim world has been neglected and has been misjudged for a long time. People want to rise up and get their human rights in any way they can and I can understand this. The West did not offer any solutions to the Middle East. They have made it worse. If you look at the role of the Americans, they are the supporters of and gun makers for the Israeli government. They are helping and financing them. This is not the way to do things. Another new generation has come to the Arab Muslim world. They are educated but they have ambitions. They want to rule according to Islam and I think they have started to. I mean if I meet a Christian man and he wants Christian rule I would not be surprised. I will be surprised if he wants another rule. I think as a Muslim that Islam is valid and it has more dynamic force than any other system in the world. Christians used to live freely in Muslim countries. They have their own churches. I will give you a small example. How long have Muslims been living in the West? For more than a century, two centuries! None of them holds any strong position in the government. There were Christians in Sadaam's government. Take Tariq Aziz, for example, he is a Christian and he was the Foreign Minister for a long time. Forget about Sadaam; look at Boutros Boutros Ghaali a Christian in the Egyptian Government. So the Christians have a role in our country. They live, they exist, and they live in harmony in our countries. But if you take my life and you kill my wife and my sister, don't expect me to say that I will be nice to you. Some people believe in *'an eye for an eye'*.

In terms of a Muslim government, it depends on where you are and where you stay. You cannot bring the Khalifah to South Circular Road. I think the Muslims are contributing a lot to Ireland. They are taxi drivers; they are businessmen; they are living quietly and they are doing well here. They never harm anybody and they never get involved with anybody in a bad way. We are contributing to the culture. The first people who brought the kebab to Dublin were the Muslims, Ishmael Kebab, in the 1980s. That is history. I used to drive from South Circular to Baggot Street in front of the pub and he was the only one who was making kebabs. The first man, who opened a restaurant 'Sidir Idris' on Wicklow Street, was a Lebanese. Now I will tell you something. I was driving a while ago in Dingle and I found a restaurant of Tandoori Chicken, the only one in Dingle. I was driving in Killybegs and I found another Arab restaurant. There are also many mixed marriages, which show that we have a strong affinity. In most of the mixed marriages where Muslim men marry Irish women, the women become Muslim. They wear the abbayah, a scarf, and get involved with the Muslim community.

What we hear about the issue of women in the Muslim world is just negative propaganda. Women are better treated in the Arab Muslim world than women in the West are. I have been living in the West for a long time; I have seen the suffering of single mothers; I see the abuse; I see the punishment. Every woman dreams of getting married. In our country, in a way it is a destiny that we are going to get married. The man comes and proposes to the woman and he is the one who pays the dowry. In the Muslim world, the woman doesn't have to go out to pick up a man. The men are knocking at the doors. She has the right to refuse if she wants. The woman doesn't have to work except at home. The man is the one who works.

If the West did not support some of those governments in the Arab world, they would not survive. Look at the choice of people in the last elections in Egypt. The Ikhwan (Muslims Brothers) exist as a political party and won 22% of the vote. They were arrested and beaten up but people still voted for them. If there is real democracy and real voting in the system itself, how will it be? Another fact is they are hypocrites; they don't want the Muslims but they are dealing with the Shii'ahs, two Shii'ah Muslim groups, Hisb Al Da'wa and Majliis Al Thawrah. Those people are puppets of the Americans. They accept the occupation of Iraq, they came to power with the help of the American tanks, and so they are OK. It is all a convenience for the Americans.

My ambition is to see more Irish people come to Islam because the Irish are great fighters and great missionaries. The Irish carried the message of Jesus Christ as a prophet. I believe like Muslims they believe in Moses and in all the prophets. They carried this message for nothing to all of Africa. I think if the Irish believe in something they will carry it out. Most of the NGOs and charity workers are Irish.

Ultimately, it all depends on us Muslims here in Ireland and how we can show our good example, how we can convey Islam and show the applications of Islam. I am working on this in my own way but it takes great effort and teamwork. As individuals, many Irish have converted to Islam but it takes teamwork. The Muslim community here is not interested in calling people to Islam; they are only interested in making euro. The euro is no good and it does nothing for you when you go to the graveyard. Among this generation of Muslims, there is some political division but I do not think it will last. If you want to talk about the situation and long term planning, we do not have it. We have not reached that stage yet. Maybe we have reached a stage of securing our own selves. Now our immediate need, our priority is a high school for Muslims, which we do not have. We have two primary schools; we have two mosques; we have the graveyard but if we could get a secondary school that would be good. There are many things to consider; there is the land and the money, the finance and the effort and actually the determination to do it. Somebody must devote himself to it for a year or two, to run around, to establish it, otherwise it will not come. Money comes first but I think manpower and people are more important.

Republic of Lithuania

*After Lithuania became a member of the EU in 2004, there was a huge exodus from the country. As far as unofficial statistics go, there may be about 100 thousand Lithuanians at present in Ireland. **Ewa** wirks in Dublin.*

I grew up in Lithuania. I spent 17 years there and then I migrated to Poland where I studied for six years. I treated Poland as my native country because my parents were Polish so even though I come from Lithuania I am of Polish origin. I studied English Philology in Poland. My first language was always Polish, which I spoke with my parents and at school. I went to an ethnically Polish school and that was great because all the subjects were in Polish. I spoke Lithuanian obviously with my friends and Russian as well with some friends. Russian and Lithuanian were the main languages when it came to official documents in the offices. Polish people were an ethnic minority.

The Polish minority and the Russian minority were more or less equal, each with about 10% of the population and the rest were Lithuanians. The majority of course would be speaking Lithuanian. I went to Poland to study university because at that time the best opportunities were actually in Poland for people who were ethnically Polish. Poland would sponsor people from Lithuania and from other countries to come and study in their country while in Lithuania if you were from a minority it was difficult to get a job or to get to university. Things were a bit corrupt so obviously if you were Polish it was not so easy.

I went to Wudz, an industrial city, in Poland. This is a big city but not as big as Warsaw. I spent six years there but I never fell in love with the place. It is not beautiful; it is just an industrial town but it is famous for an Academy where many people study. I studied there for five years and stayed a sixth year. I couldn't find a job so I went back to Lithuania. I spent three years in Lithuania, which had already been independent for three years from the Soviet Union. The economic situation was not so good even though I always had quite good jobs related to my knowledge of Polish. I worked in the Polish Embassy, in a Polish newspaper and a Polish bookstore. I could always find a job and I could manage. But obviously the economic situation was not giving opportunities to people for the future. A couple had to struggle to buy themselves accommodation. There was very little possibility to do that so everybody was living with parents and young people's marriages often ended in divorce because of this. There were no jobs and this affected relationships a lot. People just started to leave and go abroad.

Having English helped and this became the first basic grounds on which you could get a job anywhere. One of the first questions the employer would ask you was 'Do you know English?' I was doing some translation but obviously when you are living in the country that is not English-speaking you begin to lose the language. So I decided that I just had to go somewhere to an English speaking country to brush up on my English. That was the main reason why I wanted to go away; I also wanted some adventure so I came to Ireland but that was just by pure chance. I could have gone anywhere. I wanted to go to the States and actually got a visa. Europe is a bit closer and I feel more European. The American mentality is a bit different from the European mentality. Some of my friends went to live in Canada, to the States, to Ireland and to Poland. I had not many friends left in Lithuania so when I go back there now I do not have many people to visit.

Starting from the early 1990s, as soon as Lithuania got independence people started to leave to go abroad because the situation was awful in the country. You could not find employment. Everybody was getting a good education. I think it is part of our history. In the Soviet times, it was very easy to get high education and people were used to that. Many people with good degrees could not find jobs and they had to go abroad. That, I think, is why most of the young people left. I do not know the number actually, it is hard to say but thousands, maybe hundreds of thousands left and went abroad and they are still not going back. During the Soviet times, there was no way to leave the country. Poland is the neighbouring country to Lithuania and it was quite hard to go to Poland. You had to get an invitation from your relatives and your friends. It all had to be official. It was not automatic, and you could not just go to Poland, just across the border. So forget about other countries. People just did not travel in the Soviet times and as soon as the borders opened, they just flooded out.

The economy has not started to improve yet, not at all. I do not know why. I am not an economist. You take Ireland here with the Celtic Tiger; the major influence on the improvement of the economy here was foreign investment. They say now that Lithuania also needs foreign investment but the conditions are not very good so foreign companies just don't want to invest in Lithuania at the moment. The only thing that people are doing is buying property mainly because it is so very cheap there. But the country is still not growing, although there are some statistics that say the economy is starting to grow. This is not really true because people still have a lot of difficulty finding employment and they are still going away and on that basis you can say that the economy is not really going anywhere.

I did not know much about Ireland before I came except what I had learned during my English Philology course. I knew it had been occupied by British people for a very long time and just basic things about the IRA but not very much. When I saw the reality here, I was amazed at how friendly people are towards foreigners. In fact, I can say that are probably friendlier and more tolerant towards foreigners than Polish people are towards people like me when I went to Poland. This is very striking and it was very strange for me when I went to Poland because I always considered myself of Polish origin. In Poland, I did not feel so welcome and at home as I do here. Maybe it is just the nature of the Irish people. I fell in love with this country. I cannot imagine myself living anywhere else. I have been here for four years. It is a long time and I do not feel myself a foreigner. I am at home here and cannot imagine being anywhere else. Even in Lithuania, I do not feel as much at home as I do in Ireland. All my friends are scattered around the world and my family as well and I have only my father living in Lithuania so I do not have much left in common with that country. Of course, I love to go there and to walk down the streets but I feel great in Ireland and I think Ireland has loads of opportunities to study, to work and to enjoy living.

Of course, it is very expensive but there is always a chance to do something here, to buy accommodation even if you can't pay off the loan immediately but you still have the opportunity. You also have the social welfare system here, which is very good. If you cannot pay off the loan through a mortgage you can always go for some social scheme with the government. The government really takes care of people here. In Lithuania, I do not think this will happen. I remember when I was back home years ago I could not get a mortgage even though I had a job. I wanted to buy a flat but it was impossible because they would not give me a mortgage. They only gave mortgages to people who can buy the flat for cash, to people who don't need the mortgage. Hopefully, in maybe 10 or 15 years, Lithuania will be better. I think if politicians open the borders and frontiers for trade this will create a good position for them and things will grow.

There are many Lithuanians in Ireland – they say about 100,000 but it is very hard to count. I asked the ambassador before but he couldn't give me the numbers because he said officially there were about 50,000 3 years ago. Then of course there are also a lot of people who are here illegally. We do not need a work permit now but not all the people apply for a PPSI number. If the person does not apply for this number you cannot tell how many people are in the country. I do not know anybody who is working illegally but it may be that is the case.

Malaysia

*Malaysia has experienced strong economic growth over the last 25 years and has moved from being primarily an agricultural country to a manufacturing industrial centre. About 26% of Malaysians are of Chinese origin and form probably the richest section of the society while approximately 8% are ethnic Indians who moved mainly from southern India during British colonial times though there was a history of Tamil settlement in the peninsula from the 11th century. I met **Raj** in Dublin.*

Malaysia is a tropical country and the weather is hot. We have a mixed culture, western and our own local culture as well. The food is Asian and spicy. I am a Hindu but of course, there are a lot of Chinese as well as Muslims. There is work there. Many people think that when you migrate you do it because you need work but some people do it also for a change. There is plenty work in Malaysia but many people still ask me why I am here. I just wanted a change.

I grew up in the countryside where my parents have a plantation and I spent my early life there. I got a job in a hotel and worked in hotels for a while in Kuala Lumpur. I left Malaysia in 1992 and went to America. I stayed in Miami, Florida where I worked for some years. That is a crazy place. I went back to Malaysia again in 1997 for three years and again worked in a hotel. Malaysia is multi cultural and it is very comfortable to live in because nobody bothers about what other people do. Muslims do their own thing. We are Hindu; we do our own thing. The Chinese do their own thing but we all live together side by side. There are no problems and no tensions between the different groups.

In 1999, I got a job in Ireland, came here, and worked in a hotel. I was here for three years as a bar man and that was interesting. When I first came here, I found it a bit difficult because it was very different from where I used to work. But people treated me very fairly here. I did not have any problem with that. I am an easygoing person myself and get on with people. I learned a lot about the bar trade here because there are many differences between here and Malaysia. Now I work in the transport industry.

My wife is Welsh. I met her here in Ireland. We have two kids; my first boy is 19 months and the second is 8 months. I have gotten used to the culture here and it doesn't bother me. It is very easy for me to adapt to it and I feel comfortable. Maybe someone who comes from the countryside in Malaysia, may find it all very shocking. I am used to it and as well as that I have worked a lot in the bar trade and have met many people and seen a lot of drink. People treat me quite well here. I don't experience any problems and if there is anything I just ignore it. Life is hard enough so you don't make it harder for yourself. I find the weather a bit hard to adapt to because I come from a tropical area. It is not easy to get used to this weather and you miss the Malaysian food. I cook curries a couple of times a week at home. You can get many ingredients for Malaysian food here now.

The Malaysian community in Ireland is very small. It is just starting to grow. We have a consulate in Ballsbridge that opened two years ago. Movement of Asians to Ireland is a very new phenomenon and the Malaysian community is very new here especially when compared with the UK. During the next ten years, I think it will grow quite a lot. If you go to the Royal College of Surgeons, you will see many Malaysians. You may also find them in Tallaght Hospital and St James as well. The Malaysian government sponsors them to study in Dublin. It is very expensive to study here so they need sponsorship. It takes six or seven years before they complete all their studies and then when they go back they have to pay back the whole lot to the government. The money is deducted from their wages and they have to work for at least five years for the government. If everybody goes to study and doesn't return, the government will have no money. Malaysia is reasonably wealthy but not very. You can make a decent living there if you work. There is more farming than industry. Tourism is very slow; definitely not many people from Ireland but maybe a few from the UK. Many people from here go to Thailand and it is very well known. Malaysia is such a huge country but most people are not aware of it. You are the first person I have met in this country to mention anything about Mahathir Mohamed and Anwar Ibrahim.

I got a job in Ireland through the newspaper. It was all very fast. I enjoy travelling and this has given me an opportunity to come over here and see a little bit of Europe as well, because you cannot afford to come all the way for a holiday, as Europe is so expensive. I have a working visa and that is no problem to get it renewed because our company sponsors us and once a year I just get the permit stamped in my passport. My parents and the rest of my brothers are still in Malaysia. I try to go and visit once a year for a month's holiday. I don't think I will go this year because it is a bit more difficult now with young kids and 15 hours flying to get there.

There have been some political tensions in Malaysia. What happened was when Mahathir Mohamed had been Prime Minister for 10 years, Anwar Ibrahim tried to make the country more Muslim oriented. It is very hard to do that because Malaysia is a multi racial country. When Anwar tried this, Mahathir said 'No' and put him in prison. Anwar's goals would be OK if the country was 100%

Muslim but it is a mixture and has been so for over 100 years. Anwar wanted to put the values of Hindus and Chinese aside as he tried to tell people *'this is wrong and that is wrong'*. The Prime Minister said that this approach was not fair. I think Anwar was in prison for six to seven years. His wife became involved in politics but no one supported her; Muslims even don't want them because most of them believe in living in harmony with everyone else. If you followed Anwar's views, there would be many people left outside. Everybody wants to be normal. Therefore, people did not support Anwar and his wife. Anwar's wife's party did not get a single seat in the government.

The way Muslims practice their religion in Malaysia is probably more open than in many other Muslim countries. You can wear as you want. For example, a woman can cover her whole body or wear half-and-half. Nobody is going to bother her. There are no restrictions; some women cover everything including the eyes or you can dress as a modern woman. It is up to each individual how they want to practice. Mahathir Mohamed tried to impose the same fines for littering as was done in Singapore but Singapore is a tiny country and Malaysia is huge and very hard to keep control over such things as littering.

I do not plan to go back to Malaysia yet, but maybe in the future. I am not a rich man so if I went back now I would have to work so it doesn't make any difference if I stay here or go back. If I were going to retire that would be a different story. Salaries are much better here but the cost of living in Dublin is very high. It is very expensive here but of course it all depends on your salary and your expenses. Life goes on.

Mauritius

*The Republic of Mauritius is a small group of islands in the southwest of the Indian Ocean. In recent years many Mauritanian students have come to study in Ireland. I met **Jennyfer** when she was doing her teaching practice in Dublin.*

I am originally from Mauritius where I was born and raised. I completed my Bachelor's degree and all my secondary education as well in Mauritius. I came to Ireland nearly four and a half years ago. My secondary education was through the medium of English. French is also taught in the schools and is very similar to our mother tongue which is a Creole derived from French. We have Creole, French and English, which is the official language of the country. In the government sector, documents are in English. All the subjects in the school are taught in English except French.. At home, we speak Creole but there are different social classes and some speak French because this is considered higher class. But Creole is the commonly spoken language especially among the kids. It is very close to French and if someone had not studied French in school but watched a French TV programme they would be able to understand it. There are some differences in linguistic patterns but you will be able to understand.

Mauritius is about the size of Dublin and it takes only one and a half hours to travel from the north to the south of the island. There is a capital city, Port Luis and there are several quaint towns. Port Luis is the financial centre and the centre of import and export. I come from a small town in the centre of the island and we have shops, buses and such conveniences. Mauritius is a very class based society; you have Indians and Muslims, Chinese and the black African community. Those of Indian origin tend to work in the government because the government has an Indian majority. The Chinese tend to own the businesses. The black Africans tend to be the lower class, though I do not like to say that. It is a pity as they are not given the chances. They tend to work in construction or fishing. A few go to university, get good jobs and are breaking the barriers. However, the island is very segregated in terms of class.

Theoretically, it has a democratically elected government. We vote for the Prime Minister and other Ministers but it seems that they only work for themselves. I think it is one of the most corrupt countries in the world. They steal overtly. Our Prime Minister drives an Asti Martin but in Mauritius, the currency is rupees. How can he afford to buy an Asti Martin if not by stealing from taxpayers? He claims there is transparency but there is not.

Mauritius was a French colony but the British defeated the French and took over the island. That is why we have a dual heritage. I am not sure if we get foreign aid but we are an independent republic. If I want to travel from Mauritius to the UK, for example, I do need a visa and if I want to go to France, I need a visa. I think the EU does not involve itself very much in Mauritius. But people have to move out of Mauritius because the economy is very bad. I think the EU keeps its hands out of Mauritius because if they got involved the Mauritian community might think it had some rights into the EU. They might want to move into the EU. Tourism is the second biggest financial income. There are huge resorts with spas all around the island, which are of very good quality. There are lots of beaches and places for water sports so tourism is very big and it brings in foreign currency. The climate is nice. It is always bright and the beaches are lovely.

I decided to move out of Mauritius because I always felt very out of place there. The position for women in the country is still very traditional. Though they have their rights and can go to college and university, they are still expected to marry at a certain age, set up a home and have kids. Some marriages are still arranged but in general, girls can now choose their own partners. They still have to marry within their own religion and their own caste. An Indian for example would not go and marry a Muslim because this would be considered taboo. It happens but you are brought up knowing that you don't cross the borders and intermarry with a person from another religion. You are expected to marry within your own group. When I finished college at 21 or 22, I did not want to marry because I wanted to experience the world a bit. I had just finished my degree but I didn't have any money. I was looking for a country to which I could come. I applied to the UK but my application did not get approved. I came to Ireland because the visa regulations were not so strict. A Mauritian does not need a visa to come to Ireland. You just book a place in a college, take a plane, and come here. You can even come here on a tourist visa for three months and then you can change your status to a student visa.

There was an agent in Mauritius who recruits students to come to Ireland and he recruited me. Because I was already qualified with a degree, I thought I could get a job here as a teacher or in an office. But when I got here I could not find anything. The agent was a Mauritian of Indian origin and I paid him some money though not too much. I also paid a college here to come and study and then he got a commission from that college. I do not know how much he got but I do know that at the end of the day he became very rich because so many people came here through him. I applied to do a diploma in Hospitality Management even though it was not my field but it was a way to get out. I studied for a year in the college and then I

216

stopped. I registered for my Master's in UCD because I really wanted to do Women's Studies. After that, I took a year off and worked. Then I went back to UCD to do my Higher Diploma in Education.

I think one of the reasons I was interested in coming to Ireland was that women have so many rights here. I do not mean these rights are going out with as many boys as possible but the freedom to be yourself. I am, not against marriage but I think you need to know yourself before you get involved in a marriage. Even though I was with my boyfriend in Mauritius and we came here together in 2002, we only got married this year. We were ready this year but we did not want to be forced into something before that. There was not any objection to the marriage because he is the same religion as me. I would say if he had a different religion, my parents would dig their heels in. He is also the same caste but I really do not like using the word caste or class. I think we should have a classless society but that is very difficult.

I have found living in Ireland very difficult. When I came to Ireland, there were only about 10 Mauritians in the country and they were all part of our group. After I came here, I did not get a job for three months and I ended up working in MacDonald's. That was very difficult because a couple of months before I had been working as a teacher in Mauritius. The other foreign workers, mainly Chinese, were not very welcoming to new foreigners because they saw Ireland as theirs. They were here before us and they saw us as a threat. I could not do MacDonald's for long so I left after three weeks. Then I got a job in a pub. I was living in Glasnevin and the pub was about five minutes walk from my house. I have been working there for four years and still am. When I am studying, I cannot work but when I am not I work and my boss is such a lovely

217

person. He is like a father figure; I have been very lucky and he has encouraged me all the time to study. He adjusts my hours; he has facilitated my study and has helped me in whatever way he can. If I did not have this job in the pub, I would not have been able to stay here. With that job, I managed to pay all my expenses. I have had to pay foreign fees for all my courses. I paid €7,000 for my Master's and €11,000 for my Higher Diploma. All the money I have earned has gone into education. I find it very hard looking at Irish people who do not seem to appreciate education. There was a girl working in the pub with me; she came in to cover for her Mum and she told me she is dropping out of school after Junior Cert. I asked her what she was going to do because these days even a Leaving Cert is not enough. I was dumbfounded when I heard this. For these students they only have to pay €1,000 and I am here slaving in the pub, working for €10 an hour to pay for my study and there she is having all those chances and she does nothing. It is a big issue for me.

Living expenses are terrible here. When I first came, I lived with a host family and just paid rent but I had a tiny box room. It was very tight because I was used to living in a house with lots of space. You had to wait for the right time to cook and to use the bathroom. I do not think Ireland provides very well for foreign people living here - even for the students. In terms of benefits, we do not get anything. I have been working here for almost five years, paid my taxes and my PRSI but if I go to the hospital tomorrow, I will have to pay €200 – 300 to get myself checked. I do not have private health insurance. That is the big difference between here and the UK. I have an aunt who is studying in the UK and she gets all the health benefits free. As soon as she entered the UK, she was registered. It is not like you need these all the time but just in case you do it is important to have them. Here nobody cares. Mauritius is like the UK; the health care is free and it is very good.

Irish people are very nice. They are very pleasant and always smiling. They ask you how you are and where you come from. I think this varies with class though. I feel from working in the pub that I can look at the person when he comes in and tell what class he is. You know just by looking at the person but everyone is very nice. Some people tend to be racist. My husband works in a hotel at night and he was telling me about a group of drunken Irish guys who felt they could throw things around because they pay these foreigners to clean up after them. You can see that some Irish are not at ease with foreigners and they will not really interact with you.

I had a very nice time working in the school for the year and this is what I really want to do. For the last two years, I had not been able to do what I wanted and this year I did and I was very happy that I got the chance to work in the school. It is a lovely school and I had a very nice time even if you don't get paid for the whole year. I was teaching first and fourth years and this gave me a very good insight into the age difference and good experience. I did not encounter any major incidents. Students sometimes talked a bit when my back was turned but nothing major. The kids were very nice and they reminded me so much of my school days because it lets you grow as an individual.

I would love to stay in Ireland and buy a house here if I could get a job. I have applied to about 20 ads and I have not heard from any. Two replied and said they could not take me but for the rest I do not know. I renew my visa each year and now I have a visa until October. Now people who have completed a degree here are allowed apply for a work permit. When my visa expires in October, I will have six months after that to find a job and then I can apply for my work permit because I am skilled labour. They are making it very difficult because they say your salary has to be over €30,000 but what if I get a teaching job that only gives me 11 hours a week. There are so many restrictions and conditions. It seems they do not want people to come in and take jobs but still they need so many teachers. One supervisor who came in to my class was shocked to see the number of students in the class and asked how we cater for 30 kids at the same time. I think UCD and Trinity are training more teachers and the course is good. We are the best-trained teachers in Europe. The course is hard but I enjoyed every single day of it.

If I cannot find a job here I might try in the UK. An agent came to UCD from the UK and last week I got two interviews. I went there and I got the first job I was interviewed for. The school gets me a work permit and will stamp it in my passport for five years. After five years, I can apply for indefinite stay in the UK. The job I have been offered in the UK is a permanent post for full time English with housing and health benefits. I cannot afford to stay here if I do not get a job. My husband is doing his degree in Hospitality Management and is in his final year. He can transfer to a UK university and finish the last year there. In Ireland, if I am on a student visa and my husband is dependent on me he cannot work. Now we are both on separate student visas so we can work 20 hours.

In the last year, I have seen so many Mauritian people in Ireland because there are ads everywhere in Mauritius talking about the opportunities in Ireland. The realities, however, are very different. Many Mauritian families come here and move their kids from school. But in the long term how long can they continue with this? Only one person in the family can work so can they do it? I am free to work nights but not if I have kids. Here you can't get into the system but in the UK you are put in automatically because they know you are going to work and provide good services. Irish people will not do many kinds of jobs so the migrants are going to be stuck

220

in dead end jobs. They may have qualifications but they are not allowed get into the system. It is a grim reality and if Mauritian people come and ask me if they should come to Ireland, I would tell them not to come. The reality is grim here.

Nigeria

*Many Nigerians have moved to Ireland over the past ten years and are involves in a variety of activities around the country. I met **Chenidu** at his office in Dublin.*

I grew up in the Southeast of Nigeria, a predominantly Christian, Catholic area to be precise. The weather makes it a very good place to live especially at this time of the year. In fact, the weather there is always good.   In February, it is very hot and you need air-conditioning. All the drinks companies make a lot of money because of the heat. Some of the drinks are locally produced though they are owned by foreign companies. Guinness has the largest brewery in the world in Nigeria. Coca Cola is strong; Heineken is strong. You know there are so many big companies in Nigeria and when I say they are strong, I mean they have a strong foot in the country, Seven-up, Pepsi and many other drinks. Every company that produces soft drinks here can be found also in Nigeria. If they do not have a factory in Nigeria, they have a market and they export to Nigeria.

When it comes to Christmas, I think it is more fun where I come from, in the sense that the society celebrates Christmas outdoors, unlike in Ireland where it is indoors with families and relatives. In Nigeria, the celebration is extended-family oriented.   Nigerian people spend more money it seems to me than people do in Ireland when you compare the amount of money they have as their disposable income because all the family gets something for their relations.   When you have the extended-family system, there are many expenses and many financial problems.   So the way they celebrate Christmas is unique in the sense that Christmas begins a couple of months before. People, relations, friends, family friends prepare Christmas food. They cook and bring food to your house two months before Christmas. That is an invitation to come to Christmas in their house. So it is only the people that are special for whom you cook Christmas food; you deliver it and they come to you during Christmas on the appointed day. They will come with drinks, buy many gifts, and celebrate Christmas with you.

At this time, there are a lot of fund-raising ceremonies. People fund-raise for their weddings and put money together to help others. This is seen as a way of covering the cost of the wedding and sometimes people make a profit from the money raised. In Nigeria, what we have is self-help, and not the organised help you have here. The people organise themselves without the support of the government and do many things for themselves. They bring electricity and pay for the construction of roads. They pay for the piping in of water and energy. So at this time of the year there is a lot of fund-raising for such things. People coming home from all over the world contribute and organise ceremonies where you actually come and donate money openly. If you do not want to donate openly you can write a cheque and give it specifically to the fund-raising. People organise different activities on Christmas Eve and Christmas Day. There is even a fund-raising event taking place within mass after the offertory. The MC comes out and announces the way people will donate money. If you have returned from Europe, this is your opportunity to come and donate. If you have just returned from Lagos or Abuja, our capital, you know that this year God has blessed you this is your chance. It is a way of pushing people to donate money. Christmas actually ends about the 1st of January and in total there are about eight market days in my whole area. Market days celebrate Christmas one a day. One community has a market area and celebrates one day and then another community has another market day and celebrates another day. It goes on like that. Cultural dances, masquerades, acrobatics, and plays entertain people. So that is the way they celebrate Christmas and on the 31st of December, which is New Year's Eve, there are serious parties here and there. New Year's Day is usually the last day. One community will definitely celebrate that day. People also have many parties after church and church is the centre unlike here.

In my part of Nigeria, people farm and do civil service work. The system is different to Ireland. Over there everybody owns a piece of land. In our own house, we grow a lot of food and though my parents are retired public servants we still have our own farms. Every family has a farm. In my region, we have some Anglican people but we are mostly Catholic in the sense that Catholics are 70 – 80% of the population. These days there are many Christian Evangelical groups. We also have a Muslim community but it is very small. Muslims, for example Lebanese, are found in every part of Nigeria doing business.

I will say what I want to say about my journey to Ireland. I arrived here in 1997 from Lagos. I used to work in – well I have done so many things in Nigeria that I do not know where to start. I have done journalism. I have done public relations. I have done letter publishing. I have worked for an airline, many things. Since arriving here I have been working in various things but mainly in journalism; I have also done one week's factory work. I have worked in advertising. I've done consultancy work – everything.

There are no statistics for the Nigerian community here in Ireland to show that this is the number of Nigerians in Ireland. I would say it is over 15,000. Some of them are well established and others are just floating around. But I would say give or take a little in five to ten years time there will be many established Nigerians, simply because the government has been able to regularize the number of parents of Irish born Nigerian children.

The attraction of Ireland for Nigerians depends on whom you meet. There are many Nigerian doctors here. I do not know any hospital here where you will not meet a Nigerian doctor or nurse. You have people on work permits. You also have people on work visas though they are not too many here. You also have students. In any college you go to in Dublin or the main cities in Ireland, you will find Nigerian students as well as at private secondary schools. You also have those in the Diplomatic Corps; they are fewer than 15. The majority of Nigerians are refugees or asylum seekers. The attraction of Ireland for Nigerians – I would not really know. It depends on whom you meet – if it is somebody who lived in the UK in the past and today is living here, it may be because of his residence permit. He may be getting better work here. Some Nigerians have British nationality, had good work there, and have been living in Ireland for the last five years. A couple of them had family problems and they wanted to move and others just think they can do it better here than in other countries. Some of those seeking asylum have genuine cases. Some see it as an opportunity – you see it depends on whom you meet. Sometimes the authorities in Ireland recognize the difference between the two groups and sometimes they do not. It is very difficult to investigate. For example, they are going to recruit ethnic minorities into the guards but one problem they are going to face is how to get security information on these people. It is not going to be easy actually and there is no way of investigating the people once you have hired them.

Before coming here, I had heard about Ireland. I had seen it on television, heard about it on radio but what we know about Ireland is the trouble in the North. Gerry Adams is better known in Africa than the Taoiseach and the president. So that is what I knew about Ireland apart from the many missionaries who worked in Nigeria. I also knew that many Nigerian professionals were coming over here to train; the airline industry for example Aer Lingus used to train many Nigerians. Even my uncle who is a doctor, retired now in Canada, has been here several times. He studied in the UK. When I arrived here, I was the only black person on the plane. It was a bit of a shock for me. Then we were seen as ambassadors because there were only a few black people in Ireland in 1997. Today, it is not the same. I was surprised when I came here that people did not say 'hi' to others. When you said 'Good Morning', 'Good Afternoon' or 'Good Evening' to other people they would not respond. That was a shock to me. The level of people's engagement with pubs and clubs generally was shocking to me – though if you go to Port Harcourt where you have a cosmopolitan community, things like that happen every day.

I do not think I had any problems with the people in the way they reacted. Over the years, what I have come to see is that somehow it could have been better. When you compare the people here with Swedish people or people from other countries, you find that the people here are warmer and more welcoming. When I came first I wasn't terribly impressed. I expected more because of what we had been told back in Nigeria that in the foreign land in the white man's or white woman's land this is the way things are done. I came over here and it was not the way things are done. So it was a shock – to hear about robbery, armed robbery. We have this in Nigeria, in most African countries. We used to have it all the time. It is not the case now but still crimes happen here – people go and attack an 80-year-old man or woman, living on their own. That was all very shocking to me.

Sometimes in the media, all is quiet as nobody is interested in anything apart from Christmas. By January when the newspapers have nothing to celebrate, they start looking out for things and that is when it gets very bad. If you compare today with five years ago, I would prefer today; it is better. People are getting information about multiculturalism and integration; they have come to realize that look it is here with us, and we have to change. The entry of some new countries into the EU has helped a lot because those people three years ago who were seen as the order are no longer the order. They are no longer giving out about the new people because now they are the same in terms of European Union Movement. Those people in Ireland who are interested in multiculturalism are making efforts. There are also people in organizations that are making efforts but personally, they have a different agenda. I am talking about some big unions. You hear them condemning how migrant workers are treated but some of those are just publicity stunts. This feeling is not coming from the bottom of their hearts. Personally, some of them can do worse than those executives.

What we do here in Metro Eireann is publish a monthly newspaper. By the end of this coming year it will be weekly. Apart from the newspaper we bring out an annual magazine which is called 'Ireland 2005', 'Ireland 2006' and so on. Apart from the magazine, we do training, like going to conferences to talk about multiculturalism. We participate in public events, whatever people are organizing we come on board to speak about any aspects to do with multiculturalism, and ethnic issues. We also run the MEMA, which is Metro Eireann Media Awards in association with RTE. That targets people, Irish and non-Irish who are contributing towards creating cross-cultural cooperation and understanding in Ireland. We give awards every year – the selected few just to support what they are doing, promote interest, and see if we can help other people

227

get ideas from them. So those are some of the things we do. We have also tried to set up a radio station which did not work. We were not successful but there will be another attempt next year.

There is not equal opportunity here. This week somebody rang. I was not here. He spoke with Catherine and left his number. I called him back. The reason he rang me was simply to talk about some articles we have done in the past and how he had interpreted them. He is a migrant and he has not had it so good. According to him, he has done another course in Ireland to re-qualify and everywhere he goes, it has been very difficult getting a job. One particular company, a recruitment agency, gave him some advice and told him *'Look I don't think you are going to get this job – you should think about doing something else'.* But he is not interested in factory work and he says if he goes to factory work by the time he comes back he has no energy to look for anything else. He has no energy to check his internet and to look for another job so why should he keep on doing it every day. Apart from that, there are people who have tried to work, who are constantly looking for work but they are not getting it. You have some companies that are going abroad to recruit, to look for workers while there are people here actively looking for work. Take for example care work. In the last two months, many immigrants have wanted to do care work. They have done training in the area but they cannot get work. Some Dublin hospitals went abroad in the last few months and recruited care workers while there are tens of people looking for such work here in Dublin. I don't know why these people have not been able to find work. It may be that they have been unfortunate or there is no vacancy. If there is no vacancy, why do you go and actively recruit abroad? I don't really know what to call it. There are some communities, foreign communities, who believe that they are not treated in the same way that other minorities are. For example, the black community believes that some of the other ethnic nationals are treated better. So, one could say that this accounts for the lack of jobs for some groups. I actually noticed this a couple of years ago when people were looking for certain positions in shops as shop assistants. The shop owners were happier to recruit people who could not speak English because they are not black.

Employers need to know that it is beneficial for them to give work to people who are already in the country rather than going abroad to recruit. They also need to know that if the reason for not giving work to those already in the country is to exploit those they recruit from outside the country that this will not last. After some time problems will develop and eventually the company will be exposed. That area needs to be investigated. The law needs to be strengthened and I do not think the way it is now is actively encouraging companies to look at migrants who are in the country. Apart from that, migrants in the country need to keep up their education as well as training. While you have no work, you need to keep on updating and using every opportunity to improve your skills. Funding is a big problem but if someone is looking at not going into full time education, he or she can save money for it even while on social welfare. It is possible to save a couple of euro a week and at the end of the first year you have enough to pay for the first year – about €800 – for those who are interested in saving.

Right now, I am here in Ireland. I concentrate on here. I also have a home in Nigeria. That is where my parents are. My sisters and my friends are there. I have a home here. I have a home in Nigeria. Who knows, maybe tomorrow I will have a home outside of Ireland in Europe somewhere, in America as well as Nigeria. I just make the most of wherever I am. That is the way I see it. I do not know how or when this society can be provided with more information

229

about ethnic minorities. I think if they have more information, accurate information they would be in a position to know that immigrants are not a danger to them.

I met **Abimbola** *in Dublin city centre.*

I am from Lagos, the capital of Nigeria, which lies along the West African coast and is home not just to Nigerian people but to a lot of people from all over the world. I lived and worked in Lagos for a good part of my life. I was schooled in Lagos where I studied Business Administration and worked as a banker for 13 years. I quit my job and decided to move to Ireland in 1998. Ireland is a different ball game to Nigeria in many respects. In Nigeria, everybody needs to go to College if they want to have a career. In Ireland, however, people can start a career after Leaving Certificate. That is good. I came to Ireland because I had some friends here. I oversee here in the 'Studio' and help but I do not work full time.

I have four kids and I find it a bit difficult to work with four kids who are aged 7, 5, 4 and 1. I have to fit into their itinerary. My husband lives in Nigeria where he is working on a project. Life here in Ireland is different to Nigeria. In Nigeria, you create fun for yourself. There are carnivals and parties. Everybody in Nigeria is like family. Everyone is his brother's keeper. In Ireland, you feel that people have their own family but after that, people don't care. People go ahead and look after themselves. It is a selfish society.

Organizations cater for the poor in Ireland but the loneliness is great. People are very lonely and I think that is the cause of so much suicide. Even Nigerians attempt suicide because of loneliness. You never find this in Nigeria. There is a strong Nigerian community here. There are organizations here such as 'Know

Racism' which help people. There are some Nigerian organizations with Irish affiliations.

I live in a bed-sit with my children in the centre of Dublin. My 7 year old is in school and he can speak Irish. I can manage but it is not easy. Ireland has a good social welfare system and most people benefit from this. It allows people to work flexibly. I have Irish papers and my children are Irish. I plan to set up a business in Ireland. I am a Christian and I want to start a business selling Christian materials that could benefit people.

I believe that Ireland needs to refocus on Christian values. I know the Irish brought Christianity to Nigeria and gave us the gospel. But Ireland now suffers so much from so much alcohol. I would like to address that. I can do that by preaching the gospel of evangelism and through personal prayer. In the process of marketing and producing Christian products, I can reach out and preach. I am going to look into the possibility of setting up a business through Fás. Here in Ireland, the whole concept of Christmas has been eroded. All people do is buy gifts, spend money, exchange gifts and get into debt to do this. The actual meaning of Christmas is a celebration of the birth of Jesus Christ, his life and Calvary. We should reach out to people. I belong to the 'Redeemed Christian Church of Christ'. This is a Nigerian church and it has over 40 parishes in Ireland.

Pakistan

*Pakistan is a troubled country that lies in the eye of the American war on terror. I helped **Tauseef** with preparing his application for a licence for a business college in Dublin.*

I was born in Pakistan in Rawlapindi, one of the small, but beautiful cities in the Punjab. There are four provinces in Pakistan. Mine is Punjab, the biggest province in the centre. Then there is the North West Frontier Province and that is close to the tribal areas in Afghanistan, famous for its association with the Taliban. Because of its location on the border, many people cross over and back. The government has now set up a border post, checkpoint and people require IDs to cross the border to make sure that only those who have the right to do so can cross into Pakistan. The other two provinces are Sind with the capital Karachi; this is one of the biggest trading cities in Pakistan and makes up about 50% of Pakistan's trade as the main port is there. The fourth province is Baluchistan near Iran.

Pakistan is a country of four climates in one calendar year. In terms of the population, the rich are rich and the poor are poor. Now it is a democracy with an elected president who is also the chief of the Pakistan army. I grew up there; my father was in the army. He is a doctor and we spent most of the time outside Pakistan. My basic education took place in Saudi Arabia. I was in school in Jeddah from my fourth to my eighth year in both the Royal School and the Pakistan School. My father wanted us to know Urdu as well as Arabic. I was very fluent in Arabic because of being in school in Saudi Arabia for all those years. I went on the Umrah and Hajj many times. We used to go every second week to Mecca for the Umrah.

In 1980, my father was posted back to Pakistan into the air force. I continued my education to 10th class in Rawlapindi and then did my Junior and Higher Cert in Islamabad. I did a B. Comm. in Islamabad also and then did my Master's in Public Administration from the University of Baluchistan. I am a gold medallist. This was a new degree and we were the first batch to complete the course on this campus during 1990 – 1993. It was supposed to be two years but it ended up being three. My father was living there and working as a doctor in the army. He retired in 1994 and we moved back to Rawlapindi.

During my studies, I was employed by DCS, one of the largest logistics companies in the world. I started as an Accounts assistant and ended up as manager in 1996. During the next nine years, I served in many different countries and moved from place to place. I got firsthand experience of logistics working with DCS as it represents DHL the international company in Pakistan. Howard University did a study of this company and the development that took place because of their staff and the efforts of people behind the scenes. I was one of the people who grew with the company and ended up as a station and country manager in Islamabad.

I got married in 1996 and I moved on to college business. I was a director and part owner and the college did very well. We developed many courses including data courses; the college managed the junior and leaving certificate courses also. In 1999, I moved to Ireland because there was a rift in the Pakistan economy due to the army coup. The student counselling services with which I was associated had many problems so I decided to try my luck elsewhere and move away from the problems facing us.

When we moved to Ireland, we had to look at the culture because it is totally different to ours. I started working in a meat factory owned by my brother-in-law. It was a terrifying situation for me to wake up at 6 o'clock in the morning loading, unloading, and cutting up the halal meat to send it to France, Libya and Dubai. It was partly an office job but you had to be there in the factory to make sure that the killing and cutting were done in the correct Islamic way. The meat was loaded on the trucks and dispatched according to the schedules. There was a lot of accounting and management work. The weight of the animal is reduced once the kill is done because water drains out. You have to calculate the weight, send the meat to the destination and make sure they are aware of what is coming in the container and deal with the problems associated with moving meat from one place to another i.e. taxation and motorway permits. The factory closed in 2000 and then one of my associates asked me to start a recruitment company with him. We did a lot of counselling services for students while placing them in different colleges. I was one of the first people to source international students to different private Irish colleges. I brought students to state institutes like Athlone Institute of Technology and Dundalk Institute of Technology. We worked mainly as an intermediary and worked hard at getting students from abroad to come here.

In 2003, I thought of setting up my own college and with one of my so called friends I started up this college. We bought a college actually known as PQ Training; it was a technology college which had been run by a South African woman. She was unhappy about the educational system here and was always complaining. We provided her with students and then we decided to buy the college. We offered her a price; she accepted and the deal was closed. The deal was closed in September and we started operating in January. In March, we got a surprise visit from the authorities. The

234

Immigration Authorities came with questions about the running of the courses. Within 3 months we had satisfied their requirements but in June 2004 they stopped us doing any further business. But a consultant we knew helped us fight our case with the authorities and eventually after six months we were able to get a licence. I was so happy when I saw that letter saying that we could recruit students for the college. The year 2005 was a year of recovery for me. I applied for my naturalization and got it in 2006. I developed a plan that we could recruit students for CCMIT in Management and IT. The authorities did not want to give a licence for IT only but they did for the whole college. We then had about eight lecturers and 350 students from different disciplines. It is difficult to put all the Quality Assurance into practice. It takes more than a year or two. I think you need at least five years even if you are going in the right direction. We started having more visits from the Immigration Bureau asking many questions about the students especially the Chinese. There were some problems with the Chinese and we tried to help them to improve our working relationship with the authorities. But I guess it didn't work out the way we wanted and since December we have been fighting with the authorities. We also had a visit from the Department of Education and they were unhappy about certain issues. One of these was the Fire Cert issue and another one concerned the letters of protection. They removed the chance of appeal from the register and the process is ongoing.

Ireland is a beautiful country and I am enjoying myself here. The main problem if I compare it with the UK where I have a business as well is for people trying to locate themselves in another culture. People want to be a part of the society and at the same time exercise their rights and freedom, for example, to practise their religion. Integration has to take place but it has to be done in the proper way. Some minority groups find some difficulties but I have not had any

235

problems here other than with the Immigration Authorities in terms of the College. Sometimes you feel you are not being judged on your merits; you feel if you are native Irish you will be dealt with for your own merits. This is also a common complaint that I get from students while I have been doing counselling over the last five to six years. Students feel that jobs are given to EU people before them. I always advise them not to lose hope and also to remember that they are integrating into a society that is developing itself. With the economic boom a lot of expansion is going on in society and Irish people never expected to have all these people coming from countries like Romania and Bulgaria to their country. It will take time for all the different people to get settled. I think then everybody will enjoy the benefits and perks that are there for them. The reward will be fully proportional to the efforts they put into it.

Afdal is a student from Pakistan who works at a food store part time.

Pakistan is a very good country. I grew up in Gujenwala in the Punjabi part of Pakistan, near Lahore. People in that area grow grain especially basmati rice. My father is a business man and he works in Kuwait. I spent a good part of my childhood in Kuwait along with my family. Part of my education took place in Kuwait but the family had to leave at the time of the First Gulf War in 1991. After a couple of years, my father and brothers returned to Kuwait where they still work. I stayed in Pakistan and continued my studies. I took a Bachelor's Degree in Psychology in Gujenwala University. I did a course in homeopathic medicine and qualified as a homeopathic doctor. Then I did a laboratory course in chemistry in Peshawar. I did a six-month computer course in Lahore.

Some of my classmates had come to Ireland and they told me it was good here. They also said the country was beautiful. I saw ads in a newspaper for the computer college in Ireland. I applied, was accepted and came here. I have been here one year. I am in the College of Computer Training (CCT) on Upper Dame Street. My class is all foreigners, Pakistanis, Indians and Chinese mainly. Our teachers are all Irish. There are courses in Programming and Management. When I finish the course there I will go on and do a Bachelor's degree in Computing.

I work in a food shop three days a week and all day Sunday from 10 a.m. to 8 p.m. It is very difficult to combine working and studying. My father helps me cover expenses. The rent for this room is €550 and you see it is a small room with two of us living in it and the fees in the college are €4,800. I am lucky that my father is able to send me some money. He told me that I should go to Kuwait and work when I finish here in Dublin. My favourite subject is Psychology and I really enjoyed doing the Bachelor's degree. Psychology is inter-related with homeopathy. I have not practiced here in Ireland, as there are not many places for homeopathy. There are no side effects from homeopathic medicine so it is better than ordinary medicine. I wonder why the medical services are so bad here. It also takes a very long time for emergency services to come.

Living in Ireland is very expensive but everything else is fine. People are nice except those especially the teenagers who drink. It is much worse I think than other European countries. They talk too much when they drink but when they sober up they usually say 'sorry'. You don't see people drunk like this in Pakistan. We usually go to the mosque on Moore St because it is near. We go to the bigger mosque for Eid celebrations.

Poland

*According to the 2006 Census, there were over 63,000 Poles living in Ireland, most of whom are involved in the construction industry. The following four stories reflect the lives of some of the Poles living in Ireland. I taught **Iwona** English in Dublin.*

Growing up in Poland was not so difficult from the point of view of a kid. I don't know how it was from an adult perspective. However, when I was young we had martial law in the country and there were shortages of food. We did not have a lot to eat at that time. The shelves were empty and you needed special cards; for example you could only buy a few kilos of sugar every month and soap and a little of everything you needed. Later when I was 15 or so and it was still in Communist times, life for kids was very easy because everything was organised by the Communist Party. Each company organised vacations for kids and we were all very busy during our vacations and of course it was all for free. We know that these things cost a lot of money and now we are paying the government back. At that time it was very easy and parents had things to do with their kids. Comparing the present times with the past in Poland, it is much more difficult for people these days. It is not such a happy time for kids because if the parents don't have money kids have to spend their whole vacation at home. Of course, nowadays the shops are full of food from different countries but if the parents do not have money, they cannot buy anything except the basics.

I am from a small city in the south of Poland, the most polluted part of the country. It used to be the best part of Poland and many people came to Silesia to find jobs because of the many coalmines in the region. Today it is very poor. There is a lot of unemployment and the coalmines are all closed. Many men from that region work abroad and their wives and kids live at home. The guys work outside all week or all month and just go back with money. It is very difficult because of the fact that there are no jobs in Poland. There is still a lot of coal in the mines but the problem is they do not have money to reorganize the mines and buy modern equipment. That is why the mines are closing down. There is nobody to finance the restructuring of the company.

I finished university and then my boyfriend and I decided to try our luck in different countries. We knew it would be very difficult to stay in Poland. Everybody dreams of going to Warsaw and getting work but outside of Warsaw there is no work. There are a couple of other big cities where things are happening. Some companies have opened new factories but when they invest money, they do it only in Warsaw. Other parts of Poland have good manufacturing bases and good workers but the companies do not use them. In Warsaw, most of the jobs go to people from established families. Somebody knows somebody and so on and that is how you get a job. There is never an advertisement on the newspaper to which you can apply and you find you are not in luck because there are at least another 100 people looking for the same job. You need to have an uncle or father or good friend with father and uncle and then you can get a job. Otherwise, you have no chance.

There is a lot of corruption. I think this is a carryover from Communist times because then if you belonged to the party you had everything. If you were outside, you did not have anything. It is still like that; if you are part of a big family that knows somebody then you are somebody. Without these connections, you can forget about a good job even if you have finished two or three university degrees. There is also the question of salary. I am a teacher, my husband is an engineer, and even if you could get a job, the salary is very low. The European Union is investing a lot of money in Poland - building roads and bridges and I am sure he could get a job but the salary is only about €400 a month and you work six days a week for ten hours. This is completely crazy. If you get €400, you can have a better life than other people but you do not have time to enjoy your life because you are just working all the time. Most people do not think about buying a flat or a house. My parents bought a flat. They had been living in a flat that they got from the company where my father worked. So the price was cheaper for them because of a discount for workers. Without this kind of discount, he would not have been able to manage to buy a house.

In Communist times, people did not bother to buy houses or flats because they got everything from the Party. It was automatic. When they got married and were going to have a baby, they were able to get a flat. You just went and said we are going to have a baby and you would get the key of your new flat. They took care of families and decided it was not a good idea to leave them under the same roof as the grandparents. My husband and I went to Germany first but because of the fact that I am not German – he is half German- I couldn't really find a job. We stayed there for a while; he got a job but I did not. We wanted to go to a country where I could develop myself as well. We came to Ireland and we both have the same opportunities here. We can both work at our professions.

We have been here over a year and it was easy to find work if you compare it with Germany or Poland. I do not know any Polish people who have trouble finding a job here even if it is a very basic job like cleaning or working in MacDonald's. It is all very fast and even if they want to change their job or they lose it they can find a new one in one or two days. In Poland, you do not have this choice of changing jobs. If you have a job, you feel happy and you stick with this job, keep working even if you are sick of the job after a while. You cannot really change because there is no other option. When you think about jobs, Ireland is a kind of heaven. In other ways, it is not heaven.

Polish people have made a good impression in Ireland so far. The image of the Polish worker here is still someone who is always on time and does not have any problems working hard even on bank holidays. In Germany, Poles have a very bad reputation, which is why life is difficult there, and you have no friends. Here people are very open and there are many foreigners around. Some things are difficult here. People are not really organised. If you need something and you call an office, usually they do not know and they say they will call you back and they never do. Germany is the other extreme; there everything is very well organised. Poland is more like Ireland and is not as well organised as Germany. I think that is why Polish people feel very comfortable in Ireland. It reminds them of home.

I think Polish and Irish people also have a similar way of understanding Catholicism. I was surprised at the reaction in the Church when the pope died. In Germany, they did not mention the pope's death in church but here when I went to mass the priest said that everybody felt sympathy with the Polish people because of the pope's death. I found that amazing that everybody was trying to sympathize with Polish people. I think this would not happen in other countries.

Maybe one of the reasons Irish people like us is that they know we are not going to stay forever. They will get rid of us eventually because we just come here to work to take some money and then leave. We want to get some experience and then go home. Among Polish people, there are two groups. There are those people like me who want to stay here for some time, live a kind of normal life and not concentrate only on saving money. Another group wants only to save money. They live extremely cheaply, eat garbage food, and save as much as possible. They want to stay here for a maximum of two years, and then go back home and buy or build a house. Some Polish people come here without any plan. They just think of working in McDonalds and the following month changing to something else. I notice that Czech people are different. They come here with a plan. If they don't find a job before they leave the Czech Republic they don't come to Ireland. I think they are not so stressed about work in their own countries as some others.

We plan to stay here for some time but not for ever.

*I taught **Magda** English in Dublin.*

My name is Magda and I come from the eastern part of Poland near the Ukrainian border. This is the tourist and agricultural part of Poland. Of course, unemployment in this region is the highest in the whole of Poland. Agriculture is dying there and we hope that the European Union can help us. Nowadays, everybody especially the young people are leaving after they finish university and going to other countries. That is what I did. It is extremely difficult to get a job and even if you do, the money is not enough to help you become independent. You have to stay in the same apartment with your parents. With English, you can go abroad and have other opportunities.

I went to the Catholic University in Lublin and I did management and marketing. I studied for five years and I have a Master's degree.

The only work I did in Poland was the one month's practical work that you have to do as part of your course every year. After that you can work but the pay is not enough to pay for your food. I worked in the European integration office, before we joined the EU. We were preparing people especially the farmers from the agricultural point of view on how to get the required documentation. That was a good place and I wanted to stay but there was no position for me. I know that after we joined the EU, staff numbers fell in those offices.

I have been in Ireland two years and four months. My English was not so good at the beginning and that is why when we came here we had to go to school and apply first for a student visa to work legally. We went to a full time English course for 15 hours a week. I think the school helped me a lot with my English language. During the first few months, we were entitled to work only 20 hours because of the student visa. After we joined the EU, I could work full time. Working 20 hours was enough to pay for the rent as we were renting the house among six to seven people a month. We had to share a room and we had just one bathroom. It was enough to survive but nothing more. I worked as a supervisor in a bakery so I could get experience with people management and get familiar with the system. That helped me get a job in Oracle.

Now I am working as a revenue operations specialist for the Eastern Region. I am responsible for Russia, Kazakhstan and Ukraine as I speak Russian which is the language requirement. I deal with the Eastern European offices in the Moscow region. It is a very big region and covers all countries that were part of the Soviet Union, including Belorussia, Ukraine, Mongolia, Kazakhstan, and others. There is a lot of business between here and the Eastern market where the economy is growing, creating demand for computers, software and databases.

The financial centre for Oracle Eastern Europe is here in Ireland. The sales departments are in the local countries so all we have here are the financial services, accountancy and the admin management. We also have the revenue recognition department here. There used to be a lot of different departments like accounts receivable, accounts payable but they have recently been moved to India. This place will eventually fold up as there is no point in keeping just three departments here. They can save more money if they move everything to India especially in the salary section. I am not thinking of looking for another job because I am happy at the present. This move will not happen suddenly. They need time to plan everything; it will take another two years at least or so they told us. I am not going to look for another job but I would like to go back to Poland one day. I was working for the Polish market and I had an offer with Oracle Poland to go back home so maybe finally in two years or so I can look into going back.

In general living in Ireland is very nice. We have opportunities especially if you want to save some money and invest. I miss home and I miss my friends and my family but I am happy that I came. Definitely, the public transport in Dublin irritates me. I found it unbelievable that in such a growing environment and such a demand for public transport it is all so terrible. I think the Irish government has money to spend on public transport. It is not even that there are not enough trains but they are always delayed and you can't rely on the system. I found it very hard because you have your commitment and then you cannot keep it. I have my own car but with the heavy traffic, you cannot use it. It is worse even than using public transport.

Most of my friends here in Ireland are Polish and the people I am surrounded by are Polish. There is also a Polish community centre in

Dublin. Most Polish people plan to go back to Poland. We are a bit worried because most of the companies are planning to move to other countries in the Eastern part of Europe. We are afraid that the economic boom will be over soon and we will not be able to get a job in Ireland. I think there is a fear in the Polish community that things are changing. I hear a lot from my friends who say three departments are moving to Tunisia and Romania. This is especially true of the financial centres of the big companies. If there was no work we would leave.

I have gotten to know some Irish people, such as my colleagues from work. I have to say that Irish people are very friendly, open and helpful but I think they are a bit too relaxed and they do not seem to have any rules or conditions in their lives. I find it very strange that every weekend they go to the pub. This is their way of spending their free time. It is true for everybody even people from the office, the workers, the managers; drinking time is the weekend. I found it all a bit too much. Polish people drink but we do other things as well instead of going to the pub every weekend and taking that as a commitment. You can do sports; you can go visit the countryside. Polish people travel a lot around Ireland. Irish people just enjoy themselves in the pub or discos and are always drinking. It definitely surprised me when I came here. The healthcare is also unbelievable for me; you can't go to the doctor whenever you want. You cannot have a private appointment. We have Health Care Insurance at work but it depends on what you want; you have six options according to this insurance and if you pay more you get better service. The first option does not cover the appointment but it covers the medication. So it all depends.

I think that though Poland is more corrupt it is more efficient. If you have money you can do things, you can go private but even here if you have money you cannot help yourself. In Poland there is not such a long waiting period for everything; in certain things you can go immediately. The condition of the hospitals is better in Poland. There you share a room with three or four people not like here where you have ten people. Therefore, I think the healthcare is better in Poland. They take 12% from your salary for healthcare but you have it. Things are definitely more efficient in Ireland.

At work, things are very efficient and I am happy here to be honest with you. Compared to Polish companies this is much better. In Poland, there is great control over what you are doing. Here you do not have your manager constantly on your back; they trust you. In Poland, the management demands huge respect and you cannot talk to them like ordinary people on a daily basis. Here the door is always open and you can go to your manager and talk about everything. This really works. In Poland, it is stricter and more hierarchical. You are not paid for overtime and you feel you are being used for work purposes. You have to work at home to finish your projects. For example, my brother works for a very good company but he works about 14 hours a day.

*I met **Olivia** at the Polish Club in Dublin.*

My story is different, completely different to other people. When I reached my 16th birthday and finished secondary school, I decided I did not want to stay in Poland. There was something inside me that made me long to be a globetrotter to see other countries and other cultures. The feeling increased inside me so I learned English and took a course in Foreign Relations and Global Business in Warsaw. As a career, I chose to become an accountant in Poland and I got full qualifications in that field. It is a good profession because you can always find work in other countries. I decided to apply for a job outside of Poland. I applied to an Irish company. I was lucky and I got that position. Four years ago, the company invited me to come to Ireland. I had worked with an auditing company in Poland. They also had a Dublin based office so I had learned something about the Irish accounting system.

It was before we joined the EU so the company had to get me a work visa and contract. I had the job and I got accommodation so I could start my new life and see if I liked Ireland. I found I loved Ireland, still do, and never want to move back to Poland. I love Irish society. After two months with the first company, they decided they did not need me. It was a huge company and not very well organized. Something about me did not meet their requirements. I was terminated after two months but I found another job. I actually applied to the company that I had worked with in Poland but they said they did not have any vacancy. But after two weeks they called me and said one of their staff was leaving and they wanted me for the job. So I got a contract with them. It was an American company, very good and very well organized. I did my MBA while I worked with them and they covered the cost. I studied by distance learning but because that university is connected to the company the professors came to Dublin and we had many training sessions with them. I also did some courses in Amsterdam and then went to the States, to Florida, for the graduation.

I started as a sales assistant with this company but after one year, I applied for an accounting position and became an assistant accountant with them. I started doing the Irish qualifications because they said my Polish qualifications were not good enough. I am doing CIMA, the Chartered Institute of Management Accountants. I started working for an Irish company last June, located in Dublin 10 and it is brilliant. I can use all the knowledge I have gained.

I decided to leave Poland because I wanted to learn about other cultures, to work with foreigners and find out about the attitudes of foreigners and how they mix, work and organise their companies. I found what I was looking for in Ireland. I am really enjoying it because I am using my knowledge and training Irish people in an Irish company. I apply the knowledge I have gained in my current job. I want to improve the staff, productivity and the organization of the company.

It is very easy to train Irish people because they follow. If you ask them to do something, they do it but you need to give them direction. They follow you even if they are not happy about it. When they complain they still do what they are asked. Polish people are very opinionated and they sabotage your decision.

A company does not go in one direction. We are all very well educated in Poland but each one of us has different views so we do not follow well. All of us want to be chief, nobody wants to be a worker, and this is very wrong. I am working now with almost all Irish. My boss is English but he is married to an Irish girl. I have very good relations with him. He is a qualified accountant so we talk the same language and understand each other. Other people are not qualified yet but they follow and they want to learn. Irish people come and ask if the boss wants something like this or that. They also come and say if I have a job to do to let them help. The company is a waste management company and we have contracts with hospitals and doctors all over the whole of Ireland. It is a government contract. The waste then goes to another company who send all the domestic waste out of Ireland. It goes to different countries and is not left in Ireland.

Socially it is fantastic in Ireland. Irish people are very open. You meet them on the streets and in the pub and they just start talking to you. When you come back from holiday, they always ask you how your holiday was. Irish people have a great attitude to things. People work very hard but then they enjoy their free time. You work to live not live to work and this is fantastic. I think people know how to relax after work and they take a rest. They come to work rested the next day and they are ready to work for the eight hours they are there. People divide their time very well. It is very easy to meet Irish people because they are open to making new friends. Of course, there are some Irish people that are not happy about all the foreigners but that is normal.

I came here before all the other Polish people and I think since the Poles have started to come in large numbers attitudes have changed. People were much friendlier to us three years ago than now. There are many reasons for this. There are too many foreigners now and they take jobs from the Irish especially in big companies, in construction and in restaurants. However, high skilled jobs suffer from a shortage so people can get jobs in these areas. There are too many foreigners in low skilled jobs. Recently we had a vacancy in our company and we even had many Irish people phoning about this job. So it is changing and will continue in this way I think. I do not mix that much with Polish people. I come to the club from time to time to learn the latest news and to find out what Polish people think about Irish culture. I have my own views and they are very different. I have a great friend who is a lecturer in one of the universities. He is Irish and he is the best friend I have ever had. He is not looking to take advantage of you. He is a very open person and if anyone has any problems, he is ready to help. I believe that he is a typical Irish person. Because of your history, people are willing to help all the time and it is fantastic. You are not a jealous or envious people. You are not involved in politics too much and that is good in my view. I really love living and working in Ireland.

*I met **Paul** in the Polish Club in Dublin.*

My name is Paul and I come from Poznan. I finished secondary, technical school where I studied electronics but I did not work in my trade in Poland. Poznan is in the west of Poland and near Berlin, Germany. I worked first in a supermarket and then in a factory that produces seats for buses. The seats in the buses here in Dublin are made in that factory in Poznan. I wanted to open my own business in Poland but it is very difficult there because the taxes are so high. So I decided to come to Ireland. I arrived in Ireland on 29th of October 2006. There are many people from my region in Ireland and so we all speak about the possibilities here. Someone always knows someone who is already in Ireland or has been in Ireland. I heard many things about Ireland, positive things and that is why I decided to come here. If I have a choice, I would probably go to Spain or Greece because I like warm climates. At least the weather is not too bad here.

When I first decided to come to Ireland I did not have a job so I started looking as soon as I arrived. It did not take much time, about a week and a half, to find work. I found work and I am still in that job, a little factory that produces window blinds. I found it a very good place to work. I am the only Polish worker in the place; all the others are Irish. People are very friendly. They have a lot of respect for me and they are very helpful. The atmosphere in the workplace is very good and I am happy there.

I had a friend here before I arrived and I lived with him when I got here. Now I have found a place near where I work. The main difference between Poland and Ireland is the money. If we compare the person who does a very simple job, e.g. washing dishes in the two countries, in Poland it would be impossible for this person to live alone after he has paid rent, taxes and so on but in Ireland even if you work for the minimum wage you can still have a reasonable standard of life. You can pay for your house; you can eat very well and on Saturday, you can go for a pint. This is not a problem in Ireland but in Poland, you cannot afford this. I am sure I can save some money here. For one week of the month, I work for my rent; the next week I work for food for the month; I can save the money for the next two weeks in the month. That is good for me.

I really do not care what is happening in Poland or that the economy might be suffering because all the Polish workers are in Ireland. That is the fault of the government; they lost their chance. They should try to change the situation for the workers in the country but they are doing nothing. I do not care if young people are going abroad. We are in the UN and the EU and that is the problem of the Polish government. If you are feeling bad in your country, you should have the right to go. Of course, if I have a real choice, I will stay with my family and friends but if it is impossible to have a decent standard of living in my own country, I will go somewhere else. Maybe Ireland will be my new home. I would like to stay in Ireland for as long as it is possible.

I have some problems with the English Language. Irish people do not speak real English, not the English we learned in school. The only person that I can understand very well at work is from Wales and he speaks clear English. I can mostly understand the rest of the people but not very well all the time. The same situation would

251

arise for someone learning the Polish language. When he goes to Poland, he will find a big difference between what he studies in school and the way people speak. Every region in Poland has its own slang. To learn and use more English is one of the reasons I have come to Ireland.

Romania

Romania became a member of the EU in January 2007. I met **Ovidiu** *at an office in Dublin where he was doing voluntary work to help migrants.*

My childhood in the 1970s was a happy time in Romania. That was probably the best period in Romania during the Communist era. In 1968, I think it was, Ceausescu did not agree with the invasion of Czechoslovakia so he got huge support from Western Europe and the country flourished at that time. Everything was nice and rosy.

After that, we had some changes and in 1989 we just killed Ceausescu and changed the regime or we like to think we changed the regime. The Communists are still in the front row; they rule the country with only a few exceptions but we have a kind of democracy. They said in 1990 that we would have an original democracy and this is the truth. Yes an original democracy – there is nothing like it anywhere else.

I grew up in Transylvania, the northern part of Romania that borders with Hungary. I grew up in a small village about 80 kilometers from the border. I did my primary and secondary school in a town called Beius. After that, I left for university to the centre of the country to a place called Petrosani, a mining area just on the borders of Transylvania. The government funded everything including education during Communist times. You did not have to pay anything. You just had to pass the exam to be accepted into university, an exam after the tenth year in secondary school in maths, Romanian language and literature. Actually, you had different requirements for different qualifications in high school. When you passed the exam in the tenth year, you had another two years in high school and after the end of the twelfth year, you had to

253

pass the baccalaureate. When you passed this exam, you could go and take an exam at the university. The exam depended on the number of seats in the university. I passed the exam and went to university. The government usually said that it was a person's own choice about learning Russian. We started in the fifth year I think to learn a foreign language. My first foreign language was French and the second foreign language was German. Every school had three or four teachers of English, German, French and Russian. It all depended on how lucky you were – you might get English and German or French and German. The funny thing was when you went to university you were supposed to be able to choose the language but I was forced to do Russian. So I did French and German in high school and one year of Russian in university but I did not learn English.

There was very little information about the outside world at that time. You could get some information if you lived in a town near the border or if you were at a university with a strong influx of foreign students. You might also get some magazines from outside and some video tapes – these became available in the 1980s and satellite dishes in the late '80s. TV programmes were very short, only about two hours a day and most of the time were about the communist regime and Ceausescu. Occasionally, there were foreign films but you only got information if you listened to Radio Free Europe or Voice of America. If you were caught listening you might end up in jail. I was born and bred in a village and went to a high school about seven miles from my home village. I used to go in the morning by bus and return in the afternoon. In my village, most of the people were involved in a small wood factory as well as agriculture. Everybody had a small piece of land to work on and there was CAP – Communist Agriculture Cooperative. They owned the land and everybody had to work a few hours per day or a few days per year for the benefit of the state. You had your small back yard, let's say; maybe one acre or less of land which you worked for yourself and the rest was for the CAP. The main source of work was the small wood factory and almost everybody worked there. A little of the wood was exported but mostly sold within Romania.

We did not have much information about Ceausescu and the government and you just got an idea of what was really happening by reading between the lines, seeing how people lived, how the economy was doing, and comparing some information. Not everybody could do that and some people because of their level of knowledge or lack of desire did not do anything. A few good people knew that things were wrong and talked among themselves. But it was very hard to change the regime from inside if you were not involved in the army or the secret services. You could stay out of the Communist party if you wanted but if you had any position in a company you were pushed to be a member of the party. That was the way and even to have any advantages you needed to be a member. The Communist system was not 100% bad. They had something similar to the Credit Union but the easiest way to get a loan was to be a member of the Communist Party. We accepted Communist ideology. It was just there and there was nothing else with which to compare it. We accepted it. There was no desire to do anything. Nobody thought of emigrating because we knew that we were trapped with very few chances to go abroad. We didn't expect to have this revolution and the system to be changed. At that time, very few people talked about leaving Romania and it was very hard to cross a border. Many people were shot or caught and ended up in jail. If the Hungarians or the Serbs caught you, you were sent back to your country.

Life was comfortable overall. You had an average salary and this gave you the opportunity to live like a normal person. You had the chance to develop your own apartment as Romania developed vertically. Many blocks were built and you could apply for an apartment through a state company and in three years you might get one especially if you bribed someone. If you had a good position in the Communist hierarchy, you would get it early. Life was quite comfortable and much better than now. You see in Communist times we had a middle class, maybe 70% of the people were middle class. Now everything has changed. You have 5% or less who are very rich, you have maybe 20% middle class and 75% poor. Of the rich, a very few were smart and set up businesses. Most of them, in Communist times were in the secret service or communist party and they had the money, the connections, the information and the support of the new democrats. They built empires for themselves. So now, their businesses are getting bigger and bigger. They are able to buy property, land, businesses – everything was at their feet. State companies went bankrupt and were sold. These people made them bankrupt and then they sold the state companies for 1 million dollars to a Romanian connected person instead of 10 million to a foreign investor. They arranged everything to suit themselves. It was a matter of knowing people and being involved in this chain of friends and network. The Communists have now become the capitalists – almost all the same people or their sons, nephews, relatives.

I studied mining equipment in university and I have a degree in mining equipment. There is coal mining in that area but I was trained for all kinds of mines which I know now is wrong, quite wrong. You study about 12 books about mining equipment. You are supposed to know everything about all mining equipment, and you are not specialized in any kind of mining equipment. You seem to know everything about everything but in reality, you know very little about those things. In those days, specialization meant that you had a broad knowledge about everything but you really did not know anything. I got a degree in 1990 but I did not work in mining. I went to a few mines but they expected me to bribe them. That was the way and that is still the way in Romania. I did not bribe them so I did not get a job. After a year spent at home, (there were no unemployment benefits), I did a course and I trained as a driving instructor. I worked for about five years as a driving instructor in my hometown, in Beius and then moved to Oradea, a bigger city in my county. There I worked as a driving instructor and for a short while as a commercial agent and a labourer. I got a job as a manager of an amusement company – they even had bingo like in Ireland. In one night in a bingo game, you could win a car. This was just for a year and then I was fed up of the misery.

There were some problems in the company arising from the nature of the business. You have these poker machines into which you insert money and someone wins or loses. At the end of the day, a person came to collect the money and they just moved the counter and the company did not pay much to the government in taxes. In fact, actually, they did not make a profit. I was there, it was my responsibility among other responsibilities, and I did not want to cover their backs. There were also some problems with the management. I did not agree with them so I left. Instead of fighting with them without any result, I just left. There were no ethics. The only ethics with that company was money – get as much money as you can and that is all.

In 1997, I took a short trip to Cyprus and met an English man. We started a business together, a joint venture company in Romania. I worked with him for about two years. We tried to attract foreign investors to Romania, to put them in contact with Romanian companies that were in need of cash. Again, dealing with Romanians was very difficult because they do not have the right sense of accountability. They usually keep two sets of accounts – the fake one for the government and the real one for themselves. We always got the fake one so when you went deep into the business of the company you found everything was wrong and you could not do anything so we lost the trust of the investors. We switched the company to building and I left during that time.

I could not deal with that and again it was about ethics, not with my partner but with his Romanian wife. She started to be involved very much and she was not ethical. My partner would not listen to us at first but two years after I left, he realized all those things and the marriage broke up. Anyway, he had a good business. The money was all his and though I was a partner on paper, I took no money when I left. We transferred my shares to his wife, partner, whatever. He bought property and land in Romania. He had a good experience in Romania and he left rich. I think he was a bit richer than when he came. He bought land for about €1a square metre and when he left he sold it for about €16 a square metre. He had profit, huge profit. He was a clever man. The problem was that he was in Romania at the wrong time, well not really the wrong time but he met the wrong people there and he didn't understand the system. He expected the system to be straightforward and somehow fair but it was not fair. You had to bribe somebody, to pay somebody to do the job on your behalf, to lobby. We explained this to him but he would not listen. He realized later on what we said was true.

That system still exists. The EU has set conditions but it does not matter what you have on the paper what is important is what you have on the ground – who is implementing all the policies, all the laws, all the regulations. You do not bring people from the EU to supervise or implement everything in your country. Remember Romania is not a small country. This is the challenge – to have somebody on the ground doing the right job, not stealing, doing other things, bribing and taking bribes and so on. This is a huge challenge but they will change, slowly they will change. There are some improvements but not too many. This lack of ethics I think is older than the Communist system. You see Romania was under the Turks and the Greeks and so on and maybe this is in our blood. I do not know how long it will all take. I was different to the vast majority and I could not accommodate to the system while I was there. Now I am here and I do not see much difference. I went home last year after four and a half years and I could not see much difference. The mentality is the hardest thing to change. It is not easy as the people do not have a who or what with which to compare the system if they have not been abroad. Living under the same system with only small changes does not make a huge difference and it may take hundreds of years to change things. Politicians and the leaders do not have much interest in change because they are benefiting from the system as it is. They are working for themselves. They have a human face, let's say, a democracy as if they are trying to do the best for the people but that is only the surface.

I worked for the charity 'Caritas' that was under the Greek Catholic Church. I am Greek Catholic, actually, my family is Greek Catholic but I did not pay much attention to religion at that time. Now I am a bit more aware. I worked for Caritas. We started from scratch in Oradea with a small shop selling second hand clothes. We developed from that and in two years, we had a pharmacy. We usually got medicine from outside Romania and we gave them away free or sold them for 10% of the value. People who were very poor got the medicines free. We had some kind of income from the 10%. We also had an office with a computer and we got some funding from Caritas. We had a small tailoring factory with five sewing machines to make clothes for priests, as well as bed sheets and pillows. We gave some grants to Catholic high school and university students. We had a partnership for a summer camp. We had a cabin in the mountains with an agreement that we could use it for two months. We had beds, chairs, pillows blankets, everything. We also got some grants so we started to develop. I started working there as a volunteer and did this for about a month or two and then I got paid. My wages increased and by the time, I left Romania I was the manager of Caritas. Again, there were problems with humans. The machines were fine but the problem was with the humans. Human nature is so difficult to deal with.

I came to Ireland. I was involved and am still involved with an organization called Pro Transylvania. This organization wants autonomy for Transylvania, not full autonomy but economic and administrative autonomy. The politicians said we wanted to break the country apart and give Transylvania to the Hungarians. It was to their advantage to tell that to the people and to destroy our good ideas. Our idea was that if you manage your own area and you keep your resources for your own area you will be better off.

Transylvania is one of the richest parts of Romania not only for tourists but in terms of general economics and people, things are different. Their mindset is very different. We were part of the Austro-Hungarian Empire and I can clearly see the difference when I compare us with the other areas of Romania. All the money collected from taxes are sent to Bucharest which sends back a set amount. For example, Transylvania sends 100% of taxes to Bucharest and they get less than 5% back to support all the people and governmental departments and all public bodies. So, of course, we are not happy and the proposal was to keep 65% of the taxes in our area, 30% should be given to the Bucharest budget and 5% would be a kind of solidarity fund for other areas in the case of floods or whatever, they would then get the money. This arrangement would promote a kind of competition among the different areas. Being able to manage your own resources and elect your own people from your area allows you do more than if someone else imposes the CEO on you. That was the main idea but the government considered us as traitors and we got some threats from politicians, and police. After I arrived in Ireland, an officer from the Secret Service was enquiring about me in my village. I realized that I could never return to Romania without the protection of a foreign country. I was not so keen to stay and live in Ireland but the cherry on the cake was that visit from the secret service officer to my friends in my village. I decided that I was better off here.

I did not have too much information about Ireland before I came. A friend of mine came to Ireland about two years before so he told me 'Come here, it is a better life, it is a safe life'. At that time, I was still OK and I was working for that joint venture. I had a good salary and the political problems were not so bad but then it got worse and after I received those threats, I thought it was time to leave. I arrived in Ireland in March 2000. I came here illegally. I applied for political asylum and a friend of mine helped me. I lived with him for about a week until I found accommodation. He explained to me how the system works. He gave me an idea but he did not know exactly how things happen. At that time, I spoke very little English – about 40 words. I started to do English classes and I was very focused.

This government in Ireland does not want to make our lives easy. They create as much hassle as they can to make you leave voluntarily. Now I am an Irish citizen and I am working in Cairde as a community development officer. I get a salary but I did voluntary work almost since the day I arrived here. I worked with many different organizations. I did some outreach work, going to schools, colleges, community groups and even the Garda College in Templemore. I told them about the life of an asylum seeker, the programs, the stereotypes, and the real life actually. Now there are many stereotypes of asylum seekers. We explained to people what it means to be an asylum seeker, what our rights are and entitlements, what you can do and what you cannot do. We engage with people in discussions – that was the best part. We asked the 5th and 6th year students in schools 'What do you know about asylum seekers?' What they gave us was all the stereotypes from the media. We are stealing jobs; we are getting money from Social Welfare; we are getting mobile phones, cars and things like that. How can we do anything? We are not allowed to work! You get the same amount of money as an Irish citizen – nothing more. You are not entitled to study, do courses, or improve your level of education. You can only take English classes and some computer classes but nothing more. How can you steal jobs if you are not allowed to work? We do not steal houses – actually, landlords will not accept foreigners so easily. Several times, we have found that the landlord will not accept social welfare payments. We cannot get a house. Mobiles – of course, all asylum seekers have mobiles. If you do not have a mobile, you cannot communicate with your people, your community and if you have a problem with social welfare or whatever how can they contact you? It all takes a long time. Cars – who has cars? What car do you have – maybe a hundred euro car.

The Garda here have a good sense of the people. They do not wear guns and they look friendly. If I have a problem, it is not difficult for me to go to a Garda or Garda Station and ask for help. Coming from a police country, you are not keen to go and you are afraid of them but they are different here. Many people do not believe this until they have contact with Garda. Now it is a bit problematic that they treat you differently especially if you do not speak the English language. In addition, there are different kinds of people and I cannot generalize and say 'all Garda are bad or all Garda are good'. Some of them might not be too happy to help you or use bad language and are not helpful when something is stolen. They just take your declaration and that is all. The file is there and that is it. Anyway it is better to deal with Garda in Ireland than police somewhere else. We suffer from the stereotypical image of the Romanian and I will tell you what I found out in connection with Irish people. When they ask you where you are from and you say Romania, the chat stops. I am from Transylvania so when they ask me where I am from and I say Transylvania the discussion opens and they know about Dracula. Or they say 'where is Transylvania, I do not know is it in Africa?' We have a laugh, and it is something different. Very few Irish people have been to Romania. When you stay in Ireland and it is only in the past 10 – 15 years you have had an influx of foreigners and most of these were asylum seekers there are stereotypes from each region. You are somehow outside the continent because Ireland is an island. You do not have many connections with the continent or Eastern Europe. You know something about Eastern Europe from watching TV, reading newspapers or listening to the radio or maybe some movies I do not know. But listening to the media gives you Romania, gypsies, asylum seekers and bank fraud. How many times have you heard of a successful businessman from Romania having a business in Ireland? How many times do they tell the public of the number of Romanians who are employed in the IT sector? How many Romanians are professors or lecturers here? Nobody is telling about that.

The things the government tells is to their advantage. Their advantage is to misinform the public and the Irish born child is the biggest mockery of justice. The Minister of Justice led to that referendum on changing the constitution on whether to give citizenship at birth or not. The Department of Justice is leading these media channels on misinforming people about not only Romanians but also all these asylum seekers and refugees. They do not want to recognize the benefits of foreigners or refugees. There is a political advantage for them because they might get some votes from some Irish people who are xenophobic and unable to realize that they are living in 2005 and not the 1930s or the 1960s. In addition, the Minister of Justice might be a well educated guy and a bright one but he is quite xenophobic and racist. This is his problem. He made many mistakes and nobody kicked his arse or shut his mouth when he said bad things about asylum seekers and other foreigners. They do not consider the good those foreigners brought to Ireland. I can tell you that 80% of the people who call us bad names do not have our skills or our knowledge and do not know anything about our countries. They think they are better than we are but they are not. They think that just because you are Irish puts you three classes above everyone from Eastern Europe or Africa. When you work with some Irish people, they treat you like third class citizens, third class human beings and want you to keep your mouth shut. When you tell them about your qualifications and your knowledge, they feel so small like an insect. When they know about your skills and your qualities, they do not know what to do and they will do everything in their power to get rid of you. To me now it seems Ireland needs only tools and slaves to do their jobs and then to kick them out.

I have made Irish friends and again it is wrong to generalize. I have made many friends through my voluntary work and through being very involved in sport, soccer in particular. I do not have any problems and maybe because I can express myself in English, even though I am not perfect, someone who wants to understand me can understand. In the non-governmental sector and the sports sector people are more open and they see things differently than in the government. They do not belong to that xenophobic part of society. It is easy to explain things to them, and I brought some of them to Romania. I recommend people to go there and not because I am Romanian but for them to see what Romania is compared to Ireland. We might not be as developed economically but we are not from the Third World. If you look at the Romanian cities, they look better than the Irish cities. In terms of the quality of the people – of course we have our bad and good but you see a different quality. For me if you look at the stereotype here it is the Romanian gypsy selling the 'Big Issue' on the street but on the other side of the street there is the Irish guy begging. Having a strong economy and taking care of your people how can you have so many homeless and beggars on the street? Who is taking care of them? What is the difference between Romanians and Irish? I can tell you something else, which is very disgusting, but it has happened. You cannot see a Romanian city in the morning with so much vomit as you do on the streets in Dublin. Why? That is the question. You are smart and you are adults. Do you have to drink until you lose your mind and why do you drink if you are going to vomit it all up in the next half an hour? What is the point? You go for a drink to enjoy, not to get drunk and it is not only vomiting after drinking – after drinking you are not human because you cross the border to animal hood. There might also be other actions, not very nice actions.

Anyway, it is easy to see the bad side of things. We should see the good side as well of every culture and all people. For me Ireland is a nice place. I have been in contact with people, most of whom are nice. I do not have any problem. I am grateful for being here. It is good for me to be in Ireland. I am well accommodated and I even like the weather.. The system is not perfect but after a while if you are very keen to stay you learn the system and you can get by easily. You can learn how to do things, where to go and who to call. Personal contacts are very important.

Slovakia

The Slovak Republic is a landlocked country in Central Europe with a population of over 5 million. Slovakia became a member of the EU in May 2004. I met **Lucia** *in Dublin where I taught her English.*

I was born in the countryside in the middle of Slovakia, an area surrounded by mountains in a place now called the 'Hungry Valley' because there is no work and people don't have money to buy food. When I was young, we moved to Bratislava, the capital of Slovakia. My mother and I live in Bratislava but my whole family still lives in Central Slovakia. The Communist regime collapsed and after the Velvet Revolution all the big factories closed down. There was no money to keep them running. These were Slovakian factories but the Russians bought most of the goods they produced. Now Russia does not have the money to buy from us so they carry out a kind of exchange or barter. They take something valuable from us and give us things we cannot use. After the Velvet Revolution, the new government found piles of Russian goods in the country that we could not use. In exchange also for Slovakian goods, we received gas and petrol from Russia.

My childhood was similar to many children in Eastern Europe. Memories of my childhood in Communist times are of the Communist Party always taking care of the kids. Living in the capital city meant that the Party was always interested in taking the kids outside somewhere to experience nature for at least one or two weeks of the year, so we could get some fresh air. A couple of teachers came with us and took care of us. We were still learning when we went on these trips but it was more relaxed than school. Most of my holidays were spent with my grandmother in the village and I had many things to do there. In primary school, I studied

German. Then I moved to college and studied Chemistry and German. We studied through the medium of Slovakian. When I finished college, I wanted to go to the UK but I had never had a lesson in English. I applied for a one-year course and I started to learn English first in Bratislava. I left for the UK after eight months of studying English where I worked as an au pair for two years. I lived with an English family during that time. There were some good and some bad things about the experience.

I came to Ireland for a holiday and had a brilliant time while I was here. I had lived for two years in England but I found the Irish much closer to the nature and personalities of the Slovak people than the English. The way people approached us was very open minded and very friendly. It was a brilliant holiday. After I finished in the UK, I went back to Slovakia where I worked for two years. I decided I did not want to stay in the department of the bank where I was working. There is an unemployment problem in Slovakia especially in the middle and eastern part where many people have no work. Most of the people from these regions try to move to Bratislava. But rents for flats are very high in the capital and you have to share with two or three other people and try and save something. Living there is not heaven. Young people in particular want to get out of Slovakia and go to Ireland or the UK to get some experience and money. Everything is different here and you need to come to experience it all.

It took me a month to get work when I came to Ireland. It probably took this long because I did not go for the waitress job which was easier to find. I wanted to find an office job but without any experience in Ireland, it is difficult to get a job like that. Then I got lucky and all of a sudden, I had two offers. Compared with some of my friends who went to the UK and other places I have been quite lucky. Language was a big help in getting a job here. Speaking English is of course a very important asset but speaking other languages such as Slovakian and German on top of that really helps. I do not know any Russian. I am from that Slovakian generation that did not have to learn Russian. When the Velvet Revolution happened I was just coming up to the time when I should have stated to learn Russian but then it didn't happen and the class was split into learning German and English. The reason I was put into German was I was absent the day choices were made and they just put me into the German class so the decision was made for me.

I have been living in Ireland for quite a while now and of course, after living here for a while you start to see the disadvantages as well as the advantages. Being so far away from the family does not help. I still feel like a foreigner and I know I always will. That is the reason I would not like to stay forever. I want to go home in two or three years. It depends on what the situation is like in Slovakia. I have found Irish people very friendly. The only thing is the way properties are rented in Dublin. This annoys me a lot. Flats are very expensive and the quality is not good for the price you pay. If somebody went to check any of these places, they would not pass the basic check. For me some of the things I have seen do not represent a human way of living. There is no control over the quality of accommodation. I get the impression that these days, people can rent anything that has just a door and a window. This is sad.

I am also concerned with how Irish people will react in a couple of years to the number of foreign people who are coming into the country. I know that they still need foreign nationals and migrants to work and fulfil the labour requirements but I know it can get out of hand when too many non-national people come. have been here a year and a half and when I first came, I was very pleasantly surprised to find Irish people so friendly and could get on with all the foreigners. I never heard any Irish people say anything about foreign nationals. This is very surprising for me because of the way people react to foreigners back home we don't get so many non-nationals around. The concern here is what will happen if something happens to the economy and how people will react to all the foreigners. Here you do not have any skinheads who cause a lot of the problems in Europe. We find it very nice but unnatural to be in a country where nobody is hostile towards you. If so many foreigners came to Slovakia, there would definitely be a backlash against them. In Slovakia, there is hostility towards anybody who looks like an individual such as punks and hippies and who do not fit in. The skinheads are mostly young people just finishing school and nobody would employ people like that.

In Bratislava, because there are many universities you can find people coming to study. You can find black people who come to study and though unusual, you still find them. I notice now that there are whole families coming to Ireland not so much from Slovakia but from places like Russia. I have seen old couples and young married couples from the Russian regions.

Somalia

*Somalia has had a very troubled recent history and as a result many Somalis live outside the country. In his 2003 book 'Zanzibar Chest', Aidan Hartley describes Somalia as follows: "Somalia was a failed state with no government, none of the institutions that make a modern nation, not even a single proper school, laid low by famine and all-out war." I met **Fatima** from Somalia in Dublin. Her English was still quite limited and it was difficult for her to communicate her story for several reasons.*

I was born in Mogadishu in 1978. I have seven sisters and one brother. When I was a child, there was peace in the country. I went to primary school at the age of four. My father worked in the government and we were comfortable living there. When I had finished four years of primary school I moved to secondary school and I learned Somali and Arabic and all the usual subjects such as history, geography and mathematics. We studied religion after school and sometimes we were beaten if we misbehaved. I never finished secondary school because in 1991 the government fell in Mogadishu and war broke out. The fighting started while I was still at school but I did not go straight home. Like all children, we were curious and went to look. I ended up in the home of my relatives and could not reach my parents house. They left and fled to Mandera along the Kenyan border and I went with my relatives to another border town, Leboya in Kenya. We stayed there until 1994. I could not join my family.

In 1994, there was a lull in the fighting, so we went back to Mogadishu and I rejoined my family. However, in 1995 we had to leave again and we went back to Western Somalia. For three years there was fighting between Somali and Ethiopian forces. I studied nursing and then I got married while we were living in that region. My husband was not a close relative but was from my tribe. There was constant fighting but in 1998, we were able to go back to Mogadishu. My family had lost most of their belongings by this time.

There was ongoing fighting in the streets and you never knew where and when the fighting would break out. I found some work with one of the agencies in Mogadishu. At that time, there were several agencies including the Red Cross working in Somalia. One day my husband was out in the streets and got caught in the fighting and was killed. I was pregnant with my second child at the time and I decided to try to leave Somalia. We had relatives in USA and I wanted to go and join them. Some agencies helped and my family paid a man from the border regions between Somalia and Kenya about $5000 to get me to the USA.

When we arrived in Ireland I thought at first that it was just a transit stop but I am still here. I arrived at the end of 2003. At first, I was sent to a hostel in Tramore. After that, I moved to Tralee and lived in a hostel in a small village. This was very difficult because there was no halal meat and nobody to talk with. I was first refused refugee status but after my second daughter was born in Tralee I was able to become a refugee because I now have an Irish child. As soon as I got this, I moved to Dublin because a lot of Somali people live here. Of the Somalis who come here, only about 20% get refugee status and the rest are turned down. Doing the interview is difficult, the government person keeps asking questions, and it is easy to get confused. The Government knows what is right and wrong but we do not and we do not know what they want.

Life is not easy for me. I am living alone with my children and I feel alone and miss my family very much. War really affects your chances of study. I would love to finish my study in Ireland. I applied for a course as a carer's assistant but I was too late. It is difficult also because my daughter is too young to go to school and I have no one to take care of her while I go to study. I really need to take English classes but that is difficult.

I don't understand politics but right now Ethiopians are killing many people. I want to try to help my family because right now they have nothing but trouble in Mogadishu.

South Africa

At the Nobel Prize Giving ceremony Nelson Mandela, a great South African citizen, said: "There must be a world of democracy and respect for human rights, a world freed from the horrors of poverty, hunger, deprivation and ignorance, relieved of the threat and the scourge of civil wars and external aggression and unburdened of the great tragedy of millions forced to become refugees." **Shaheed** *is South African and lives in Dublin.*

I come from South Africa, from a family with a long lineage of saints, from the Arab side. Some of my family on my father's side came from Yemen, from the Hadhramut. On my maternal side, my granny's family were Irish by the name of Connolly. On my mother's side, there was Indian blood and that brought the intellectual influence. I am a mixture of religiosity and academic. My grandfather was a school principal and his brothers were school principals. On my father's side, they were all sheikhs and imams.

I have had a very intense political journey because I was part of the black consciousness movement in South Africa. My friends and I were called the famous five in high school. We suffered a lot under apartheid, from a very young age, I fought against apartheid. Before the security could get hold of us, we were shipped out of the country but unfortunately, for me my father took me off that truck that was taking us to Pakistan. I could not go so I had to finish my high school in South Africa and went on to become a Muslim lawyer. I opted for Shari'a, Islamic Law and that was one of my ways of getting out of the country. I was sent to Saudi Arabia to study Shari'a in Medina for which the Saudis paid. I was very young when I graduated; before I left South Africa I was already a graduate in Islamic Law and I could speak Arabic. Even under apartheid, Islam was not oppressed as a faith.   Many of the militants came from the Sunni community.   In my era, in the early 70s I was one of those young fires but have mellowed now. Islam was never under attack and prospered under apartheid and under the democracy of Mandela.

At the same time, we had people in South Africa who invited the Islamo-fascist element into the country. I did not run out of South Africa at first but ran all over South Africa to different parts of the country.   You see one of them gave an order that I should be killed; more than 300 people were killed.   They call themselves People against Gangsters and Drugs (PAGAD).   They started labelling everybody as gangsters but they are actually the ones who are the gangsters as they took over all the drug cartels and funded themselves with drug money. I condemned them in my sermons, on the radio, TV and all over the newspapers. I condemned them for killing children, for killing the children of drug dealers. That is not Islam. They are Shii'ah, a brand of Islam. Maybe the Shii'ahs that you find in Ireland are not that militant. In South Africa, Iran is pushing them, funding them though they are not Iranians. They are South African Trotskyites turned Shii'ahs. I have a big mouth and I don't care what I say when it comes to the truth.   You see the Prophet Mohammed (pbuh) said you must speak the truth in the face of oppression and I am not afraid to speak the truth in the face of that oppression.

The South African regime did not take me. I could have died in a South African prison but the South African regime did not put a price on my head. It was in the fledgling democracy that the so-called Muslims put a price on my head. This all happened after the end of apartheid in 1995. When I graduated from Medina in Saudi Arabia, I did not go back to South Africa. I was very young, too young to go back. I was 21 and I went to another university at

Mecca. I studied, married and had children in Mecca. I married a South African girl, a librarian. We lived in Mecca for quite a while where she also studied. I went back to Cape Town, primarily to teach the Black Muslims because Islam has been taken over by the Indians. They believe that they are the Muslims, even though they are non-Arab. Non Pakistani Muslims are not recognized. There is terrible racism among Muslims. If you cannot say which tribe you come from then you are not a Muslim in their view. In Ireland, it is difficult for the Arab Muslims to understand that I am not Arab even though I have Arab blood in me. I think they resent the fact that I am a qualified Sheikh and they cannot accept that. They do not even question the fact that I speak Arabic very well. They think anybody who goes to Saudi Arabia for a couple of years can learn Arabic. That is the attitude and it is racist. If you are not an Arab, if you are not a Pakistani then you are nothing. Now this is what is happening to the non-Arab, non Pakistani Muslims in Ireland. They are becoming the marginalised community, groups such as the Bosnian, Indonesian, South African and African Muslims. I think there are great Muslims in Africa, as well as the Indonesians and Malaysians.

Back in South Africa, I became the principal of a college of Islamic and Arabic Studies. Students from all over Africa, in fact all over the world came to study there. South Africa is quite advanced as far as Islamic learning is concerned. In my family, there is a tradition of spreading Islam. South Africa has more Islamic universities than any other Western country. There are Islamic universities in Cape Town, Johannesburg, Transvaal, and Natal. Muslims opened the National Peace University in South Africa. South Africa is very advanced and there is an Egyptian Al Azhar primary school there. I did not like the school though. I had a son in one of the schools but I took him out. My eldest son was studying at the same

276

university as I had studied; he went to South Africa on holiday and he became a teacher in Port Elizabeth in the Eastern Cape. I am from the Western Cape and was born and bred in Cape Town. My son became a teacher but I took my other son out of Al Azhar because these Arabs are not teachers. They might be qualified but they come with their wild culture insulting and abusing the children. My son became a nervous wreck; he did not like school. I took him out, put him in the normal school, and he improved. He is now in high school in Cape Town.

I am a refugee in Ireland but my family is not. I preached to the Black Muslims for quite a while and then I got into trouble with the murderers and had to run. I was in Saudi Arabia for a while with my friends but my family was still in Cape Town. I went there from time to time. I have been running for my life for ten years. I provoked them because they gunned down some children and I told them that was disgraceful. They killed a drug dealer by burning him alive. That got them international news coverage which pleased them. You see they do things for news coverage because they want publicity; it does not matter what type. They publicise themselves as a cleaning society for gangsters and drugs but at the same time, they took over the drug cartel.

Back in Saudi Arabia, I was working and studying. When 9/11 happened, I was in Mecca but I went back to South Africa. The Muslim community became very militant and marginalised. No, I should not say marginalised; it was more polarised. They became very militant and pro Bin Laden. I could not understand this insanity. I started talking against this polarisation and tried to get back some sanity into the community. That was not good for me, condemning the Ahmed Qasims and Qiblas, those Islamo-fascists. Ahmed was a Trotskyite turned Shii'ah and that combination is very scary. You get this among the Muslims here in Ireland also, this Trotskyite Shii'ah combination. They invited Ahmed Qasim here. Some of them are not Shii'ah but they do not know which agenda they want to follow.

In 2001 when I went back to South Africa, I brought them back to sanity. I became public enemy number one to Ahmed Qasim and they wanted me dead. I am not the only one. I planned to go back to Saudi Arabia after 9/11 because I was just on holiday and still had my return ticket. My wife decided otherwise. Ireland has the Health and Social Welfare Board programme that South Africa was going to implement in 2007. She wanted to learn about that and about 200 social workers from South Africa came to Ireland as the country needed social workers. My wife was part of that group. I was planning to come and assist her because she needed to rent a house. She came alone at first and when I knew they wanted to kill me I immediately booked a ticket to Ireland. I joined her and about six months after that she went back and brought the children here. The five children came; we now have six as one was born here. She works with the Northern Area Health Board and specialises in child protection and child abuse. She had a very good job in Cape Town. She was running an institution but she decided to come to Ireland. She has a work permit but she cannot get a mortgage because she only gets a one-year visa at a time. I do not understand that. She was also subjected to some racial discrimination. She wears a scarf and she is the wife of a sheikh. Wearing a scarf has brought her some pain. The children are in school. The eldest one is in high school and four of the children are at North Dublin Muslim School, the school that made headlines.

I have been granted refugee status here. My family is on my wife's work permit but I am here as a refugee. I have the right to reside here and have the same rights as Irish people. I will eventually get a passport and I have travel documents now. It is not a complicated process to become a refugee but it is very long. I think my case is very solid. Everybody knows PAGAD; you can Google and find it. They kill and murder people. They are people against gangsters and drugs but that is not the case. Everybody knows about PAGAD, the Islamic Revolutionary Council. They killed my brother. They bought the mosque where I was the resident Imam.

As a Muslim in Ireland, I do not have any problems. I have more Irish friends than I have Muslim friends. They say the Irish are not racist but nationalistic. I am involved in many things here and I make myself useful to the Irish. I volunteer. I am a lecturer at the Free University. I run my own radio programme on a volunteer basis. I deal with drug addicts on a voluntary basis. I write for Metro Eireann on a voluntary basis. I approached all these people because I have something to offer. I feel grateful that Ireland has granted me refugee status. I appreciate that but I have many skills and know how to give back to this society. It is not only what Ireland can do for you it is also what I can do for Ireland. I saw the need especially in the ethnic minority communities and I can give something back.

I see Ireland erupting within ten years. I see London bombs going off here because of the type of Islam here. The government needs to support the idea of the Muslim Council where I can unite all the Muslims and get a controlling body going. The Council should be recognized by the Irish Government to help bring some sanity to this whole situation. You see some of these people want power and they are moulding the youth as they want. I give Ireland about ten years. The Irish Government and the Irish people are not aware of what is happening and all you get is people like this Ahmed Chowdry; he came some two years ago and he attacked Yahya who could not answer him. They challenged Yahya and these people are now banned in Britain. Ireland is a free country but they should close the borders. They should get rid of those who abuse the hospitality of the Irish. They had a conference and they brought all these Islamo-fascists, Trotskyites and Stalinists here. I do not think Ireland is aware of nor does it have a list of undesirables. The Supreme Muslim Council of Ireland will have to sort out the problem and then have a meeting with the Minister of Justice. Maybe I should write to the Minister for Justice and set up a meeting about all this. There is a major power struggle going on between Clonskeagh and South Circular Road mosques; they even ended up in court at one stage.

The Maktoums of Dubai bought the mosque in Clonskeagh and appointed a Sudanese Imam but then decided to take it over themselves. Bitter hostility arose and some rumours have spread that the Clonskeagh mosque is funded with racehorse money, a kind of money in Islam that is forbidden. There is a double standard within this extremism. These mosques are financially independent. Clonskeagh is funded by the Maktoums and South Circular by someone in Kuwait. They also have businesses producing halal meat.

Spain

*Spain, on the southwestern tip of Europe has had close associations with Ireland for centuries. A common religious heritage, the Catholic Church, created both religious and political bonds in the past and the Irish search for sanctuaries in the sun cemented this centuries old link in recent times. I met **Monica** in Dublin and went to hear her play her very special style of music.*

I was born in Galicia on the north coast in a place called Lugo. I have always been attracted to sea places because I was born so near the sea. My family were teachers. My grandmother spoke five languages as well as knowing classical Latin and Greek. She spent a lot of time in the USA, in New York when she was young. She always encouraged my sister and me to learn different languages and to have an open mind towards people and cultures around the world. She visited Hong Kong, China and the Indian Ocean at the beginning of the 20th century. We do not know exactly how she got around to those places. She was single at the time and was still living in New York. We know that she went to the Indian Ocean with the family that she was living with in New York. She was an orphan but her aunt was married to a very wealthy Italian man and they took her to New York when she was about 12. They lived in Morristown and she went to a school in Long Island called Saint Elizabeth. She always encouraged my sister and me to be interested in people around the world and to learn as many languages as possible.

She used to speak French and English to my sister and me but I do not know why but I never liked the sound of French. In fact, when I was young I was sent to a French school, but they had to take me out because I sat on the stairs with my fingers in my ears, crying until my Mum came. They told her I had spent all day like that because I did not want to hear that strange language. I really had a clear mind about it; I hated French but loved English. The sound of English has always appealed to me. My grandmother had beautiful books in English about fairies and she used to read to me so maybe that is why I became hooked on English. When my grandmother was about 22, she left the States and went back to Spain. Several years later, she married my grandfather who was a vet. They settled in Lugo in the north of Spain. Neither of them was from there originally. My grandmother was Galician but she was from Orense and my grandfather was from Leon beside Galicia, the neighbouring province. My grandmother had two children; my mother and a son who died in the Civil War, in the bombings in the last days of the war. He was only 21.

When I was born, my Mum was already a teacher and a writer and she had to do conferences here and there. She always encouraged my sister and me to go with her if we wanted. We went many times to different poetry readings and lectures that she was giving or to art exhibitions. Our house was always full of painters and writers. I have two Dads actually; my biological Dad was a writer and poet and belonged to the Royal Academy of Galicia but my Dad who brought me up was not an artist.

My Mum was transferred from Galicia so when I was five years old I went with her to Badajoz in Andalusia very close to Portugal. I loved it there. The climate was warm and people were open and friendly. Galician people are a bit reserved and it is difficult to connect with them. People from the south of Spain are quite open in general, though of course there are exceptions. I loved the heat; it was December and we were dressed as we are in Galicia in the summer. I have very good memories of the south of Spain. When we went back again to Galicia I got really sick. It was winter and my memories are of a sky that was as black as pitch, raining non-stop, fog everywhere. My Mum was afraid that I would die; it was some kind of stomach bug. It might have been something from the water but they did not know. I lost a lot of weight but I overcame it and survived.

My hometown in Galicia was small compared with other towns but I was happy because we knew everybody. When we came back from the south of Spain, we moved to La Coruna and this was a big trauma. I never liked that city from the moment I set foot in the place, maybe because I idealised the place I was born. I wanted to go back; I was not ready to let it go and start a new life. I did not feel comfortable. Before I had been very light-hearted but in La Coruna I could not integrate. I had to start going to school; it was a nun's school just for girls. I did not know anybody and the weather was depressing. My sister was fine with the place. My Mum was very helpful and she knew that I was going through some kind of trauma. I got throat infections and very high temperatures. So my mother often let me miss school but she kept an eye on me and made sure I was studying and doing my homework.

I continued like this until I was 10 years old when I started secondary school. I integrated perfectly but I was very lucky that my Mum understood my psychology because other mothers might have forced me to go to school. I spent most of the next years in Galicia. I did my Leaving Certificate and then did the exams for the university and did very well. I attended university, did a one-year course in early history and enjoyed myself. I had many other things going on in my life at that time and I could not concentrate and had to leave the university. I had always loved music and had been in choirs so I joined a band. I started singing, gigging and rehearsing, playing piano and doing backing vocals with this band. At home, there had been a lot of music; my Mum's first career was piano but she did not teach piano as a career. She played Chopin, Liszt; you name it she played it. When my Mum played the piano I used to dance around and we often had great parties. I loved music and I used to entertain myself trying to learn Beatles' songs.

When the first band folded after a year or so, I started my own rock band. At the same time I was working with a newspaper and also with a radio station and ended up having my own radio programme about music in the Top 40. I introduced the Top 40 songs during the day but at night I had my own slot with another girl for which I could choose my own music. The programme was called 'La Frontera' and we could talk through the programme as well. It was very interesting. In Spain at that time, you just got a contract for three months at a time and I think I spent about a year with that radio station. Then I moved to national radio in Galicia and at certain times, it linked country wide to the national radio. I had my own music programme and I played the music I liked all the time. I sometimes had to introduce some artists who were at the summer festival in Galicia and I interviewed some famous bands at times. I loved playing the music I liked. I never played the music of my own band because there was this kind of morality that if you were in a band you did not play the music of your own band. Some people did but I also thought it was not the right thing to do.

In 1987, I saw an advertisement in the newspaper 'El Pais' for a grant to go to the Netherlands for a mass media experience. I applied and they called me. I went to Madrid for an interview and a short time later, I got a letter saying that I was chosen. So I went to the Netherlands basically to see how the mass media worked in that country. We went for a month with all expenses paid and there were many other young people there. This was my first real contact with this type of multimedia and multi-nationalities. There were some very talented people; I remember one Scottish guy in particular and I think he went on to have a very successful career in the media. We went for a month and observed how the media worked in Holland and our visit included visits to the Parliament. We saw how the major TV channels broadcast; we visited their studios and it was a brilliant experience. We also had a chance to see a new country and we stayed with Dutch families so we had even more contact with people of the country. This was better than staying in residential student places and we got to see Dutch society.

I continued working with my music and always had my band. By this time, I had it in my head to come to Ireland and see how the country was. In 1988, my sister phoned me and said a mutual friend who was a group leader with students from all over Spain for a trip to Ireland could not go because her Dad had had a heart attack. They were asking me to go instead of her. I thought it was a miracle because I was really short of money by then and though I had a plan to come to Ireland there were all the expenses. At that time, you still had to take two flights to get here so it was awkward. The chance of coming here, bringing students and working, I thought was brilliant. I just jumped at the opportunity so I went with the students from Vigo in south Galicia to Madrid and there I joined another group and we brought about 40 students to Ireland. We were based in Portmarnock and the students went to the National School. The other group leader and I talked with the families and made sure that everything was fine. We had a chance to go on trips at the weekend. We went to Newgrange, Kerry, Wicklow and many other excursions during our month. It was a very good time. I saw Dublin City and Ireland as it was and I thought *'Oh my God this is really similar to*

Galicia'. I decided I wanted to live here to get to know the place better, to learn English and to understand the culture at first hand.

In 1990, I decided to move to Ireland. In 1991, my biological father passed away suddenly. It was a traumatic time because he had been planning a trip to Dublin with my Mum. They had been planning to spend a certain number of days in London and then come on to Dublin. A week before the trip he died and as always, the person who dies is fine. He died of a heart attack and went very quickly but for the rest of the family it was devastating. He had been very healthy and perfect and nobody was expecting that he would not be with us. He passed away on the 28th of April and I decided to go back in May because my Mum was devastated. I went and spent a full year with my mother. I came back to Ireland then and have been here ever since since 1992.

You might say Ireland is home. I was born in Galicia but I do not feel Galician at all. The Galicians appear to be friendly but you have to know them for a very long time before they open themselves to you and invite you in. I almost felt myself more like a person from the south of Spain. Climate wise and the personality of people and their way of being in the south of Spain seem more me. The Irish are more similar to the Galicians but I always think there is no perfect place. The Galicians are very conservative; they hate change; they do not like anything new. They are very reluctant to take on new ideas and new projects. We had a conservative government for over 10 years and they did not like changes at all. I do think the Irish are a bit like that. They don't like to say *'this is a new idea so let's go for it'* ; they are more like *'yes, it's a good idea but I don't know – so I think I will stick to the original idea'*. This is the same mentality as the Galicians and this makes it difficult to move forward and bring about change and be open to different options.

Irish people are very friendly. If I am waiting for the bus or the DART people talk, ask you where you are from and there is a little conversation. When I say I am from Spain, they ask me what part. Sometimes they know Galicia and sometimes they do not. Everything goes well until I ask them back and I say and what about you? Then the conversation is finished. They get their information and they ask their questions but if you ask them, they don't like that. The Galicians are like that also. They don't mind hearing about the other person, they like to hear what is going on and I understand this perfectly. This is the result of the trauma of being invaded. It is like a kind of protection and they need to know who these people are, who are coming and why they are coming. They want to know what the other person wants and what his business here is.

In Galicia, we have many South Americans who speak Spanish and some Chinese also and we are aware of this reaction. People say for example *'Why are these Chinese coming here – there are more places in the world?' 'What is their business here?'* They are curious about all that. I think it is a normal reaction because after being invaded and repressed for so long and the attempts made to kill their culture it is a kind of defence. I think the Galicians are the same. We were repressed in the 15th century by Ferdinand of Aragon and Isabella of Castile who unified Spain and the first thing they tried to do was to kill the language. This was one of their weapons of control and this was not just in Galicia but also in Catalonia and any other language in Spain. It was a real stigma to talk Galician; you had to talk Spanish. I think in the 1920s during the time of the Republic, the country was very enlightened and they recognised every language and also the rights of women. So it was a very advanced time. Then of course Franco came and it was a sin again to talk Galician. I have a vague memory of seeing a notice in a bus station in La Corona saying *'Don't speak Galician; don't be a*

287

donkey'. Franco had the same policy of unifying all of Spain and standardizing everything. There was only one language, Castilian Spanish. So you can understand why people are sometimes on the defensive.

I have seen many changes in my time here in Ireland. I came in 1990 and I did not know anything about this city. I found a place to live in Crumlin, a working class area in Dublin. I remember seeing a horse and cart delivering coal to houses with dogs and kids running after them. It was very romantic and cute but you do not see it any more. This rural Ireland in the middle of Dublin was amazing to me. My natural hair is very dark and when I came, it was very long and the children used to run after me and knock on the door and say *'oh we never saw such long hair, can we touch it.'* They had not seen many foreigners and were not used to such black hair and for them it was very unusual. When you looked at the cars, you could see the economy was low.

I was looking for a job when I came and I panicked one day and stopped a priest who was coming down by Christchurch. I just jumped on him; I think I gave him the fright of his life. I was really crying and I said to him' *Please pray for me, I can't find any work'* and he said to me *'My child, what are you doing coming here to Dublin when most Dubliners are getting out of the place? We don't have any work here and you are coming here for work. Don't worry I'll pray for you'.* I am sure he prayed for me because I got work right away teaching Spanish in King's Hospital School in Lucan for transition and leaving cert students. It was brilliant and the principal was adorable. The students were amazing; they were very good. I also taught in Holy Faith in Clontarf. I lived in Crumlin and travelled to Lucan and Clontarf. The traffic moved a little faster then. I came in 1990 when the economy was low and there were not

288

many foreigners here. Ireland was still quite rural even in the capital. Little by little, I would say by 1994 you could see the economy building up.

My brother is interested in economics and he said before the Celtic Tiger began that Ireland would have an economic boom. The microchips industry started here and then the multinationals came. The changes were massive, huge cars, parties, luxury everywhere. Being in Ireland in the 1990s was I imagine like being in Spain in the late 1940s, in a psychological sense because there was no divorce as that only came to Ireland at the end of the 1990s. I saw women in this country who found it difficult to talk to men. I think Spain was like this in my mother's generation. My brother is much older than I am and he grew up in the 1960s but he had normal relationships with females. There were women politicians and everything. I think as far as men were concerned when I came here they would prefer if the woman did not know anything. If I was a bit dumb, I think they would find it better and nicer. I found this very strange and it was like going back in time. The economy boomed but the social scene was quite backward. There was discrimination against women but I think that has changed now. Women can now take the same jobs as men but I think there is still a lot of work to do. Even still it is difficult for some men to deal equally with women; I have had this experience in my band. There is sometimes a sense that women are not supposed to be intelligent; it is very strange but of course there are differences. I think there is more development to be done.

My Mum is a writer and since my childhood, I have seen her writing. Of course, when I was young I wanted a housewife Mum and not a writer; I wanted a normal Mum like everybody else. Sometimes she would read us her poems and ask if we liked this one or that. We did not really pay much attention. I like poetry myself but I do not think it is a genre that I really relate to. I like novels better. Now she has just been nominated for the Nobel Prize for Literature 2007. It was a great surprise and she could not believe it. She was the first woman to become a member of the Royal Academy in Galicia. She is not an ambitious woman in the sense that she said to herself that the Nobel is a prize she can get. We all have dreams and I am sure that she dreamed of getting in to the Royal Academy but it was not an obsession and I never remember her mentioning it. When she got membership, she was on top of the world. She never expected to get a nomination for the Nobel Prize. Of course, she is extremely honoured and we celebrated at home.

I get on very well with her because we think alike. My brother and my sister are very different. They are more like my father, the father who brought me up. But my Mum and I like the same things; in personality we are outgoing while my brother and sister are more reserved. My Mum and I love the Humanities rather than Mathematics and Science. We also believe in God and we have always talked about religion. We talk about the teachings of the Catholic Church; my mother does not say anything bad about the Church but she has her own faith. Of course, we all have our doubts but we talk a lot about the meaning of life, what we are doing here and our destiny. We talk about philosophical and spiritual things whereas my brother and sister are atheistic and as soon as my mother and I start talking about Buddhism or spirituality or whatever they go crazy. In my view, it does not matter whether you believe or not; the discussion is what is interesting. Even if they do not believe, they should debate it. Sometimes we debate but the debates can be very vicious. My brother and sister are very analytical and even though my mother is very analytical and has all the awards, they still think she lives in a fantasy world. It is amazing and I am the lunatic who lives in another world completely. They do not want to hear anything I say; they think I live on another galaxy.

I remember these debates when I have to talk in public and sometimes I feel incredibly traumatised speaking in public. Coming to university and presenting in front of the group gives you amazing confidence. You have to research so when you stand up you are not saying random facts. I feel more confident now about my own thoughts. I had many intuitions always but when I study I find facts to back them up so I am not so crazy after all. So it is wonderful and amazing to develop myself as a human being by taking these courses.

It is interesting to see the similarities between the Galician and Irish cultures because I have always felt that they are connected. My music has a strong South American influence because in Galicia we are at a type of crossroads. Galicia was a very poor area of Spain and many people had to emigrate. A lot went to Germany, Switzerland and England. But many went to South America to Mexico, Cuba, and Venezuela and in South America they call all Spaniards wherever you are from 'Gallego' for Galicians because so many went there. My grandfather lived most of his life in Cuba; in 1949 he came back to Spain and passed away in 1955. We also have a strong connection with Latin America because of the emigrants. Galicia is a cross-cultural place for music because when the emigrants come back they bring all the mambos, cha-chas and salsa plus the local music from Galicia, which is Celtic with harps and pipes. So this is why I am doing my Latin band because I remember listening to all this music when I was a child.

I think Irish people like any kind of music because they are very musical. One of the reasons why I wanted to come here was because I read that there are more musicians per capita in this country that anywhere else. When I came to Ireland, I joined Latin jazz at first. The musicians I worked with encouraged me to do my own band. I go to venues all over the country and the Irish love Latin music, some of them because they have already been in the Caribbean in places like Miami, Cuba on holiday and this music reminds them of holidays. Others like it because it is an energetic country music. You have to do something when you hear that. It is a very contagious music and light hearted and the Irish like that. One problem here is there are no Latin music record companies and no Latin radio stations. If you do not have this kind of backup, you find it hard. My CD is with one of the top record companies in Madrid and I am waiting for an answer. I have worked very hard on this, 11 years work with my band here so I am praying they will accept it. We work from our hearts on this music. We must do our own web page and sell the album that way. We want to let people download the music from the internet.

One thing I notice about the Irish and the Galicians is that when something goes wrong they don't sit down and try to analyse the problem or take a constructive look they try to blame someone else. Take the Eurovision, as soon as I heard the Irish song I thought it was a good song. People voted for that song but the Dervish singer did not sing it well or get the right pitch. At the Eurovision Festival, I thought the song was not delivered well and her voice did not come up strong. But people blamed the Eastern countries that they voted for each other but they didn't ask *'what went wrong with the performance?'* Maybe people are a little scared of saying the truth. In general if you suggest that something can be improved, they just say *'no everything is fine'*. They do not like any changes and both places are similar; they want to stick to their ideas forever but we can look at nature and ourselves and see changes all the time.

Sudan

*Sudan has a long and fascinating history but its recent history is muddied with the stories from the south of the country and Darfur. The war in Darfur is a situation that has been taken advantage of by a number of Sudanese who claim political asylum though having nothing to do with this province. The following stories reflect some of the diversity of the country. I met **Oliver** at a centre for migrants in Dublin.*

I was born in Wau in Bahr Al Ghazal. My early life was great and we were all very happy. My parents had nine children including five brothers, three sisters and me. My mother had been married and then divorced and then married my father. However, they divorced and my mother remarried her first husband but she and my father remained good friends. We lived very close to each other and if there were any problems, we sat down and discussed them. I went to a primary school that was run by the Catholic Church, St Mary's Church, and they organized lots and lots of activities for us including learning English and singing in the choir. We spoke Arabic and out own local language from our tribe the 'Fartibe'. My father had his own shop and mill in which he ground sorghum, known locally as 'durra'. My mother was well educated and had a good job. She finished secondary school; at that time, nobody went to university. She got a job as a secretary and eventually she went to work as a secretary in the University of Bahr Al Ghazal. She also worked in different public services and worked with the UN and UNICEF.

The south of Sudan at that time in the 1980s had closer contacts with Uganda and Kenya than with the north. Some people were Muslim but tribal loyalties were very important. We belonged to a tribe called Belanda Fartibe and we had our own tribal language. While the largest tribe 'the Dinka' were cattle raising people, the Fartibe were agriculturalists and we did not have any animals like sheep, goats and cows. The land around Wau was very fertile and people were able to grow all their own food. We also lived close to the river and had plenty of water. When I went to primary school, I studied through the medium of Arabic. This was a colloquial Arabic and we did not have to learn classical Arabic. However, while I was still in primary school in the 4th grade, I think, in the early 1980s the war started between the SPLA and the northern army and the school closed down. At that time, there were Italian nuns in Wau who ran a school in English. I started to help them in the school and the nuns let me enter class where I began to learn English. We had our own language ' Belanda' that had two dialects 'Bor' and 'Viri' and these were the languages that were used in our daily lives.

At that time, more and more members of the northern army came to Wau. The people who tried to help the village people were mainly the Italian nuns and priests. One day, four friends and I were with one Italian priest coming back to Wau from a visit to a village. The security forces of the northern army stopped us and arrested us. The priest was accused of being a spy for the SPLA and was deported to Italy. The rest of us, all teenagers were kept in prison for 11 days and then released. During those days, we were beaten and forced to confess untrue things about our involvement with the SPLA. When we got out of prison, my friends fled to Kenya along with many other young boys while I went to El Fasher and eventually on to Khartoum.

Life had changed very much for people in my hometown by the mid to late 1980s. The northern army, which had moved south to fight the SPLA forces, set up their own industries in our town and took

294

any timber they could find. The commander of the army set up a timber factory and exported timber to the north. They stole timber from people and from their homes as well as cutting down any trees they could. They also stole goats, sheep and cows from the Dinka tribes, brought the meat into Wau, and sold it to people there. The security forces also encouraged division between the tribes and in 1986/7, tribal war broke out between the Dinka and Fartibe. The Dinka usually supported the SPLA as John Garang was from this tribe. The northern army encouraged the Fartibe to fight against them. They supplied the people with weapons to fight against each other. I am not sure of the real cause of the war but I think people quarrelled about timber. The army armed the people and often the police, gamekeepers and prison wardens were Dinka who were much more political than the Fartibe. The army rounded up people that they thought were against them, shot them in the town square and just dumped the bodies. They also gave guns and grenades to the children. Women carried grenades on their way to work to protect themselves. There were no mines in the towns but out in the countryside on the way to the villages there were often mines. There was a German hospital for lepers and one day a group of four doctors coming back from the hospital after helping the people were blown up by a land mine. The Dinka often rounded up young people at night and shot them. The army encouraged the fighting between the two sides and tribal war became worse in the late 1980s.

From El Fasher, I eventually made my way to Khartoum where I found my relatives. I lived with my uncle and our extended family. After some time I was able to continue my education, went to Comboni College for three years, and finished my secondary school certificate. I was able to make money by trading, moving between El Fasher and Khartoum and selling fruit, cloth and curtains that came into Western Sudan through Libya from Dubai. I then had to join the Popular Defence, which all young people had to do before they could go to university. This meant 18 months training in defence and the possibility of being sent to fight against the SPLA in the south. We lived in camps in the desert and life was very hard. I was a Christian but I had to attend lectures on Islam, go to the mosque, stand, and watch Muslims pray. Though we were all Sudanese, we people from the south were treated differently. The northern Muslims called us 'kafir', which means unbeliever, a non-Muslim because we were not Muslims. They also called us 'abid' that means 'slave' because we were darker skinned than them and were not Arabs.

After we finished the 18 months in the Popular Defence, the army wanted to send us to Juba to fight against the SPLA. I was afraid this would happen to me and decided that I would have to get out of Sudan. I heard of a Chadian guy who was in the International African University in Khartoum who could help me. I bought a Chadian passport and air ticket to Damascus in Syria for $1000. I flew to Damascus sometime last year. Syria is the only country that allows anyone from an Arab African country to enter without a visa. When I got to Damascus, I heard from people that Ireland was a good country to go to because there was lots of work there. I had some relatives in Damascus, found them, and stayed with them for a while. I used to go around Martyr's Square in the centre of Damascus and try to find out how I could get to Europe. I felt nervous in Syria because if you got into any kind of trouble you could be put in prison and nobody would ever know. I managed to get some money from my sister in Australia and brother in the USA. They wanted to help me get to the USA but it was very uncertain. In the end, I bought a Dutch passport and a ticket to Ireland for $2700. A relative had the money that had to be paid to a man when

I arrived safely in Ireland. I travelled with a white man who spoke broken English from Damascus to Warsaw and then onto Dublin. I do not know the nationality of the man.

I arrived in Ireland in July 2005. I travelled to the city centre with the white guy and when we got there he took me to a restaurant, bought me a cup of coffee and we called the people in Syria. My relative paid the money and was able to go home. The man then took the fake passport from me and told me to go to the police and look for asylum. He left and I found myself alone. I had €47 in my pocket. I went to the police station and they told me I had to go to the asylum office but it was Saturday and everything was closed. They gave me a phone number and told me to call it to find a place to stay. I could not get any answer and returned to the police station. This time the police called another number and then told me to go to this place for the night. The first night I slept in the place organised by the police and on Monday morning, I went to the asylum office. They did not believe my story and said that I was lying and was a Nigerian from England. They checked my fingerprints and sent me to a hostel in St Margaret's Road. This was very crowded and eventually I was sent to a hostel in Camden Street, a centre for the deportation of illegal immigrants. I have been there ever since. The hostel provides all our meals and every Friday I get €19 and 10 cents.

I had an interview with the Ministry for Justice in September. The man who talked to me kept laughing at me and made rude signs. I complained to my legal adviser about his treatment. This man told me I would have to come back again and to write 10 – 15 pages about the peace process in the south of Sudan. This is very difficult for me as I am not a politician and do not know all the details. I had another interview after a month and saw the same man who this time was more polite to me. He asked me for the writing and I gave him the five pages I had written. I am still waiting for their decision. I check about Sudan on a web site by using the computer in the library. It seems the Dinka now control the South. There is a new government in Bahr Al Ghazal but this may be cancelled. The new leader Sal Fakiir is more popular than John Garang I think.

The hardest thing right now is all the time I have to think and I think too much. I cannot work legally but sometimes there is security work with a Nigerian company that pays €6 an hour. I also go to the Church and am involved in the Legion of Mary. I go to the library to prepare myself to take the ECDL. I last saw my mother in 1997 and talked to her last year. I talked to my brother in the States a couple of months ago.

Most of the time I just wait.

Yahya *is Imam of the South Circular Road mosque.*

I was born in a small town in Northern Sudan, called Al Nubia. I started my schooling there but continued my primary school in Port Sudan where my sister was living. I started learning English in the Middle School. You know the system in Sudan; we have primary, intermediate and then secondary school. The government has changed the system now but I started learning English in the Intermediate School.

From there I went to the University of Khartoum where I first studied science. After that, I entered the Faculty of Agriculture. I did five years, four in Agriculture and the first one in Science. During my time there, I started to memorize the Qur'an and that took about two years. There was a centre where I used to go on weekends and holidays with some students from the Faculty of Medicine. I would often spend weekends there and when I graduated, I had completed memorizing the Qur'an.

After graduation, I went to work on Al Raha scheme in central Sudan for two and a half years. Then a major change happened in my life when a friend of mine who had been studying in Dublin came back to Sudan in 1983. He was the Imam of a very small mosque in Harcourt Street. When I came in 1983, this location in South Circular Road had just been bought. Almost all the money for the mosque came from the Gulf because there were a good number of students here from Kuwait, Qatar, Saudi Arabia and United Arab Emirates. Then the other major change was that we started the school here. We had two classrooms at first. This was my office. I remember we changed it into a classroom and I moved downstairs. We followed the Irish Primary Curriculum.

The nature of the community started to change. There were children by this time in the community. We started a school with 14 children. The Maktoums from the Emirates sponsored the Clonskeagh centre. At first, this was a school and then it changed to a catering institute. The school was set up in 1993. After some years, Hamid Maktoum decided he wanted to build a mosque in Clonskeagh because there was a lot of land and we were only using part of it. At that time, I was Sheikh of the mosque. The Maktoums wanted to run the mosque themselves and make all the decisions. However, we have a council here and elections but they did not want that. So we moved back from Clonskeagh to South Circular Road. There are still legal things to resolve. These events took place in 1997. There were some difficulties in the community at that time. The current Imam in Clonskeagh used to be an employee here but was appointed to Clonskeagh by the Maktoums.

In the early days in Ireland, life was much better. You will be able to see the difference more than I will. It was more peaceful before. It is very awkward now especially because of the media. I remember in the early days when we were not here very long everything was very positive. We have a voice now and yes, our voice is heard. Sometimes it is not OK but everyone has his or her bad share of the media. The problem is only from individuals. We do have contact with the government and when we wanted to open the school, it took us only two or three months while in England it took years of campaigning to get state recognition. We are very small but we got permission for our school years before the British did.

The parents would prefer if there were a Muslim secondary school. We all know each other here because the community is very small. Our biggest difficulty is with the mosque in Clonskeagh. We do not think too much about American soldiers passing through Shannon. We have our own difficulties to solve. When we see images of what is happening in Iraq we feel disturbed. I was back in Sudan in July and August. It is slightly better than it was but our problem is the peace agreement with the South. Ireland is home now for one who has no home.

Magdi, *an architect, contributes to the development of architecture students in Ireland.*

My name is Magdi Mustafa Mohamed Rashied and I am Sudanese. I was born in Wad Medani where I grew up and went to primary school. I moved a lot during my primary school years and attended two schools. I went to three different schools for both Middle and High School. I think I just liked moving. The schools were not all in the same town; they were in different parts of Sudan. I finished my school certificate in Sudan in 1981.

My dream was to move somewhere else out of Sudan. I did not come from a very rich family; my father was an electrical engineer and my mother was a teacher. Firstly, I travelled to Baghdad where I tried to study but the Iran Iraq war was on. The Iraqis decided that as we are all Arab and that we should all go to war during our holidays and that was why I went back to Sudan. At that stage, I had two choices to go either to Japan or to Germany. Finally, I decided on Germany. The main reason was that it was cheaper and I did not have to pay any fees. I went to Germany in 1982 and I had to learn German. I went to an institute in a small city between Bonn and Frankfurt. I had a problem because I had entered Germany on a visit visa and they said I would have to go back to Sudan. I went back and then returned to Germany after nine months. I started searching until I got my first offer in Frankfurt. It took a while for me to prepare myself and I had to take a lot of courses. I had to take almost two years of high school to prepare myself for university. I found my study very slow because I also had to work to support myself.

I moved universities a few times and ended up in Bonn, then went on to Berlin and finally Stuttgart. I started in Berlin I think it was 1987 and I first got a place to study Mathematics but I thought this was too hard. I changed to Architecture. Mathematics is a science, science needs a clear head and you have to think all the time. I found Architecture was better for me. I started to study at a Technical Institute in Berlin where I finished my first degree. I moved from there to Stuttgart because I found a job in an architect's office. I worked with them for about four years and then did my Master's degree in 1995. I had good experience in the offices there.

I did not have any difficulty getting a job. After my Master's I found a professor who asked me to work with him. I thought I would like to work in Vienna in Austria and this man took his phone and arranged a job for me. I spent about six months working in Austria. After that, I went back to Germany and worked with the original professor who had found me the job in Vienna. I taught with him until 2000.

I was not just teaching at that time; I was also working in a practice in Germany. I moved between the two worlds of teaching and architectural practice. I found it hard to move around for work in Europe because I had a Sudanese passport. I applied for German citizenship and it took me about two years to get it. The German passport was important for me if I wanted to stay and travel in Europe but it is not true that if I go to the Gulf or Sudan that they treat me like a European. I worked in Dubai and I was seen as a Sudanese.

In 1991, I married a German lady; we were both students at the time. She was studying medicine and now she is a doctor. Her father is Iraqi and her mother German. We have three kids and she works in Germany. To go back to my family in Sudan – we are three brothers and two sisters. One sister died in 1997 and the other is in Sudan with my mother. I have one brother in Berlin and one in Saudi Arabia.

My reason for coming to Ireland was work; in 1997, I was working in a university in Stuttgart and at the same time in a practice in the city. I also had a third job with a company doing some work in Cork. This was the first time I heard about Ireland. At that time I didn't have any problem finding work in Germany. In 2000, I finished my contract in Stuttgart and I had to think about what I was going to do. The employment situation in Germany was shocking and it was difficult to get a job. I moved to London where I worked for two years. I didn't find this a great city to be in. I thought I would have to go back to Sudan but this did not appeal to me. I couldn't find any job in Germany. There were a lot of areas in which one could not get a job. At that time I was back in Berlin visiting a friend, I applied online to an agency, and within five minutes after sending my email, they gave me a ring. It took one and a half months to sort out all the papers and then I came to Ireland in 2004. I did a couple of interviews and in the meantime, I searched on my own and found a job in DIT where they were looking for someone to teach computer architecture. The same day someone gave me a ring and arranged an interview for the next day. I had an interview with the head of department and I felt that I would not get the job because it would require a lot of English. I got a job teaching ten hours a week in the College. I also got a job in an architect's office and I worked 75% in an office and 25% in the college. That was very good but very hard and when the college increased my hours I gave up the other job. With a full time job I did not need to do both.

Living here in Dublin is difficult if you have to move around a lot. You lose a lot of time going from one place to another. I am very happy working in the College. The people are very nice and friendly. I lived in Germany for a long time but it is very hard sometimes. I don't want to say that all German people are arrogant but sometimes you get this feeling. I know there are economic problems in Germany but the Germans themselves are a bit difficult to live with. In Ireland, it is different, you can see the difference between here, there and how they treat people, and I am very happy here. The big problem for me is that I am not just between two worlds, Sudan and Germany but between three, Sudan, Germany and Ireland. My family is still in Germany and they do not want to come to Ireland. Another family, my mother, is in Sudan. I cannot change it but I really do not want to go back to Germany. I would prefer to go back to Sudan.

I know many immigrants here but it is not like in the UK or Germany. Here there are many Libyans, Sudanese and I have met a few Palestinians. There are also a few Egyptians. The refugees who are here can be divided into two groups, doctors and their families and many of whom came from Saudi Arabia. They live in Ireland in a physical sense. They work here but they do not have any relationship with Irish people. The other group is the political asylum seekers and there are a lot of them. Many of them have Irish documents. Time moves very fast and you need to do something or else five, six years have passed and you have done nothing. Most of these people get this welfare benefit and live on it. They don't want to study or do anything else. Even in other parts of Europe, they are like this.

When I saw the Sudanese community here in Ireland, I was upset. They move to Europe and they bring a strange mentality with them. Their way of doing things is not Sudanese. I have never seen any mixing between Sudanese and Irish families.

Turkey

*Turkey is classified as a Eurasian country and forms the bridge between Europe and Asia. The Bosphorus intersects the city and the two continents. . **Serhat is a** professional from Istanbul and works in Dublin.*

I was born in Turkey in 1972 in Ankara, the capital city of Turkey. My parents come from Eastern Turkey from a border state called Igdir, which is on the Russian border. I mention this because the people from my parents' hometown are Azeri in origin. The Azeri are a Turkish tribe from which both my parents come. This illustrates the fact that Turkey is a mosaic and a mixture of many different tribes of people. I grew up in Ankara and studied primary, secondary and high schools there. I studied in Science high school so I got a kind of scientific education. Later on, I wanted to be a computer scientist; I went to university in Ankara and graduated in 1996. While I was studying, I also worked at a part time job. I earned my own money because I did not want to be dependent on my family. I had almost ten years in the computer IT industry in Turkey. Later on, I decided I wanted to move abroad. The main motivation, as for many young Turkish people, was to go abroad for a while, study and improve my English level, gain something from other cultures and then come back to Turkey. But this doesn't always work out because when you go abroad, or when you sail long distances it takes you to a very different point sometimes. I think this has happened to me. I was not sure which country I wanted to go to but destiny took me to Ireland. I was looking for a job in the US.

The motivation to improve English or technical skills or enjoy other cultures was not enough in itself. It is very hard to leave your own home country and go somewhere else, especially to a very different culture such as Western culture. But the event that pushed me to make the decision was the earthquake in Turkey in 1999. The epicentre of the earthquake was very close to Istanbul and we were affected by the results of the earthquake. My wife was especially affected and she could not stay at home for a couple of months because of the psychological effects of the quake. She had been very resistant to the idea of emigrating because she would miss her family but after the earthquake, she had a very deep fear about living in Istanbul. So we decided to go live in another country and we thought in particular of the States. I started looking for a job in IT because there were so many jobs in that area at the time.

I applied for a couple of jobs but did not have positive feedback. My English level was not so good at that time. One day I saw an advertisement in the Turkish newspaper about Microsoft Ireland. They were looking for a Turkish localizer but I ignored the ad because my aim was to go to the States where the technology and everything looked better than in the other countries. I thought also that living in the States would be easier for a foreigner than other countries. This was all before September 11th. I thought it would be easier than Europe. But my wife had also seen the ad in the newspaper and she suggested that this was the time to go and if we wanted to go to another country why not Ireland. It was closer than the States and we had seen the Daniel Day Lewis movies about Ireland. It was a very exciting idea to move to this country – green and as a Turkish youngster, in the subconscious we feel that we are closer culturally to the Irish. This may be because of the tourist movies because we did not study Irish history in school. We did not study anything about Ireland but these movies made us feel that this nation had been oppressed, had been occupied by other people. They resisted and they were brave and they seemed like us. I think our subconscious was telling us this. So why not go to Ireland. I agreed with my wife but I did not like the job description of localizer and it did not fit very well with my skills. My wife said 'what will you lose if you apply?' I applied and failed but later I told myself that I should not give up and that I could check the other jobs in Microsoft. I had decided to go with Microsoft to Ireland because this would be good for my career. A long interview process took over six months and the visa process was very long and complicated in Turkey. This killed opportunity for me because colleagues in Europe did not need visas and they could come quickly for interview.

I succeeded in the interviews and Microsoft decided to hire me. But I couldn't make up my mind to come to Ireland. In one way, it was a kind of dream job for me – Microsoft, another country, a green country, and an English speaking country – many benefits. However, after the negotiations the salary offered was less than my salary in Turkey. I am emphasising this point about salary – this was five years ago and then I was earning $3,000 in Istanbul per month and in Microsoft Ireland the salary in Irish pounds was less than my previous salary. So I came to Ireland for less than my Turkish salary and to a much more expensive life style. The rents here are much more expensive. For example, for the same rent you pay in Dublin for a small flat you can find a very nice apartment in the Bosphorus area in Istanbul, in fact a spectacular place and the houses are considered to be very expensive in that area. So it was a very tough decision to come but I decided to take this opportunity because in my personal view about life, money is not everything. There are many things other than money and as you get older, you will not have time to enjoy these things. As a Muslim, I also believe in the afterlife so there is no need to spend too much time in search of money. I think it is Moliere who said, 'Eat to live and not live to eat' and I like the spirit of that. Initially, my wife thought it was a good idea to move to Ireland but when she heard about the salary that they would give she said 'No, we cannot go there'. We had a big argument for almost a whole week. The company was waiting for my final decision and wanted to know if I would take the job or not. I was trying to postpone and after a week I convinced her but it was very difficult. I told her that we could go there and try and that if we did not like it we could come back. I said it would be good experience for us. She disagreed and thought that we would destroy the life we had in Turkey. We would have to vacate our house and leave our furniture so going back after a year would not be easy. I do not know but I had a feeling. Instinct was controlling me and it was not the money or the standard of living. Something pushed me and we came. I have not regretted coming up to now even though I have had some difficult times during these five years.

We came in 2001. I am planning to apply for Irish citizenship, for naturalization. I moved from Microsoft because of the money. I want to stress the place of money. We need money for living. We need to live in a decent house, go to other countries especially in Europe and you need money for tickets. This depends on your earning power so I decided to look for another job after three and a half years. I believed that I had paid my debt to Microsoft in the three and a half years. I gave a lot of effort to Microsoft but I also gained a lot from the company and it was time to leave to improve my career. I did not rush because I wanted to find a proper job. After six months job searching, I moved to Citrix- another American company in Clontarf Business Park. I am doing a different job to what I did in Microsoft. For the last one and a half years, I have been working in Citrix. I am not planning to change this job as I enjoy it.

My son was born in Ireland in 2002. This was another turning point in our lives and at that time, the constitution allowed for any child born in Ireland to get Irish citizenship immediately. I would like to gain the benefit of citizenship because Irish law and Turkish law allow for dual citizenship. In Turkey, there are some restrictions. You cannot be elected to parliament, to the National Assembly. In Germany these days, there is a lot of discussion about the status of Turks. They do not allow Turkish people to carry dual citizenship and they want the Turkish people to give up one. In Ireland, this is not the situation. My son automatically became an Irish citizen because he was born here and at that time, they were giving status of change. A person was eligible to live and work in Ireland without any working visa. I was pleased with that knowledge because I came to Ireland on a working visa and that makes you a bit dependent on the company for which you work, Generally speaking, and I am not targeting any company with these comments but some of the companies take advantage of the employees. After my child's birth, we became independent of the company because we didn't need a work permit. From this perspective, gaining Irish citizenship does not have any advantages for me because I am already eligible to work and stay in Ireland. However, if I live in a country I want to vote because while I am living in this country I am using the hospitals, the roads so I want to be able to vote. I know I can vote in the local elections but I also want to be part of the country. I want to feel that I am part of this country. In these last five years, it has been a kind of mind evolution for me. I see that patriotism is not an absolute thing and you can describe it in a flexible way. You can be true to two countries with the same values, the same humanitarian values. But if two countries' football teams play each other you will probably support your home town. But when your second country plays against another country as happened when Ireland played Germany I supported Ireland of course. I gave them my allegiance the same as Turkey.

Living here is easy. Occasionally small incidents happen but these happen everywhere and in Turkey maybe more than here. In my opinion, Ireland is one of the best countries for Turkish people to live in. There are many similarities between the two cultures, both positive and negative similarities. For example, time keeping and being prompt – we are the same but maybe this is more so in the new generation. This is not the case in the older generation as I see many Irish senior citizens who are very prompt. They also dress up and they look very well. I think the generation of the Second World War know the value of life because they earned it through hard work. I think for us life has been a bit easier. Generally, Ireland is a very good place for Turkish people. Irish people are very hospitable and they want to share with their neighbours, their friends and the people who need something. For example, if you ask for direction from someone on the street, they do not just say 'I don't know' or 'Go straight along' but they may take you to your destination even if they are not going there. I have experienced this several times. I have not seen similar behaviour in other European countries. However, living conditions are not very good often for some foreigners. When you come as a foreigner, you start from a minus position and then you need to climb to zero and on to positive levels. For example, take the case of getting a mortgage. When your family lives in another country, you simply do not have your own house and you have to rent for three, four, five years. Before they decided to give 100% mortgage, it was impossible to get your own house even for IT workers because the deposit you needed to pay was too high. So these are the disadvantages. According to my philosophy of life, I can handle it but it can be distressing for a family. Another point is homesickness. For all of us it happens from time to time. Even my son, who at three and a half years old has spent 4 – 5 months in Turkey, misses uncles and grandparents. You can understand these issues.

From a Muslim perspective, I can say from things I have heard from friends who have lived in other countries and when I compare with what I have seen on TV and read in magazines Ireland gives a lot of freedom to people from other religious backgrounds. I do not find any difficulty in practising my own religion and I do not have any difficulties in expressing my beliefs. I do not like the idea of propagating because it is a kind of political thing when you know something is not true but you are trying to convince people it is. I do not have any problem expressing my own views, my own beliefs without criticism. I cannot say this is true for everybody but you find this in every country. It depends on people's educational levels and their own personal perspective. Everything is fine and the government supports the issue of minority rights. I can say that we do not have any problems.

As far as the size of the Turkish community is concerned, there are official and non-official numbers. I believe you can find the true figures in the Immigration Office. I have heard from the Turkish Embassy that there were 700-recorded Turkish people living in Ireland. Those figures were for 2004 but I know there is probably more than this because it is not compulsory to register at the Embassy. Many people are lazing about going to the Embassy. The number I think includes the Gama workers, you know the Turkish construction company and after the problem with this company some of the workers returned to Turkey. About 4,000 Turkish people live in Ireland.

Over the last two years, Irish people have started to buy houses in Turkey for many reasons but in particular the sun. Like us, they like the sun in summer and wintertime. They like the Mediterranean and Turkey has both Mediterranean and Asian as well as Middle Eastern. There is also European culture in Turkey; it is a real mixture and an amazing place to have a property. Another fact is they are candidates to become members of the EU and if Turkey can join, property prices will increase as has happened in the accession countries. Therefore, this is a good place to invest money. I was talking with a member of the Turkish Society who buys and sells property here and he said that over 6,000 Irish people have bought property in Turkey. They have bought all over Turkey and not just in Kusadasi, which is of course a very popular destination for Irish visitors. Irish people have been going to Kusadasi for the last twenty years. This is a very well known place and it is here that the relationship between Irish and Turkish people began. However, Kusadasi alone does not give you the whole picture of Turkey but 6,000 Irish people in Turkey is a fantastic number especially when you think of the size of the Irish population. When they stay in Turkey in their properties, they will get to know the Turkish culture as I have done with the Irish culture. This will be a very great advantage for us Turkish people who live in Ireland.

It is difficult to make Irish friends. When we first moved here, there was no Turkish society or organization – nothing. There was only the Embassy but no NGO – that was five years ago. We started this NGO work, volunteer organization almost two years ago now in May 2004. The same people who began the organization are still involved. Some people have joined and the numbers are increasing. It has spread to all the Turkish community and the good thing is that it has also spread to our Irish friends. In 2001, my wife and I decided that we needed to have Irish friends to visit our house and to visit their houses because we live here. We did not try to find Turkish people at the beginning because we wanted to integrate. I use the term integrate as opposed to assimilate. We wanted to integrate into this society but to keep our own values. The easiest way to do that was to have some Irish friends to learn from them about the culture. We wanted to know what they cook at home, how they live and at the same time improve our English. After a year, I realized that there is no common practice in Ireland for home visiting. People like to meet in the pubs and unfortunately as in Turkey now both people are working. It suits my wife because she works also. Socialising in the pub was very hard for us and not because we do not drink alcohol – this is not a barrier. It is very noisy in the pub – you cannot speak; you cannot hear and you cannot concentrate. We could not manage this type of socialising so we decided to do nothing. We met other foreigners who are here in Ireland. I have a good Polish friend who works in Microsoft, his family invited us to their home, and we invited them to ours. We also have Romanian friends. We learned a lot from them about their cultures and about Ireland because they had lived here longer than us and their experience was greater than ours.

After the establishment of this Turkish Society, we made Irish friends because of our shared common goals. These were not our friends at the beginning but as time went on and we got to know each other better some of them became personal friends. Nowadays in the modern world and not just Ireland, in metropolitan areas it is very difficult to develop friendships.

From an amateur perspective and remember I am not a professional sociologist, I see the value of this type of society and the good that it does every day. Today we have seen many people here (Eid celebration). Organising this kind of event takes almost three

313

weeks. If the people do not come, you can feel frustrated. Our name here is Turkish Irish cultural educational society. We need to do something because we are getting many things from this country. We are getting our money and if I lose my job, I can get social welfare. I contribute and Irish people contribute to this pool. They will support me and if I retire here, I will get my pension. These are some of the money benefits. It is also a free environment with many opportunities. We are also getting a good welcome. Perhaps there is a little racism but this is normal in today's world. We believe that our Islamic values are common humanitarian values. What are they? If we see someone who needs help, help him. If there are senior citizens try to make them comfortable and try to make them happy. Most importantly, do not just say but live what you say. Live what you believe. Convince people through your work and not your talk.

We took the first step by visiting some houses in Ireland. We went together with some people from the city council, the community development group for the Christmas celebration. We told them that we would like to visit some senior citizens' houses. They thought this was a very good idea and they thought we wanted to visit the Turkish senior citizens in Ireland. Of course, there are not any Turkish senior citizens in Ireland though there are a lot in Germany. They were very surprised when we explained that we wanted to visit Irish senior citizens. These people need visitors because sometimes their families do not visit them. We thought it was a good idea for them to be visited by foreigners so they can see who we are and what we are doing in Ireland because they have plenty of time to listen to our stories. For us we do not have any grandparents here and our children miss them so we thought why not visit these people here in Ireland and make our children feel as if they are at home with their grandparents. We did this three times.

The first couple of times, the Turkish Society organized the event and the third time the people from the city council did the organization. The senior citizens were very happy. A kind of synergy happened, a kind of good feeling because they smiled and it made them happy. This kind of work is part of our integration ideas. When the members of the Turkish society get involved like this it is good for them also because they remember their own grandparents, their own relatives and they know we are all human.

We are all the same. Maybe our religion and culture are different, our early environment was different but we are all human. We all get upset, we become happy and we share everything so why look on others as foreigners and strangers. If we take this direction, integration will not be so difficult. My son also should go to an Irish school and through the educational system here. At the same time, he must acquire scientific knowledge and universal ethics but as a Muslim, I would like to raise my children as Muslims. As far as I know in Ireland this is possible. We can tell the school management that we do not want our children to go to religious courses. I can take this way and I can see that many Turkish people in Ireland do not feel that it is necessary to send their children to the Muslim school. In the case of my son, he also has to study Qur'an but in his spare time at summer school or at weekends.

Let me explain – people like us immigrate to other countries and we want to do some local work for the countries in which we live for humanitarian reasons. Establishing this situation fits in with the ideas of Fatullah Gulen. He is the person who suggested opening schools all over the world. These are modern schools with a local curriculum, giving education with the curriculum of the local government. They are not Islamic schools but obey the curriculum of the country they are in. They provide education in the way that some of the international schools e.g. American schools in Turkey do and give a humanitarian and universally ethical education, thus giving a modest peace contribution to the world. In my view, education and poverty are the two main issues in the world. We would like to have this type of school in Ireland. In the UK, they are already preparing to set up such schools. I would prefer this type of school for my son. If we can have complete infrastructural works one day we can consider setting up this type of school in Ireland. Until that day I can send him to an Irish school and give our ethical values at home.

Turkmenistan

*Turkmenistan literally means "land of the Turkmen" and describes a Turkic country in Central Asia, surrounded by Afghanistan, Iran, Uzbekistan, Kazakhstan, and the Caspian Sea. Most of the country is desert and forms one of the world's largest sand deserts across which nomadic tribes roamed until well into the 20th century. **Azat** is one of two Turkmen living in Ireland.*

My name is Azat Tagamov. The name Azat means 'freedom' but I cannot explain the meaning of Tagamov in English. I am from Turkmenistan, a country in Central Asia, which was part of the old Soviet Union but is now an independent country. It got its independence on 27th of October 1991. It is a neutral country and was the last country to separate from the old Soviet Empire. The transition was peaceful. Some countries in Europe were more seriously affected by the fall of the Soviet Union but Turkmenistan was the last country to get independence.

I am from the city of Merv, the last capital of the Seljuk Turks who existed 2,500 years ago. There were three capitals in the Seljuk Empire; one was in Turkey, one somewhere in the Middle East and the last one in Merv in Turkmenistan. There are many historical places around Merv and archaeologists found the old city that lies below land level. A couple of houses from that ancient city are now open to the public but they want to open the entire city, which is believed to cover about five acres of ground. If the government is willing to invest in the project, it could be an unbelievable place in the future. If you go there, you can visit very ancient places and really enjoy yourself. Even in my lifetime, I have seen different periods. Firstly, the period of the Soviet Empire; in this time the Soviet Union was very strong. There were 14 small countries inside

317

the union. In the eastern part of Turkmenistan there is a city whose Russian name is Kurki; this was the easternmost area of the Soviet Union. There are five areas in Turkmenistan; the first one is Ashgabat, the capital city. This is in Ahal region, the second is Mary, the third Lebak, Dashoguz, and the last is Balkan. There are many natural gas and petroleum reserves and in parts of Turkmenistan, you can see the hard version of the petroleum on the land.

I am the second Turkman to come to Ireland. The first was here and did an MA in Cork but I am the one who has stayed the longest so far. I came in October 2005 and I am now working in the Turkish Irish Educational and Cultural centre as an administrator. The Soviet Union realised the extent of the wealth of natural gas in our country and both Turkmenistan and Uzbekistan became the main producers of natural gas during the Soviet times. Turkmenistan now ranks as third or fourth in world reserves of natural gas. Our president who died recently did not want outsiders to know about our wealth because he wanted to protect the country. If we look at the Middle East, for example, we see a lot of petroleum wealth but we see a lot of others who have eyes on that land. Therefore, our president did not want to open these reserves to the outside world. In the last couple of years, BP has come and done explorations and now they say there are three trillion cubic metres of natural gas in the country. It may be first in natural gas reserves in the world. In terms of petroleum reserves, the country is 19th or $20^{th.}$ The regions of Mary and Ahal are full of natural gas. The petroleum is very close to the Caspian Sea in the Balkan region.

During Soviet times, the Turkmen people were not told much about the gas reserves in their country. In Soviet times, they said everyone was equal and whether you were a director or worker you had a

318

salary and that was enough for you. There were no private sectors or companies so people could not be rich. For example, if you look at IBM, Microsoft, or Bill Gates one person runs the companies, he gets the money and is very rich. In Soviet times, there was no privacy but now it is important to go in that direction. Our last president took the first steps towards privatization. The new president has only been in office for one month and we shall see what he will do in terms of education and with the old petroleum projects. Life in Soviet times was easy. At the time of the demise of the Union, I was about eight years old. I went to a Russian crèche. In my family there are seven children; my mother was at home and my father was a businessman, not probate but in the government sector. He started in Tashkent in Uzbekistan because at that time you could go anywhere within the Union. By 1963, he had done his MA; this was unusual for this time but he had a good brain. He was a director in the Merv region but now he is dead. He died when he was 58 but he directed all his children to study and now all of us have good jobs and we are all well-educated.

I went to a Russian crèche and my second language is Russian. At home, we learned and spoke the Turkmen language which is somewhat similar to Turkish. My Russian is still good because I learned it as a child though I do not remember how I learned it. For two to three years after the crèche, I studied in Russian in the primary school. The next three years were also in Russian but this was after the collapse of the Soviet Union and life for everyone in the countries in my region was very hard. In the time of the Soviet Union, everything was good but there was a disadvantage because you had to ask Moscow for everything. You could not do anything without their permission. We did not have any infrastructure in our country. Turkmenistan, for example, produced cotton, very good quality cotton as well as natural gas and petroleum, but all of the products were for the central Soviet government. Each region produced different commodities for the Soviet Union. The Soviet system was good but it did not let people practise their own culture. As we know, culture involves religion and in Russia, religion meant Christianity. In Central Asia it is mainly Muslin but there are some Christians and everyone lives in peace with each other. All my teachers in primary school were Russian and that is a mistake anywhere.

Nobody could practise his own religion. Take Islam, when a person dies there is a special procedure to prepare the body but the Russians did not allow that. Circumcision was not allowed; people did these things but in secret in the villages. For people whose family had a good position in the government like my father it was very difficult to follow these practices. In my case, I had a problem with that procedure and was in hospital for a week. Praying was not allowed and there were no mosques in Turkmenistan as Muslims and Christians were not allowed to practise their religion. Of course, people in the villages heard about religion from their grandfathers and I heard about it from my mother. My father was very influenced by the Russian culture and everyone at that time in Turkmenistan became a little Communist from the age of eight or nine. Around the age of 12, you became a kind of pioneer for the communist party and then at an older age there was a special role for the person. People had to pay a price to be a communist. If a person was working as a tractor driver in a small village, you were considered lucky and the children in the village did not have ambitions to be an engineer; they all wanted to be tractor drivers or to be the one collecting cotton.

To be getting an education made you an outsider. This was a strategy of Russia to keep people uneducated not just in

Turkmenistan. Some people were educated but they were working for the Russians and they did not know about this strategy. Of course, we understand that now but the older people, for example my mother who stayed at home feels that life was easier then. They see it is not so easy these days because earning enough money is hard. People now say they want those days to come back but truly, they do not know about the reality of those times. They did not know about the wealth of the Soviet Union. Even now, there are people in the government who were there in communist days and they do not know anything about the outside world. They do not know about the age of technology and there are still people who just want to be tractor drivers. It is very interesting. Some people still want that life because they were given everything by the government. Everyone was equal and got the same wage but they do not realise that the government kept a lot of money for themselves.

When we move to the years after the Soviet Union to Turkmenistan, we see very difficult years because there was no grain for flour and bread. It had not been grown in our lands during Soviet times and we had to start growing it for ourselves. We had to learn all the technology that was available that would help us to grow our own food. This continued for three to four years. For me it was not bad because my father was in a good position and he did not let these difficult times hurt his children. But of course not everybody was in our situation. For example, there were people from my city going to the capital to take bread for their children.

But it is not like that now. One of the positive strategic steps that our president took was to send students to other countries especially Turkey, which was the first country to recognize Turkmenistan after independence and later helped with everything. For example, they sent investors to Turkmenistan and nowadays if you look at

321

business, you can find many Turkish companies. Their businesses are well established. Another country that gave a lot of help was Iran but now the relations with Iran though normal are not as good as those with Turkey. After the breakup of the Soviet Union, the loss was Russia's. The Turkmenistan president had worked and been the Turkman representative in Russia for about 10 years so he knew their strategies very well. His approach was to cut relations with Russia. However, relations are good at present and we need them because our natural gas can only be exported by pipeline through Russia. During the Soviet times, everything was organised so the gas went through Russia. Our natural gas still goes through Russia and there is no choice. In fact, my Master's dissertation is about the technological, economic and strategic factors for pipelines in developing countries in exporting natural gas.

Turkey in particular helped us and we might try to explain this support by looking at the Ottoman Empire. But this was not a real empire if we compare it with other empires e.g. the British Empire because the people of the Ottoman Empire came from our regions, Uzbekistan and Kazakhstan. Groups of people came from our regions to the Middle East and those are now the Turks in Turkey. When the Soviet Union drew the borders of our countries, they made some mistakes. Five million of our Turkmen people were left in Iran for example and there is part of our area that originally belonged to Iran. I do not remember the new name of that area because our President changed many of the old names in the country. I think he did this for the sake of the children, to give them a sense of a nation. Thanks to him, children now have a sense of nationhood.

If we look at Irish history, we see there were a lot of wars and because of those people understand the importance of independence.

They cannot forget about the blood that was shed or the people who died for independence. The Turks are the same because there were many armies that tried to overtake their country. For us it was a major disadvantage that there was no war of independence. Therefore, the government has to work hard to convince people of the importance of the national anthem and the flag. The flag of Turkmenistan is one of the hardest flags to draw; it is green like many of the Arab flags as a desert people longing for the green. Five figures represent the five regions of the country; there are differences between the people of each region. For example in the part of the country near Uzbekistan, there are many Uzbeks. There is also a crescent moon and five stars in the flag. The five stars represent the five senses in the body and the five elements.

Turkmenistan is very famous for its cotton and a few years ago, Turkman cotton was voted the best in the world. This is because of the incredible summer heat; even in the shade, it is about 40 degrees Celsius. In winter, it is minus five to minus ten but often not as cold as this. Turkmenistan is also famous for its horses. In the middle of the star in the flag, there is a horse, which is a symbol of the country. Our horses are famous for their beauty. They have some Arab blood in them. The investment in the horse industry is very high now and there are many competitions. Carpets are very important also and the biggest handmade carpet in the world is from Turkmenistan. It is a product of Soviet times and is now in a museum. You can find a picture of it on the internet. Many carpets are exported from the country. The women continue to make the carpets by hand both in the home and in factories. In the film 'The Godfather', you can see a carpet from Turkmenistan. Turkmen silk is also famous and now we are exporting to the world.

In general, people are good. They are sensitive and they care about older people. My oldest brother has three children and the oldest one is in the army. My brother is a doctor, he is 44, and I am 24, a difference of 20 years. My twin is 10 minutes older than I am and I am the youngest. When I meet them, I do not talk much because I must show them respect. I listen, not like in Europe where individualism is high. In those countries, people live together and the most important thing is the family. The thing that will take me back to Turkmenistan immediately is if there is a problem in my family and I need to do something to hold them together. Of course, there are good business opportunities there but the main goal is to keep the family together. Perhaps when you are in Turkey you can see the same kind of respect for the family but you definitely cannot see it here in these European countries. I think people need this contact. I heard that here in Dublin city 200,000 old people live alone. Their children do not care about them. The Turkman tradition is that the youngest son stays with the parents and takes care of them. Now my mother lives with my twin sister; we are the only two in the family not married.

The first year that Turkmenistan sent students to Turkey, 2,000 went. The education system in Turkey was much better that that of Turkmenistan. Many people think that education in Turkey is lower than the average EU but if we compare with Ireland, the primary system is Turkey is twice as high as here. The difference is that in these countries in Europe and in the US, investment in research is high but not so in Turkey. It is very difficult to get into university; about 1 million students sit a difficult exam each year to gain entry. To take a BA degree there takes four years and not three as in Ireland. Of the 2,000 Turkmen students who first went to Turkey, only about 200 finished their degree. The others because of the poor quality education they had had in their home could not succeed. Another problem of course was the language.

The most important educational development in my country was the opening of Turkish high schools; the first one was opened in our capital in 1992 and in 1993, eight or nine were opened in different cities. The first high schools were only for boys and they had to pay a fee but after 1996, the schools were free. The Turkmen President went to visit all the Central Asian countries and brought many businessmen to invest in the countries. He also brought teachers from the Felan Gulan School to establish them and in 1995, I went to one of those schools in my city. This educational system believes that tolerance grows through proper education. I studied for five years in the school; the first year we learned English, Turkish, Turkman, and Russian. Then we took science and Math and we had teachers from the famous Istanbul University and Ankara. Those teachers came to help us, gave us a hand and we are grateful to them. If we compare my education with any other, it was excellent. They took only 64 students and there were 5,000 applicants. Everybody wanted to send his or her children but I was lucky. This changed my whole life. I finished my studies in the year 2000; we had one student from my school who took a first medal in education and for Biology in Turkmenistan. I went to Turkey to Istanbul to study mechanical Engineering.

I came to Ireland in February of 2006. At first, I studied English in Atlas Language School. I took a 6-month course and then took the IELTS exam. I scored 6 and my speaking score was very good as I got 7. With this score, I could apply anywhere because in Engineering this English score is adequate. I applied to Portobello College in Dublin and I started to study for a Master's in International Business. I went back to Istanbul in May 2006 to

325

repeat the subject I had failed and I did and got my degree. I decided to defer for the second term and will begin next January. I had a very nice topic in the first term and I did very well. It is a combination of business and engineering, about petroleum and natural gas reserves in Turkmenistan. It was a familiar subject to me and so I was able to get a really high mark.

Portobello is a private college. Of course, it would be better to study in a national university like UCD and I would like to apply there if I decide to do a PhD. However, the financial costs are much higher and it would be necessary to have a scholarship to study as I had in Turkey. I have applied to some places and I shall wait for a decision. I am paying for myself in Portobello and I shall continue to do that until I get my certificate. I have a part time job and I am able to cover my own expenses.

Living in Ireland is expensive. As we know Dublin is reported to be the second most expensive city in Europe; I do not know which city is the most expensive, maybe Moscow. It is difficult especially for students from Central Asia because of their financial situation. But living in Ireland is good. Irish society is different from other European countries. I have met people from many European countries and I have been in the UK but I think Irish culture is similar to our own. In our culture, your neighbours, your friends and your family are all important. Here in Ireland these relations are not as strong as in our culture but if you compare the different European countries, Ireland is the best. We can see this in the relationships between friends, family members and in the way people smile at each other and help.

In terms of myself, whether I should stay on here and continue to study or go back home are some of the decisions I have to make.

These decisions concern family; at my age in Turkmenistan at least 90% of the people are married so maybe I will marry. Of course, I will choose whom I marry. You can ask your family to choose someone for you but these days, people generally choose for themselves. It will be very easy for me to find a job back in Turkmenistan because I took my degree in Mechanical Engineering and I am one of the first Turkmen to do this. Science and Engineering departments are not so well developed in Turkmenistan and not so many people have a Master's or knowledge of English so it should be very easy to find a job. In the last three to four years, Turkmenistan has opened to international companies especially in petroleum. I remember in the 3rd year in university I had four job offers. So after my studies here and my knowledge of English it will be very easy to find a job. However, when I go back I will have to do my military service because in my country you have to do one and a half years in the military but maybe because I have an old mother I may not have to go and do active service. During the years that you are studying, you are able to defer the service. Turkmenistan is at peace with all its neighbours except perhaps for some local problems over petrol with Azerbaijan near the Caspian Sea but the new president is trying to improve relations.

The new president is really trying to improve things. He called all the ministers and spoke to them and told the Minister for Education to research all the educational systems around the world especially countries such as UK and USA and I think he plans to send students on scholarships to these countries. Now the country sends about 150 students to Turkey every year. I think we will also send students to Malaysia especially in the fields of science and economics but probably in all subjects.

The infrastructure in Turkmenistan is very good and the hospitals have modern equipment. There is a joke that there are no doctors to run the new equipment because they are not trained for it. But everything is good. Everything is free especially in healthcare. But you can say that development is not equal because much more goes into the capital than into other parts of the country. The capital 'Ashgabat' is forecast to be the next Dubai of the region. The climate is very good there because it is in the mountains. The city is very clean and many of the buildings are made of white marble. Like Ireland, there are about five or six other big cities and they are developing too but the main investment is in Ashgabat.

When I first came to Ireland, I got a lot of help from Turkish people and from the Turkish Irish Cultural and Educational Society. I am happy with some of the things that the society does. I work with the society as an administrator and this helped me a lot to improve my English and to learn about the society. I am grateful to the society; they helped me with everything down to a place to live. I am the only Turkman here; there was another but he has gone back to Turkey but because of the help I got from the Turkish people, I have felt comfortable here.

The organization (TICES) is a charitable organization which was established in April 2004 to help establish the Turkish culture in Ireland and to serve everybody irrespective of race or religion. It was established by Turkish businessmen trying to do business in Ireland who realized that as the Turkish community in Ireland they needed an organization to support each other and to celebrate Turkish events. They try to help people who are having problems integrating into Ireland. There are many mixed families here where the man is Turkish, the woman is Irish, and problems can arise in these families especially after the birth of the children. The woman wants the child to follow the Irish culture and the man wants the child to follow the Turkish culture. If the problem is not dealt with in the early stage, it could end up in divorce. There are many examples of this so it is very important to educate the children especially when they become teenagers. If the child is taught what is best in both cultures he or she will be able to make their own decisions. We visit these kinds of families and advise them to be tolerant of each other and to think of their children as well as themselves.

We also organise conferences and celebrations for important events. We try to show that Islam is a normal religion because people may have negative views after 9/11 and 7/7. We think like normal people and we are not terrorists. For the last two years, we have also been visiting the sheltered house especially in the south side in Ringsend and Rathmines areas where we visit three shelters. People often come together in these places to share their loneliness. We go with our Sufi music group and read some poems. We also visit some old people who are lonely because their children do not visit. There are Turkish and Irish volunteers who go on these visits. We do this work in cooperation with Dublin City Council. At the beginning of 2006, about seven of our members got awards from the Mayor of Dublin as part of the Unsung Heroes. I was one of those people and the interesting thing is that this was the first time the award was given to foreigners.

We are also conducting language courses because there are many Irish people who have houses in Turkey and who go there every year on holiday. People want to learn Turkish if only to communicate with their neighbours. Now we have Turkish language classes at three different levels. We also have English language classes especially for the garment workers who have had many problems here. We are trying to help people with integration so language is important. We also run a weekend school for children mainly to help with the Turkish language but sometimes also with school subjects. The society is supported by Turkish businessmen and we shall also apply for some grants from the government. We organise parties and picnics with families to raise funds for the school. We also work closely with the local politicians and the local county council.

Women in Turkmenistan have the same rights as women in Ireland but they are not so free. Men and women are treated equally in the country and if either wants to be a politician, they can. In terms of dress a woman is free to cover or not as she pleases. It is a democracy and it depends on the individual but the freedom is there. In the past, not too many women went to study but nowadays there is an equal number of men and women in the universities. Many people are Muslim but Russians living in the country are free to practise their religion. In Soviet times, people did not think too much about Islam but with the arrival of freedom, people have begun to pay more attention because it is part of our culture. About 95% of the country now is Muslim.

It is easy to get a visa to visit Turkmenistan. I can write you a letter of invitation and you can take it to your nearest embassy and get the visa. You can also fly directly to Turkmenistan and get your visa at the airport.

Ukraine

The word 'Ukraine' means 'the borderland' explaining why the country was often referred to as The Ukraine in the past.   Perhaps one of the best known more recent facts about Ukraine is the Chernobyl disaster in 1986 when a flawed reactor design caused the worst ever nuclear reactor accident in history resulting in many deaths, ongoing cancer cases and the movement of 350,000 people from their homes. **Inna** *lives in Dublin.*

I am from Zaporozhia, an industrial city famous for cars. Many people may think of it as a boring place. There are many factories and it is quite polluted. I lived in the outskirts of the city but the city centre is quite dirty. I studied in school through Russian. There were only two Ukrainian schools in our city but we did not really speak Ukrainian at home. My Mum can speak Ukrainian and Russian very well because she finished school in Ukrainian. We speak Surjek at home, a mixture of Russian and Ukrainian. Most people in the cities speak Surjek. The sisters of my grandmother in the village still speak pure Ukrainian.

I tried to enter university but failed because I was not well prepared. I wanted to study English but we had not studied English language in school at all. It was always a problem to find a teacher and several years we had no English classes. I took some private classes but we could not afford as many as I needed. When I failed, I decided to do something else because I did not want to waste my time. I did a bookkeeping/ accountancy course and started to work as a bookkeeper. I was 19 by then and it was difficult to continue studying because the system had changed and you had to pay for everything. Nothing was free anymore after the fall of the Soviet Union. The only place where you did not need to pay was the

331

Teacher Training School so I went there. My Mum is a teacher in kindergarten but before I went to Teacher Trainer College, I could not imagine myself as a teacher. I went to the College only because of English. I finished Teacher Training College. My results were good, and that allowed me study in university free. However, I decided to take a correspondence course because you need money to study. I started the correspondence course and started working in the school. I went back to the same school where my Mum and I had studied, and I became a teacher there. My teachers became my colleagues.

I taught English for half a year and taught everything including Maths and Religion. Our school was quite a famous place and every year we had visitors from places like Canada. It is famous for its German architecture and it was originally built by German Mennonites. When I worked in the school, I tried to organize some concerts for the children. I taught them some songs and poems in English. I was doing a correspondence course but it was not very good. It was in a city about two hours from my city and I was taking English but you cannot really study language from a distance. I graduated from the course but I was still not happy about my level in English. That is why I decided to come to Ireland to study.

We did not really have money to send me abroad to study. When I was thinking about a place to go, the travel agent said that there was a better chance of getting a visa for Ireland than the UK or other countries. I had even thought of going to Malta but the information about the course in Ireland sounded very good. I really loved what I read about the college in Ireland but we still did not have money. I thought I should forget about it but my Dad got money through a business that he had. He decided to invest money in me and so I came to Ireland. It was for an academic year consisting of three months General English; three months work experience and three months preparing for the First Certificate. I took that course and that is how I ended up here. I got a student visa and that allowed me work up to 20 hours a week. I started working in Arnott's coffee shop doing whatever, cleaning, washing dishes. I was so happy to find a job because I had spent two months searching. I have worked in different places since then at any job I could find even if it meant filling in for a friend. I did that for a friend who was cleaning in the Bank of Ireland and she went home for a month so I took her place. So I would do the cleaning in the morning around 6 or 6.30 and then go to college after that. When I finished in college at 1 o'clock, I would go to work in Arnotts. That was only three to four days a week but anytime there was overtime I would do that also.

For the first month in Dublin, I lived with a host family in Clontarf. I liked them but the first month was hard because I had never been away from my parents in my life. The maximum I had been away on my own was for two weeks. Even then, when I went for two weeks I felt extremely homesick. My Mum had warned me to think carefully before I went because she said I did not know what it was like to be away from home. I wanted to go because I thought my English level was low. Of course, in the teaching situation that I was in nobody would know that. My strength was that I knew the pedagogy very well and I could organize my lessons in a way that could hide my language inadequacies. Most of my students were kids. We would play and it was not too demanding. Everybody knew me in the school but I felt that I had to get more knowledge and I told my Mum this.

The first month in Ireland was very difficult for me but I was very happy about the school. Two very good things that I got from the school were knowledge and the fact that I met Ollie. I met him when I had been here three years as I was doing an evening course in the school to keep my grammar going. People who went to the school in the evening all went for different reasons. I wanted to do the CAE exam and that is how I met Ollie. But in the first month here I really felt like I was on a different planet. That was in November 2002. Everything was different for me – the layout of the city, the transport system. There were two other students living with the host family: one from Italy and one from Korea. The Italian guy had been here before and at that time I thought his English was better than mine but I realized later that I just did not have confidence in my speaking ability in English. I was very shy and I could not start a conversation until I was 100% sure that my sentence was correct. Otherwise, I would not speak at all.

When I first came, I would go to school every day with the Italian and wait for him going home because I was afraid of getting lost. I do not really have a very good sense of orientation and that is why I would wait for him or I had a piece of paper with me with the address written on it. I would stand near the driver with a piece of paper and ask him about the address. A couple of days later I would still be standing by the driver with the same piece of paper. One day it was a different driver but he asked me *'Are you from the Ukraine?'* I said *'yes'* and asked *'How did you know?'* But a few days earlier the other driver had contacted him to find out exactly where the address was in Clontarf. That was how he knew. It took me at least two weeks to get used to it all. It would take me up to an hour to find a bus stop if I was alone. I could not see the name of the street and the map did not help me.

I moved into a flat with some Belarusian people after that. I stayed with them for a month and then I moved and shared a room with a Polish girl. There was also a Ukrainian guy who slept in the living room. After I had been in Ireland for nine months, I went home for two months. I decided to come back to Dublin and do a Business course. I wanted to continue learning. I had taken my First Certificate exam and failed it. I do not know why because I had studied hard and I did not find the exam difficult. I decided to repeat it again and when I came the second time, I found a job in Ranelagh in a florist shop. I was the junior florist and I was very happy with that because I was familiar with flowers as we used to have a family flower business. When I was finishing school, we moved from our flat to an old house. We needed money to rebuild the house and there was loads of land so we grew flowers and sold them. I was quite happy to get that job in Ranelagh because it was something that reminded me of my house, my family and my life in Ukraine. I spent about two years working there and I really enjoyed it and met some very nice people. I improved my spoken English a lot because I worked with five Irish women. I met a very nice woman that I am still friends with and we still meet from time to time. She became almost like a second mother and she was very warm towards me. She was very kind and invited me to her house for Christmas and times like that. I also started hill walking with her.

I fell for Ollie a couple of months before I started going out with him and I could not imagine any relationship with him because he was a teacher and I was a student. He lived in Rathmines and I lived in Donnybrook at that time. We would go home together after school because it was quite late in the evening. We started out as friends. We would just talk to each other, and he was into hill walking also so we would go walking together. He was very nice to talk to. A few months later, I moved into a flat on my own and this was my first experience living alone. I had lived with Chinese, Polish, Slovakian, and Spanish and so this was my first experience to go out on my own. I was 28 and I felt I needed my own space.

Even though it was expensive to live alone I felt it was better. You feel like a different person. Ollie would spend most of his time with me and then he moved in with me and we spent about a year in that flat.

We decided to get married because I wanted to move back to the Ukraine to be near my family and friends. I had planned to go back in December 2005 when my visa was up. I had known Ollie for about six months and I did not know what to do; stay here or go back home. In November, I had to make a decision and I remember telling my Mum that if nothing happens with this man I am going home and I am going to join a convent. I was quite serious about that and my Mum was shocked. I felt if he was not the one it would not be anyone else. I decided to extend my visa but I had to continue studying. We got married in August but it takes a very long time to organize all this. My Mum was going to come for the wedding but they only had dates in September. We already had tickets to go to Ukraine in August. We told the people that we had tickets to Ukraine for the 24th and there was a space for a wedding on 23rd evening. Nobody knew about this date but we got married. Then we found a job in Ukraine in Daniesk a town four hours from my city. Ollie was a teacher and I was a secretary.

The money was very good for Ukraine but conditions were not. I did not really have time to visit my family and friends and that was the main reason for moving back to Ukraine. It was quite hard work. We started in the morning and sometimes did not finish until nine at night and often we had only one day off a week. We decided to move back to Ireland but spent two months in my city before moving. We came back to Ireland in March 2006. I started to mind a baby who is bilingual in English and Russian. Her Mum is Irish and the father is Russian She was born in Dublin but she lived in Russia for 3 years and when she came back to Ireland her Russian was really good, better than her English but now it is getting bad. The parents are divorced and the father speaks on the phone to the child sometimes but not very often. I am the only person she speaks Russian with and she hates Russian now. She likes being with me because I play with her and I do everything she wants. I think if you are with a child, you have to give them all your attention. I never stop speaking with her. Last summer I spent time travelling to Ukraine and Russia with her and the Mum who was doing work there. I spent more time with her than her mother. When she was in Ukraine and Russia, she was fine speaking Russian. But all her constructions are English. Russian words on English syntax and I try to correct her all the time.

After I met Ollie, I felt more comfortable in Ireland. I used to have many jobs because I felt that if I worked all the time I would not have time to think and be homesick. I worked in the florist and then I would go work in a restaurant. Anytime I had a day off, I would go clean house. I did this for six months or so. It was very hard and I wanted to travel and visit other countries because it is very difficult to travel from Ukraine. I went on a trip around Europe, by bus from London around six countries. I travelled to England on my own and stayed with some friends and then I went to France, Holland, Germany, Austria, Italy and Switzerland. We stayed for two to three days in each country. It was nice but very tiring. When I met Ollie, I did not want to work at all. I had only one job and then it became part time.

My Mum came here once. When I go home, I have to get used to living there again. You have to change how you think. People are the same everywhere but the way they live is different. The things they talk about are different or maybe talk about things in a different

337

way. They have different worries and lifestyles. So you have to think about how to organize your words and the subjects you should touch and avoid. Sometimes it is hard. When Ollie and I went to work in Ukraine, it took time to get used to it. I felt stressed being there. To be honest in some ways it is easier to live here. People do not interfere in your life and they do not judge you. In Ukraine, people talk about you. They want to know all your personal details and you feel they interfere and it can be difficult sometimes. It is rude not to tell something but in my view, the working place is separate from family place.

Here you do not need to try to please people all the time. At the same time, I feel that my life has stopped here and that it is only when I go to Ukraine that I will lead my own life again. It is fine here but the life style is different. I participate but it is a kind of contradiction to what I have just said but nobody notices me and nobody cares whereas in Ukraine many people know me and expect something from me and I want to live for them and to show them what I can do. I feel I have a community in Ukraine but not here. When I started teaching in Ukraine, I realised that it is the job for me. When I first came to Ireland I asked myself why I had come; what did I not have in Ukraine that brought me here and what made me come here? I had a job in Ukraine. I had a good family. What else did I need? That was when I faced difficulties. But the job in Ukraine had been very demanding, always correcting exercise books and no time to relax. Even when I went out somewhere, I was always thinking of the work I had to do and planning classes. Then when the chance came to travel it came quickly and no one in the school knew. I am thinking of doing some more courses in education.

Venezuela

Venezuela is situated in the northeastern side of the South American continent and in addition to the mainland consists of numerous islands. Its current leader, Hugo Chavez reflects the diverse history of the region as his ancestry includes Amerindian, Afro-Venezuelan and Spanish connections. **Rafael** *was a secondary school student in Dublin when I taught him English .*

Venezuela was a beautiful place to grow up in but if you are a foreigner, it is not that good because all Venezuelans live within their family group and you will feel like an outsider outside the group. I lived in a flat with my brother and parents. The standard in schools in Venezuela is not that high, not as high as here in Ireland but my school was one of the best and my grades were good. I am not from the capital Caracas; I am from Purto Ayacucho, which is in the middle of the country and about eight hours by car from the capital. Caracas is very polluted and so is my city because it is in the middle of an industrial area. My father is a system engineer and works in a factory. My Mum is an architect but right now she is not working because of the government. She stays in the house and takes care of my brother. He is two years younger than I am. I decided to come to Ireland because of the things that are happening in Venezuela and I have aunts here, which is a big advantage for me. I came first to study English and then to see if I could study here. It is very good living here and it not difficult to study through English because the information is the same as in Spanish.

For me Hugo Chavez is the basis of the problem in Venezuela right now. When I was 10 years old, he came to power, about eight years ago. I can see the difference now to the past. In terms of the media, he holds very strong control. The economy has also suffered because Chavez stopped all the industries. Unemployment has increased a lot and there are many problems.

Venezuela is a very rich country. We have gold, oil and even some diamonds. The problem is the way these are all being managed because now the government has all the power. Chavez says something; it happens; he acts like a dictator. Every seat in the Parliament is pro Chavez so he can control everything. I think there was cheating in the election because the names of some people who were already dead were used for voting.

The currency has lost a lot of value and so it is very bad for us when we come here or go to other parts of the world. When Chavez came to power, $1 was equal to 700 bolivars and now it is 3,000 to $1. It is very difficult to travel around the world because you have to ask for permission to get euro or dollars. In the past, you could just go to the States and change the bolivars anywhere you liked but it is not like that anymore. You can also take only a certain amount of money. The first time I went to the States, it was easy and prices were normal for us but now it is almost impossible and very expensive.

We still have some tourists coming to Venezuela but only in certain areas such as Angel Falls, Margarita Island and another mountain area near Merida that is very high and very cold. The mountain peak Bolivar is the highest in South America. Development is not as good as it was 10 years ago because of government control.

I like living in Ireland for many reasons. In Venezuela, you cannot take a bus or a train; we just take a taxi when you want to go somewhere and only then if you know the taxi driver. There are many kidnappings. So if you want a taxi you must phone and make sure you know the person. If you stop someone on the street, the driver may kidnap you and then look for money. These are called 'Express Kidnappings'. Things are dangerous for taxi drivers also. For example, last year more than 50% of taxi drivers were killed and as a result, all the taxi drivers changed. The good ones were killed or gave up and the worst people took over the job. Most of them now are criminals. Sometimes they kidnap just for money but sometimes they act like contract killers and kill because someone is paying them to do it. Sometimes they may kill just to get something you have.

There is another thing. If you go to the city centre and someone hands you a paper it is better not to touch the paper and to run away. Nobody touches perfume now because of a plant called burandanga that grows in Columbia. If you touch that plant, it has a hallucinogenic effect on you. Someone puts it on paper and if you touch it, it can control you. You go to the bank with the person who gives it to you and you remember nothing. You go to the bank, give the number of your account, remove the money and give it to the guy and you remember nothing. This drug from a plant is very bad. You do not remember a thing.

Sunset happens every day between 6.30 and 7 in Venezuela and after 7 you can't go out in the street because it is too dangerous. There is no curfew but it is just too dangerous and if you go out you are crazy. This is all over the whole country. My parents like Venezuela very much and they do not want to leave. I told them it is much better here but they do not want to come. I told them that you can go out and go everywhere but they think Ireland is very poor. I told them that this is not true. I have an uncle who is politician in Caracas. He is pro Chavez and the rest of the family hates him. This is happening a lot in families; they are divided over politics into pro

341

and anti Chavez. He says good things about Chavez all the time. My uncle works with Chavez and so he likes him.

People in Venezuela think of Ireland as that country with all the farmers. It is like here; some people think that Venezuela does not have technology or anything. They think we live in very small houses and very simple lives. Venezuela is a very wealthy country but now there are just two classes: the rich and the poor. Chavez says he is helping the poor but he distorts the truth. He says he is going to put everybody on the same level but everybody is going down and not up. The poor people are still poor and he is able to buy their loyalty by offering them about ∈10.

I want to stay here and do my Leaving Certificate and I hope I can stay on after that. I want to convince my parents to come here as well but I do not know if they will. I came here because I do not see any future for me in the country but the people who have helped to construct the country like my parents do not want to leave. For example, my Dad has a very high position in his company and they are happy with their lives. My Mum does not have to work and they have enough. I want to become an engineer but if Chavez decides one day that everybody will earn the same money, I will get as much as the guy sweeping the street. I do not want that.

In Venezuela I played soccer and studied a lot. I also went to parties with my friends. Here I don't go out very much. Secondary school in Venezuela is five years but here it is six and it is harder than my country. Here there is a national standard but in Venezuela it depends on the school. My school was one of the best there. Students choose between science and humanities and I went for science. There are only three to four good schools and the rest are just normal. The government puts a lot of money into a few educational projects, for example, giving classes to adults who can't read and write. These people can finish primary school in two to three years; then they do secondary school in another three years and they can do university in three years. This makes for very poor quality education. The government is putting money into these projects and also building schools but not into regular education.

Here it is good. I do not need a car to get me to school. I come by myself and I know that nobody is going to kill or kidnap me in the street. I live with my aunt, her husband and my cousins here. I have another aunt and cousins in Celbridge. My uncle is Irish; he worked around the world in engineering and met my aunt in Venezuela. He is working for a pharmaceutical company here and he loves his work but he is very supportive of his family. He loves the family.

Zimbabwe

*Zimbabwe has known much trouble in recent years and on March 6th 2008, the Zim dollar dropped to an all time low of 25 million Zim dollars to one US dollar. Under Robert Mugabe's rule, any criticism of the government is dealt with in a very harsh manner and there are ongoing accusations of serious abuses of human rights. Many international media groups including BBC are banned from entering to report on the country. Consequently, many Zimbabweans have left the country. **Dambudzo** lives in Dublin now.*

I was born in Harare, Zimbabwe where I went to primary and secondary schools and then went on to College. After College, I got a job and I worked in a company in the city. Then around 1999, a political issue forced me to leave the country. The behaviour of the government and its attitude towards people drove me out. We were forced to attend meetings, rallies and there was a political party MDC that was in opposition to the government party. Mugabe's party forced people to join and carry cards to show you belonged to their Zanu PF party. Most of the people living in the urban areas, Harare, did not want Mugabe because of the way he was treating other people. I think the majority of people belonged to the opposition party, the MDC. Mugabe was so angry about this that he started using military force against people to force them to join his party. There were soldiers going around checking identity cards and if people didn't belong to the government party they were taken to prison or beaten up. They used so many ways to convince people to join their party. This went on through 1995, '96, '97.

Around this time, the government started to confiscate farmers' lands. In my case, I am not politically minded but I was motivated to join the opposition because of what was happening in Zimbabwe.

Every person who belonged to the opposition party was in danger. Mugabe did not want anyone to join and he could even have you killed. I think it was towards Independence Day in 1999 and Mugabe was trying to force everybody to go to the rallies to celebrate our independence on April18[th]. Most people did not want to go because they knew Mugabe was going to address the rallies. They went to the opposition party's celebration. After the rally, government party people and opposition groups clashed during the demonstrations and people started to fight. The government people had the power because they were armed. Soldiers had all the equipment and all kinds of guns. I was involved and was taken to prison. It was not a prison as such but a dark room; I could not see and did not know where I was. They covered my eyes when I was taken there. Then they questioned me about what was going on and they wanted to know everything about the opposition. They interrogated me but I did not say anything because we were told even if we were ill-treated or tortured we should not tell anything. These were secrets and we should not tell. I was beaten up because they wanted me to say something. They tried to scare me by showing me dead bodies. Of course, I did not know much about this opposition party either because my aim in joining the party was simply because we were supposed to join one or other of the political parties. If you continued without joining any party, it would be a problem because you would have no protection. Each party would ask you where you belonged and if you did not belong to one then it was a problem. That was why I chose to join the opposition party.

I was beaten but eventually I was released because the room was too small and there were too many of us to occupy this small space. We were sent back home and warned that if we continued going to the opposition we would be beaten again. The well-known members of the opposition were not allowed go free. I think they were sent to another prison; I am not sure what happened to them. When I was released, I went to my pastor and I told him everything. He suggested that if I had any way of leaving the country I should do so and go to Botswana, South Africa or anywhere. It was not safe to go to a village in the country because they were operating everywhere. So I was told that it was better for me to go somewhere out of Zimbabwe. I had no money. I had saved a little when I was working but not much. My pastor told me that since they had already taken me to prison they could come back. I had a niece here in Ireland and I told her everything. She told me that I could come over to Ireland and that she would give me money for the ticket. That evening the pastor came to where I was staying and told me the government soldiers were looking for me because they wanted to ask me more questions. Luckily, I had seen the government people around because there were demonstrations and slogans so they did not find me. I went to the pastor's house where I stayed. From there I went to Bulawayo, the second city of Zimbabwe, and stayed for a couple of months. I found some work and saved some money. I put that money with what I already had, my niece sent me some money, and I got a ticket and came over here. That was 2001. Unfortunately, my niece was not here when I arrived. She is married to an Irishman but he works in America so they had already gone. They had been in Ireland on a visit only when I talked to them and they had gone back to America. I knew nobody here when I arrived. Someone had told me that when I came to Ireland or England I could tell the immigration what had happened and people would help me. I told them and they took me to a hostel.

From there I was sent to Galway. I lived in a hostel in Eyre's Square for almost a year. I was called for an interview and after three weeks, they granted me refugee status. I was told that I could look

346

for a job, which I did for three to four months. I started working in Galway, washing sheets and pillowcases. This was a contract job and then I had to look for another job after a couple of months. I worked for Supermax in Eyre Square in Galway. This was contract work also. From there I went to Dell in Limerick where I worked for almost a year. It was not a permanent job so I worked for about 10 months and then was laid off. I was called back after two months and worked for a few more months. The work in Dell ended and so I had to look for another job. I found one in Galway and moved back and I worked for a company that does carpets.

At the same time, I realized I had no qualifications and I thought it was better for me to do some training so I could get a permanent job. I applied for some CAO courses and I got a place last year. There were some complications because they wanted me to pay for my accommodation and everything but I did not have any money. They told me I could apply for grants when I started the course in Blanchardstown. When I was told I had gotten a place I left the job in Galway and moved here because I wanted to go to College. Then I went to Social Welfare and told them that I wanted to go to College. It was September 2005. I wanted to come to Dublin and settle here; it was my first time in the capital city. When I went to Social Welfare, they told me that they could pay for my accommodation and food while I was waiting for a place in college but as soon as I started college, they would stop everything. I would have to look for a job, go to school and do everything on my own and social welfare was not going to assist me. The time that I was working, I was supposed to save a lot of money to go to college. I discovered that the money I had saved was not enough to keep me going. They referred me somewhere to ask for assistance but when I went, they told me that they could not give me assistance unless I had been one year out of work. I think Fás is the name of the organization. All that I could do is apply for grants. I found this all very difficult so I deferred going to college this year. I re-applied again and they told me they have my application but I do not know if I have the place or not. They said getting the place should be automatic and I hope this is true. I want to study computer and electronic engineering. I have a good idea about computers because when I lived in Zimbabwe I used to help my friend who had a shop for HI FIs, TVs and computers.

When I came here, I tried to find a job. I got a job in Blanchardstown with IBM computers but I was there for only two weeks. It was a short contract and I hoped they would renew but they did not. They said they would call me back but they have not. I was assembling computers but after two weeks, it stopped. I am looking for a job again but it is very difficult. It was not as difficult as it is now when I first came. This was before people from Poland started coming here. Now it is very difficult and it seems that they prefer the Polish to the African people. Even when you look for a cleaning job, they promise but they never call you back. I have been trying now for six months so going to college would be very difficult. I am going to apply for grants and probably social welfare is going to assist me because I am long term unemployed. I will keep on looking for a job but it is very hard.

I am always busy here trying to sort out my life. I have tried many things but I have not been successful in most of them. I was thinking that when I moved from Galway to Dublin it would be easier because this is the capital city and employment would not be a problem. Now I am starting to realise that I made a mistake. Galway was much better than Dublin and as well it is much more expensive in the capital. Most of the people that I know from my country are in Galway. Here there are only a few Zimbabweans.

Some of them are doing well and some are just struggling. For those who have children, life is very tough. I used to go to church but the majority of people in that church are from Nigeria. The way they pray and worship is quite different to the way we do in Zimbabwe. I stopped going to church because I could not understand their accents and even though they speak in English I cannot understand often what they are saying when they preach. Sometimes they even preach in their own language. It was not a bad place but the language was the reason I stopped going. In Dublin I sometimes go to the Methodist Churches and some other Irish churches. I do not have one particular church to which I belong. I am still looking for a church where I can feel I belong.

Getting an Irish passport is another major issue. I applied for naturalization three years and they replied to me just last year and said that the laws had changed. They told me I had to make a new application and that I should collect the form from immigration. I went there to get the form and I have to get three people with Irish citizenship but I only know two people. I have been looking for another person since I came here to Dublin. I do not know how long the process takes and I do not know the reasons why they reject some people. My friend from the Congo who came here at the same time as me got a red (Irish) passport. We applied the same time, the same day in 2002; he got the passport but they told me I have to reapply. I do not know the reason why. The interview was fine and the person was very nice. I think the interviewer was not Irish, perhaps from Britain. He told me that he is not Irish and he knew a lot about Zimbabwe. He asked me certain questions and it amazed me that he knew these things. It is over three years now since I got refugee status so they said I can now reapply for citizenship. There is no transparency in the system here. When I came, they granted me refugee status and they told me that I was going to be treated like an Irish citizen. They said that wherever I went I would be as good as an Irish person. But my experience has been that the response towards me has not been as good as towards Irish people. Travelling is a big problem. When I got my travel documents, I decided to visit England because I was quite curious to see what England was like. When I arrived, it seems that people did not understand what the travel documents were. The immigration officer in London asked me where I got that piece of paper and I explained to him that I had been granted refugee status in Ireland and was given these documents so that I can have access to travel whenever I want. The British immigration people told me that they knew nothing about this and they had never seen papers like this before. I asked them if they did not have refugees in the UK. They said they did but they did not use those kinds of documents. They have a card that refugees use and it looks like a driver's licence.

They took the papers from me and I waited. They rang, I think, immigration in Dublin and after waiting about one hour they gave me back the papers and told me I could enter the country. They told me that next time I should bring all my papers with me. I was not able to communicate with the person who was waiting for me. As he did not know what was going on, he left and by the time I left the airport and rang him he was on the way to Bristol. He had to come back again to pick me up. The British Immigration caused all this delay. I do not know if there is any communication between the Irish and British. I think it is better now. Being an African in Ireland is a problem. I think the government has to do something about that. When I moved to Dublin, I found things changed a lot. I do not know if it is always Irish because I cannot tell the difference between Irish and British and others but often when I meet people, they say to me *'go back to your own country'*. *'Our country is a nice country and you go back to your bush'*. This can happen when I am

350

walking along the street and someone stops his car and shouts at me. *'Go back to your country. What do you want here?'* Now I have gotten used to this and I ignore it. It is not everyone. Some people seem to like you when they are talking to you but later on, they start to behave badly. When I work in a place, people talk to you but as soon as you leave, they start to talk about you behind your back and say bad things about you.

I am a foreigner and I cannot do anything. I cannot retaliate because I am living in their country. Teenagers and men are the worst but girls are usually alright. Men are bad when they are drunk and they can say whatever they like to you. The police seem to be very idle, should I say. If you tell them that there is a problem, they don't take you seriously. When I was working in Limerick, one of those people who live on the street came to me, beat me and even broke my glasses. He put them on the ground and smashed them. I had to buy a new pair. I asked him why he was beating me and he said it was because I was black and he did not want to see a black person in his country. He continued beating me and I did not fight back because I was afraid other people might join him and beat me. Finally, I managed to run away. I went to the police and told them what had happened and said that this person was just round the corner. They started to laugh at me and said *'you are lying'.* I asked them to come out with me because I was afraid and wanted to go home. They told me to stay there until that fellow went away. But I asked them *'What if he sees another black person and does the same because he said he did not want to see any black person in Ireland?'* But they just told me that they have more important cases to deal with and that mine was just a minor thing. I stayed there for about two hours. I asked them to drive me home because I was still afraid but they said they did not have enough cars. The police did not do anything.

However, even with all this bad treatment, it is much better than living in Zimbabwe right now because my country is very dangerous. It is my country and I love it but now it is too risky for me to go back especially if they know I have been here. I am sure that if I go back, they will take me to prison, interrogate me and even torture me. So the problems here are just minor problems compared to what I have there. I have been through far greater hardship than what I am experiencing. Here it is all harmless if I do not retaliate. This is the principle by which I am able to live, not to retaliate or fight back.

Irish people in general are very nice but these youngsters are terrible. One problem is the media because they do not show the good part of Africa. This kind of publicity influences young people and deters them from going to Africa. They have the idea that Africa is all bush. Everyone who asks me about Africa all ask about animals, the bush and such wild things. I grew up in Africa in Harare; I am 38 years old and I have never seen a lion in the wild. I have watched them on TV. I have seen elephants in the zoo and seen other animals in the natural park reserves. Many people who live in Harare have not had the opportunity to see the animals even in the parks. This means that they do not know the animals. The impression that people have here is that Africa is just a long stretch of bush land with no houses or anything. The media have to take the good parts of Africa and show them. Of course, they have to show how people are suffering but they also need to show the good parts, the beauty of Africa. Some of the negative things they show are exaggerated and I have never seen them in Zimbabwe. These things may happen in remote areas but in general, people are not like that. They should show that we have nice buildings, and roads. With the programs they have, they are jeopardizing tourism in Africa. If an African, for example, wants to invite a young Irish person to his home that person will not want to go because he has such a bad view of Africa.

Zimbabwe and South Africa are quite similar though South Africa is larger. If you think of the infrastructure in both places you will find that some of the facilities are much better than in Ireland. There are buildings that are similar to those in California and other American cities. Even when they show South Africa, they do not show those beautiful places, beaches and other such places. The things that are shown just discourage people. When Europe is shown on TV in Africa, they show all the beautiful things here and everybody in Africa is very eager to travel to Europe. Before I came to Ireland, I imagined it would be like heaven but when I came I was disappointed. Building wise, Zimbabwe is much better than Ireland, beaches even my father's house where I was living is a four-bedroom house and we are not squashed the way people are here. Many people have a lot of land and swimming pools in their homes. When I came here, I was surprised at the poor quality of the roads. Before I came, I thought I was going to see wonderful things but I was disappointed.

If the political situation was OK it would be a good idea for Irish people to visit Africa. It would be good for them to mingle and to see the world. The media show only hunger, aids and poverty in Africa and they never show the good things. There are white people living in Zimbabwe who do not want to leave the place. Our only problems are political. Many Europeans go to South Africa on holiday, to live and buy property because it is a good country. It is very hard for people to respect us after they have seen all those negative pictures on TV. They degrade us and do not see us as people. We are educated just as Europeans are. I went to school; I have a diploma. It is not my first time to see a white person. In school, I shared a desk with a white British kid. We were about half white, half black in the school. There were also some Indians and Chinese in the school. It is not a new thing for me to mingle with white people; we are used to it.

According to the way African people live here, they can budget and save money if they cut out things like going to the pub. If the Irish see the Africans driving a car they seem annoyed as if they don't want to see the black person doing well. If they are driving a 07, 08 car, the police will often stop the car and ask you how you managed to buy the car. I remember being with my friend in his car in Galway. The car was not very new but a policeman followed us and when we parked he stopped beside us and asked for insurance and tax. We showed them and everything was in order. We asked him if he was following us because we were black but he just left.

To tell you the truth even if you went to Zimbabwe now you would find people interested in you. We are happy to see the foreigner. If you came to Zimbabwe with me now, my relatives would be very happy to see you and they would respect you.